Actor–Network Theory i

Actor–network theory (ANT) has enjoyed wide uptake in the social sciences over the past three decades, particularly in science and technology studies, and is increasingly attracting the attention of educational researchers. ANT studies bring to the fore the *material* – objects of all kinds – and de-centre the human and the social in educational issues. ANT sensibilities are interested in the ways human and non-human elements become woven into objects. They examine the particular connections and translations that assemble all of these objects, processes, concepts and institutions into presence, and they follow the movements and politics of these objects as they assemble to order everyday practices and places in particular ways. Most ANT studies trace all things as enactments that are *effects* continually produced in webs of relations. Since its first introduction, actor–network theory has undergone significant shifts and evolutions, and as a result, it is not considered to be a single or coherent theoretical domain, but as developing diversely in response to various challenges.

This book offers an introduction to actor–network theory for educators to consider in three modes. One mode is the introduction of concepts, approaches and debates around actor–network theory as a research approach in education. Another mode is a showcase of educational studies that have employed ANT approaches in classrooms, workplaces and community settings, drawn from the UK, USA, Canada, Europe and Australia. These work with ANT in highly diverse ways, often bending and twisting ANT ideas to better approach the educational question at hand, whether it focuses on policy critique, curriculum inquiry, engagements with digital media, change and innovation, issues of accountability, or exploring how knowledge unfolds and becomes materialized in various settings. A third mode is conversation with recent 'after-ANT' inquiries. These open an array of important new approaches to trace the ontological politics of socio-material phenomena in education, its messy and fluid objects, and its ambivalences and non-coherences. Across these diverse environments and uptakes, the authors trace how learning and practice – as assemblages of activity, actors and spaces – emerge, show what scales are at play, and demonstrate what this means for educational possibilities.

Tara Fenwick is Professor of Professional Education at the University of Stirling, UK. Her research focuses on knowledge and education in workplace and professional practices, for which she won the Houle Award for Outstanding Contribution to Adult Education Literature, awarded by the American Association for Adult and Continuing Education.

Richard Edwards is Professor of Education at the University of Stirling, UK. He has researched and written extensively on post-compulsory education and lifelong learning and has an international reputation in the field.

Actor–Network Theory in Education

Tara Fenwick and
Richard Edwards

Routledge
Taylor & Francis Group

LONDON AND NEW YORK

First edition published 2010
by Routledge
2 Park Square, Milton Park, Abingdon, Oxon OX14 4RN

Simultaneously published in the USA and Canada
by Routledge
711 Third Avenue, New York, NY 10017, USA

Routledge is an imprint of the Taylor & Francis Group, an informa business

Typeset in Galliard by GreenGate Publishing Services, Tonbridge, Kent

British Library Cataloguing in Publication Data
A catalogue record for this book is available from the British Library

Library of Congress Cataloging-in-Publication Data
Fenwick, Tara J.
Actor-network theory in education / Tara Fenwick and Richard Edwards. -- 1st ed.
p. cm.
Includes bibliographical references and index.
1. School environment--Social aspects--Cross-cultural studies. 2. Distance education-
-Social aspects--Cross-cultural studies. 3. Curriculum planning--Cross-cultural
studies. 4. Actor-network theory. I. Edwards, Richard, 1956 July 2- II. Title.
LC210.F46 2010
306.43--dc22   2009052313

ISBN13: 978-0-415-49296-6 (hbk)
ISBN13: 978-0-415-49298-0 (pbk)
ISBN13: 978-0-203-84908-8 (ebk)

Contents

Acknowledgements

Intertextuality and interstanding are integral to authorship. Such is the case with this book, which is the culmination of many forms of personal and textual connectedness that we feel it important to acknowledge.

Tara Fenwick is indebted to funding provided by the Social Sciences and Humanities Research Council of Canada for studies that have contributed to this book. Among these are *Learning Social Responsibility in Practice-Based Networks* (SSHRC 410-2004-0076), *Knowledge Networks of Portfolio Workers* (SSHRC 501-2001-0020), and *Knowledge Creation Practices of Older Professionals* (SSHRC 410-2009-0071). Many colleagues and graduate students supported these projects and deserve thanks. In particular, grateful acknowledgement is extended to Anne Zavalkoff, Tara Gibb, Lee-Anne Reagan, Lesley Farrell, Kathryn Church, Elizabeth Lange and Kiran Mirchandani. Tara is also grateful to the University of British Columbia which was not only her university home during much of this book's development, but also provided library resources and some research funding. Certain chapters here draw upon previously published work, including Fenwick (2009), Fenwick (2010a), Fenwick (2010b) and Fenwick and Edwards (2010), and earlier formations of ideas that have continued to expand and grow in this book were published in Fenwick (2007, 2008, 2009a, b).

Richard Edwards has drawn upon a number of Economic and Social Research Council (ESRC) funded projects in which he has participated in contributing to this text. These are the *Literacies for Learning in Further Education* project (RES-139-25-0117), the *Cultures of Curriculum-Making in School and College* project (RES-000-22-2452) and the *Ensemble: Semantic Technologies for the Enhancement of Case-based Learning* project (RES-139-25-0403). He would like to acknowledge the support of all colleagues from these projects, but, in particular, Roz Ivanič, Greg Mannion, Kate Miller, Mark Priestley and Sanna Rimpiläinen. Intellectual debts rest with too many to name, but he would particularly like to acknowledge Julia Clarke who introduced him to the scallops of Michel Callon. In addition, he would like to acknowledge resources provided by the Carnegie Trust for the Universities of Scotland and the Stirling Institute of Education, University of Stirling, which enabled him to complete his contribution to this text while on research leave. Parts of certain chapters have drawn upon previously published work, in particular, Edwards (2002, 2010), Edwards *et al.* (2009b) and Edwards *et al.* (2009c).

Tara and Richard would both like to acknowledge the wonderful contribution of Dr Anne Zavalkoff at the University of British Columbia who served as a post-doctoral researcher in this project. Anne tracked down, in published and fugitive literatures across diverse fields, as many studies in ANT and education as could possibly be found. We also wish to acknowledge Dianne Mulcahy and Jan Nespor whose explorations in actor–network theory and education have inspired and provoked our thinking in ways too numerous to name.

Preface

Around the edges of educational research a body of unsettling and rather auda-
cious work has emerged, in studies that draw upon what has come to be known
as 'actor–network theory' (ANT). These educational studies often rupture central
assumptions about knowledge, subjectivity, agency, the real and the social. They
bring to the fore the material – objects of all kinds – and de-centre the human and
the social in educational issues. They trace all things as enactments that are *effects*
continually produced in webs of relations.

But what is actor–network theory, and what use does it offer for educational
research? The risk in explaining ANT is to treat it as an 'it' or 'thing' that can
be known and contained. In a recent mini-history of ANT's development, John
Law (2009) emphasizes the openness, uncertainty and revisability of ANT-
inspired studies. He even suggests that we talk of 'material semiotics' rather than
actor–network theory, and offers a stark warning: 'beware ... of any text about
actor–network theory that pretends to the objectivity of an overall view' (Law
2009: 142). So readers of this text may consider themselves warned – and the
authors duly reproached for any attempt to synthesize or authorize particular
accounts of ANT. Perhaps the safest way to talk about ANT is as an array of practices for approaching complexity in the world and its problems.

Actor–network theory can be traced in a lively trajectory through the social
sciences since its emergence in the early 1980s at the Centre de Sociologie de
l'Innovation (CSI) of the École Nationale Supérieure des Mines de Paris. Largely
associated with its progenitors in science and technology studies, including
Bruno Latour, John Law and Michael Callon, ANT analyses trace how all things
that are taken to be natural, social or technical are more accurately some messy
mix of these which are enacted in webs, how they associate and exercise force,
and how they persist, decline and mutate. Nothing is given or anterior, including
'the human', 'the social', 'subjectivity', 'mind', 'the local', 'structures' and other
categories commonly taken for granted in educational analyses. Throughout the
1980s and 1990s, ANT figured prominently in studies published in sociology,
technology, feminism, cultural geography, organization and management, environmental planning and health care.

We are among those who believe that ANT approaches can open useful insights about the dynamics and objects of education. We conceive education broadly as intentional processes for producing knowledge, practices and subjectivity that involve purpose and pedagogy. These processes unfold in schools and post-secondary institutions, but also in community agencies, social movements, agricultural extension, training centres, work organizations, union initiatives and a host of other settings. ANT's usefulness to education is in spite of, or perhaps because of, its mutations in the past three decades into a highly diffuse, diverse and contested set of framings and practices. Its own key commentators refuse to call it a 'theory' as though ANT were some coherent explanatory device. It may be more accurate to think of ANT as a virtual 'cloud', continually moving, shrinking and stretching, dissolving in any attempt to grasp it firmly. ANT is not 'applied' like a theoretical technology, but is more like a sensibility, an interruption or intervention, a way to sense and draw nearer to a phenomenon. For educational researchers, ANT approaches can enact questions and phenomena in rich ways that discern difficult ambivalences, messy objects, multiple overlapping worlds and apparent contradictions that are embedded in so many educational issues.

This book offers an introduction to actor–network theory as a source of research practices for educators to consider in three modes. One mode is the introduction of concepts, approaches and debates around actor–network theory as a research approach. While these are well-worn through many discussions of ANT offered since the 1980s, we suspect they may be new to some educational researchers. In our own explanations, we try to approach these concepts and their language lightly – as provisional rather than authoritative formulas. We also try to show these concepts where possible through empirical studies, some which have by now become classic, from the broader ANT literature in the social sciences.

Another mode is a showcase of studies in education that have employed ANT approaches. Compared to fields of sociology, human geography and technology studies, there are relatively few educational studies drawing from ANT. Those that we could find work with ANT in highly diverse ways, often bending and twisting ANT ideas to better approach the question at hand. We do not know of any other place where these ANT-inspired educational studies have been collected together, and we hope that their gathering will introduce some interesting juxtapositions and new questions. Educational settings and situations may be argued to offer a unique site for examining a research approach such as actor–network theory. While most sites for social science research are dynamic and emergent, education in particular is about prompting dynamic change, and examining a future imaginary existing within the immanent present.

A third mode is our inclusion here of what some call 'after-ANT' developments. A range of conversations have leapt from the original ANT propositions to explore ontological politics in socio-material phenomena, messy and fluid objects, partial connections and topologies of gels and webs that explode traditional notions of network pipelines. They also challenge some presumptions and limitations of ANT research. Explorers among these terrains of material

semiotics and science and technology studies may well reject any direct association with actor–network theory. However, they continue to share an interest in
the ways that human and non-human elements have become woven into objects,
in tracing the connections and translations that bring objects to presence, and
in following the movements and politics of these objects as they create everyday
practices in particular ways. For us, these after-ANT studies offer particularly
rich territory for educational researchers, and they make little sense without the
trajectory of thinking that catalysed their emergence. So we have included them
all here, unapologetically, as part of a general 'cloud' of scholarship. While the
book appears to be about actor–network theory, we use this term only as a tentative organizer, a quick way to refer to a cloud that in fact escapes any attempt to
grasp it. Generally, we follow Law's (2009) cautions about not getting caught up
in what is a real account of ANT, or what should be included or not, or whether
ANT is actually dead or not. Our focus is whether and how ANT sensibilities are
useful for our further work in research and indeed for education at large.

ANT is not presented here as a new grand narrative to replace other
understandings. In fact, ANT, like other approaches to research, has limitations
and preoccupations that render it more useful for some questions and less for
others. Its modest usage so far in education means that important fields of
contemporary inquiry in educational research have not yet worked with ANT.
Much uptake of ANT in education was at first most visible among those
interested in science education (Roth 1996, Roth and McGinn 1997, Fountain
1999, Verran 1999, 2001). This is understandable given ANT's close links with
science and technology studies. While in the past ten years there has been a
wider proliferation of ANT-associated studies in literacy, curriculum, educational
reform, policy and educational technology, there is as yet little published ANT-
related research that explicitly explores issues of identity politics, inequities and
exclusions. In this respect, those perusing this text for ANT-analyses of gender,
race and multiculturalism, indigeneity, sexual difference, dis/ability, class issues,
transnationalism and other complexities of inequity and identity are likely to be
disappointed. This may point to ANT's inherent limitations as an approach, or to
the fact that experts in these areas have not had opportunity to work with ANT-
related approaches. We believe that ANT's potential for analysing the dynamics
within questions of diversity and social justice is vast. ANT-related approaches are
well suited for tracing and naming complex politics, hybridities and métissage,
non-coherences, absences and problematic representations of presence, dynamics
of assembling and disassembling powerful interlinked entities, embodiment, and
materializing processes that are so often unmentioned in educational accounts.
We maintain that this potential has yet to be fully explored by educational
researchers in the many domains where it offers useful resources.

So why did we choose to write a book rather than edit a series of contributions from different authors? Why not many voices and many versions of ANT
rather than one? Arguably, an authored text presumes to capture in one singular
account one peculiar version of something. Usually this is accomplished without

signalling the many ways in which the writing of that account is creating a world, an 'it', precisely what Law (2009) points out does not exist in relation to ANT. This world is a particular enactment, particularly in the academic convention of a smooth and coherent narrative that grinds down or ignores all the jagged edges and non-coherent mismatches that burble behind it. This is fair critique. In our case, however, we decided to risk the problems in order to offer the widest possible glimpse of the educational uptakes of ANT. Rather than limiting the voices to a few selected authors, we decided to bring into presence the dozens of commentators and researchers who have worked with ANT in the past 25 years or so. This choice was made for two reasons. First, to push the point that actor–network theory, broadly understood as a sensibility infusing many approaches, is enjoying widely diverse uptake in researching many educational fields. Second, to open an array of possible entry-points for readers: examples, questions, language and compelling non-coherences that might open useful possibilities for their own research practices, possibilities that we do not presume to anticipate.

We do not pretend to tread any new ground. Nor do we purport to be comprehensive or authoritative in our selection of educational studies included here, other than pointing to research in a range of areas that we believe asks some useful questions. We certainly are not trying to define and nail down actor–network theory, nor to privilege it above other perspectives and approaches. Overall, our intent in this book is to suggest some openings and networking potentials for educational researchers that this ANT-ish cloud of rather unique approaches can offer.

Chapter 1

A way to intervene, not a theory of what to think

Actor–network theory is not terribly familiar in the study of education. This book examines its uptakes in educational research and the potential it offers for fresh and productive interventions within educational issues. Its routes in the 1980s from post-structuralism, the sociology of science and technology, human–computer interaction and feminism are still apparent. People still engage within it in these domains but it has dispersed and developed since then. Some people in education have taken it up over the years, but it has been sporadic rather than sustained. This book aims to provide a basis for a sustained engagement with actor–network theory and to take forward fresh agendas for intervening in educational research, policy and practice. Our use of actor–network theory is not for telling us about educational issues; it is a way of intervening in educational issues to reframe how we might enact and engage with them.

It is extraordinarily difficult to write or talk about actor–network theory without either destroying or domesticating it. Many of its more recent contributors would call their work 'after-ANT' or 'post-ANT', or for example, explorations of complexity, material practice, material semiotics, feminist science and technology studies or the sociology of science and technology. Often they avoid using explicit ANT-associated terminology at all. We say these things not to mystify ANT as some rarefied or sacred site permitting only elite knowers to draw near, but to declare at the outset our recognition of the essential difficulty – and possible heresy – of setting forth some explorations of ANT. After all, ANT's key contribution is to suggest analytic methods that honour the mess, disorder and ambivalences that order phenomena, including education. As Law (1999: 10) has warned, the worst thing we could do is to re-establish and impose a purity of ANT-ness: 'only dead theories and dead practices celebrate their identity'.

However, we are committed to engage educational researchers in ANT insights and approaches because we have experienced profound possibilities that these afford in our own work studying educational issues and conditions. We will undoubtedly suffer some missteps and become caught in contradictions and incoherences along the way. We also believe that, for the purposes of this book and for those unfamiliar with ANT ideas, it is helpful to represent with the single term ANT a constellation of these ideas that have associated themselves with

ANT at some point. Our hope is that we can employ this term in the spirit of a temporary marker, an organizer – if a precarious one, as we hope to keep reminding readers. The term is also a handy reference to help distinguish ANT approaches from the many other available conceptions of socio-material practice and interobjectivity that have captured interest among educational researchers, such as post-structuralist geographies, complexity theory and cultural–historical activity theory.

Why do we say that ANT is difficult to write or talk about? ANT cannot accurately be described as a single, stable or identifiable theoretical framework. While the same thing could be said of many social scientific and philosophical theories that find their way into educational research, ANT has been particularly slippery and diffuse since its first appearances in the 1980s. Indeed, many of its progenitors such as Bruno Latour, John Law and Michael Callon have either struggled to avoid defining it as a set of theoretical ideas, or have distanced themselves from others' efforts to do so. The frustration expressed by the most prominent ANT commentators is that many ANT uptakes have solidified particular models of analysis, have reified concepts such as networks, and have colonized their objects of inquiry in representational ways that ANT approaches were intended to disrupt. A landmark volume of essays, entitled *Actor Network Theory and After* (Law and Hassard 1999), was premised on the assumption that ANT ideas proliferating throughout the 1990s in various studies had largely run into an impasse. At that time, leading scholars associated with ANT declared various approaches that included eliminating or replacing certain naturalized ANT language and models, delimiting ANT's claims and opening its conceptual scope.

At the time of this writing, ten years on from the publication of *Actor Network Theory and After*, there has been a remarkable profusion of ANT uptakes, critiques and hybrid theoretical blends as ANT has travelled across a number of disciplines ranging from scientific innovation to cyber-punk semiotics, from anthropology to the sociology of the everyday, from literacy education to organizational change, from urban planning to art history. Recently, Law (2007: 595) has referred to ANT as a 'diaspora', a disparate set of:

> tools, sensibilities and methods of analysis that treat everything in the social and natural worlds as a continuously generated effect of the webs of relations within which they are located. It assumes that nothing has reality or form outside the enactment of those relations.

This diversity and these uptakes have each helped to extend and reconfigure ANT ideas, opening new challenging questions and ways of intervening for educational researchers. The *After* in Law and Hassard's (1999) book title did not signal the end of ANT, but that there was more to be done. This book is an attempt to explore what has and can be done in education.

ANT offers an unfamiliar take on many familiar issues. It invites us to avoid making a priori distinctions and then making these the foundations upon which all other knowledge builds. Distinctions, such as those between the social and natural, between the material and cultural, the human and non-human, and between the technical and social, are taken to be effects rather than foundational assumptions. In particular, they are taken to be network effects, as subjects, objects, agency and actions are taken to emerge from the particular networks through which they co-emerge. In ANT, therefore, society and the social are not seen as a pre-existing object of enquiry, but as emerging through enactments of various forms of association, as network effects. Here, the social is viewed as assembled and only becomes possible through its own enactment as a separate domain. Actor–network theory examines the associations of human and non-human entities in the performance of the social, the economic, the natural, the educational, etc. The objective is to understand precisely *how* these things come together – and manage to *hold* together, however temporarily – to form associations that produce agency and other effects: for example, ideas, identities, rules, routines, policies, instruments and reforms. In educational discourse, such an approach leads us to question common categories and distinctions, such as teacher and learner, curriculum and pedagogy, formal and informal learning. This includes the notion that there is an a priori domain that we can identify as education as separate from not-education. Each of these distinctions can be examined as themselves network effects.

A key assumption in ANT analyses is that humans are not treated any differently from non-humans, because 'without the nonhuman, the humans would not last for a minute' (Latour 2004a: 91). Humans are not assumed to have a privileged a priori status in the world but to be part of it. This position, first suggested by Bloor (1976) and then elaborated by Latour (1987), is called *symmetry*. In ANT, a generalized symmetry is enacted in relation to different things, and approaches are adopted for 'levelling divisions usually taken to be foundational' (Law 2007: 597). Everyday things and parts of things – animals, memories, intentions, technologies, bacteria, furniture, chemicals, plants, and so on – are assumed to be capable of exerting force and joining together, changing and being changed by each other. As they assemble together, they form associations or networks that can keep expanding to extend across broad spaces, long distances or time periods. In the process, such networks can become more or less durable. For example, think of a mathematics textbook for children. That one object, the textbook, embeds a network of curriculum development (policy-makers, computers, teachers, maths experts) with networks of publication (writers, editors, reviewers, text drafts, pilot testers, print machines, ink) in a network of distribution in schools and classrooms across a country, or further. All are linked together such that a very particular maths concept presented in one particular way can be experienced at the same time by thousands of children in far-flung contexts. We therefore witness how networks can become more durable by being both supported and promoting standardization across space and time, a theme in relation to education to which we will return throughout this book.

ANT is an approach that enables us to trace the ways that things come together, act and become taken for granted, or 'black-boxed'. Latour (1987) uses the example of a camera to illustrate his understanding of a black box: it is made up of many elements but is taken to be a single entity with properties, and acts in a certain way. ANT can show how things are invited or excluded, how some linkages work and others do not, and how associations are bolstered to make themselves stable and durable by linking to other networks and things. Further, and perhaps most interesting, ANT focuses on the minute negotiations that go on at the points of association. Things – not just humans, but the parts that make up humans and non-humans – persuade, coerce, seduce, resist and compromise each other as they come together. They may connect with other things in ways that lock them into a particular association, or they may pretend to connect, partially connect, or feel disconnected and excluded, even when they are connected. We are in a world of precarious correlations rather than cause and effect. ANT analyses try to trace these negotiations and their effects, and in the process show how the things that we commonly work with in educational research – whether classrooms, teachers, curriculum, a policy, standardized testing, racism or evidence-based practice – are each in fact assemblies of myriad things. These assemblies order objects and actions, flows of movement and choices in space and time. Yet these assemblies are precarious and require a great deal of ongoing work to sustain their linkages.

ANT analyses can show, therefore, how such *assemblages* can be unmade as well as made, and how counter-networks or alternative forms and spaces can take shape and develop. Networks can never be complete or totalizing; there are always gaps, holes and tears, and multiple networks vying to be effective. Further, ANT analyses show how knowledge is generated through the process and effects of these assemblages coming together. In this approach, learning is not simply an individual or cognitive process. Nor is it simply a social achievement. Learning itself becomes enacted as a network effect. ANT does all of this by drawing attention not only to the importance of things, to the non-human, in all educational endeavours, but also to the intimate associations between objects and all human attributes, capacities and activities. Life, in education as well as other spheres, is never only about the personal and the social. It is about what we will refer to as the socio-material.

Working from these assumptions, this chapter has been shaped to speak to those who may be newcomers to ANT ideas and approaches. In an introductory spirit, we do not intend to be comprehensive in breadth or depth, but to explain what we have found to be particularly helpful concepts for education. At the same time, we try to do justice to certain complexities and critiques around these concepts that have emerged, and to indicate some questions that gesture to interesting possibilities for educational analyses.

The rest of this chapter and the next represent our desire to explore what we believe to be certain useful ANT interventions for studying educational practices and dilemmas. Our objective is simplicity without dishonest simplification. Our challenge is to be clear without smoothing out lumpy complexity to purified clarity. We will discuss how ANT writings help us to consider the following issues in education: 'things' and why they are so important; 'translation' as a way to think about how things come to be and how they change; 'networks' and how they grow to constitute educational practices and ecologies; and 'effects of networks' in terms of agency, power, identity and knowledge. We also show some limits of ANT, what it does not seek to address and what it cannot, nor should be asked to explain in education. These limits do not diminish the power of what ANT can offer to educational analysts. ANT commentators have been clear that its ideas are best utilized as an approach, a sensibility and a method for understanding, not a totalizing theory of the world and its problems. For us, ANT is a way of intervening in or interrupting education rather than simply a different way of representing education.

Things – why are they so important?

> I have sought to show researchers in the social sciences that sociology is not the science of human beings alone – that it can welcome crowds of nonhumans with open arms, just as it welcomed the working masses in the nineteenth century. Our collective is woven together out of speaking subjects, perhaps, but subjects to which poor objects, our inferior brothers, are attached at all points.
>
> (Latour 1996: viii)

Chalk and textbooks, tests and databases, student portfolios, playground equipment, desks, bulletin board displays and math manipulatives: education could be described as a set of material things or artefacts that are continually distributed, managed and employed (Lawn and Grosvenor 2005). And things are themselves assembled or, in Molotch's (2005: 1) term, 'lashed up' from numerous elements; 'to understand any one thing you have to learn how it fits into larger arrays of physical objects, social sentiments and ways of being … each element is just one interdependent fragment of a larger whole'.

Pedagogy centres around, and is constantly mediated by, material things. Pedagogical encounters change radically when its things change, for example, when a PowerPoint presentation is used instead of a textbook, or field trip to show how a pumping station works, or when desks and chairs are removed for learning activities to explore democracy or relationships. In one study, McGregor (2004) traces how things in a school science department office – from laboratory preparation materials and filing cabinet of students records to wall displays of timetables and humorous photos – drew teachers together in a distinct network of materials and conversations that reaffirmed particular practices and values, and that organized specific associations of materials and information. Her ANT analysis shows how the science department comes to be an accumulation of particular forms of knowledge that orders people, things and teaching identities and flows in space and time. This is taken to be qualitatively different from the physical education department.

However, schools constitute only one type of the many environments addressed in educational research and throughout this book. Things are central in vocational learning. Novice cooks, electricians, nurses or managers, for example, explore the nuances of how all the tools and substances of their work behave, what they can produce, and how these things act upon them as much as they act with them. Educational policy processes, workplace learning, curriculum-making, technology implementation and evaluation activities are all fundamentally shaped by the material things with which they associate and are associated, as much as by the human ideas, desires, meanings and actions that are entangled within them.

The simple recognition that things are ubiquitous in educational practices does not go far enough. Social scientists, including those working with ANT, are now emphasizing that things are integral to such processes. Things exert force themselves. They do not just respond to human intention and force. In fact, things change and shape human intentions, meanings, relationships, routines, memories, even perceptions of self. Miller (2005) reminds us that in our everyday lives, our material things can possess us as much as we possess them. Things in our homes can take up space we might not necessarily have, or compel memories and associations we may not wish to make. From food in the fridge to plants in the garden, things have demands and needs. People associate with these according to their own emotions, intentions and desires. Things exert attachments that enact identities.

Consider the struggle of many people to de-clutter their homes, offices and classrooms by giving up attachments to certain things. Knorr-Cetina (1997: 9), whose conceptions of intimate objects in professionals' knowledge has influenced a whole body of scholarship, emphasizes that '[t]o understand the binding role of objects, personal object ties, object-centred traditions and collectives, and object-created emotional worlds all need to be considered'. Consider how a teacher actually comes into being as a teacher. This is not through force of individual will, nor through the conferring of a certificate alone. It is rather through the myriad things that she designs, selects, organizes, stores, evaluates, maintains and responds to, as well as the humans with whom she interacts every moment. Furthermore, things themselves embed complex histories of events and forces that produced them and continue to change them. To view things as either the products of human design or as brute tools controlled through human action alone is to underestimate the power and contribution of things themselves in enacting events. It is to overlook the complex effects that these non-human entities produce through associations with other (human and non-human) things.

Waltz (2006) is one who argues strongly for ANT-like attention to things in educational research. He claims that material non-human things are often analytically subsumed by human intention, design and drive and treated merely as representatives of human ends. As tools, the role of non-human things is typically limited to extension, transportation, distribution and prevention. Overall, this subjugation of things to humans obscures their own particular contributions and hides the qualities of the entities themselves. One example Waltz uses is the course textbook. This is typically treated as a tool even by critical theorists who present texts as ideological vehicles for control and oppression. However, textbooks exert force themselves. Depending on their form, they can enact certain pedagogical activities and sequences, align curricula across space and time, limit the teacher's academic freedom, affect student funds, and generally can function as 'co-conspirators, law-enforcement officers, administrators, racists, quality control agents, seducers, and investment advisors' (Waltz 2006: 57). In another example provided by Waltz, school playground equipment combines with children's behaviours to produce particular activities, speech, social groupings and exclusions, injuries, even gender identities. The point here is that material things are performative; they act, together with other types of things and forces, to exclude, invite and regulate particular forms of participation. What, then, is produced can appear to be 'gender identity' or 'expertise' or 'knowledge' or a social 'structure', such as racism. A focus on things therefore helps us to untangle the heterogeneous relationships holding together these larger categories, tracing their durabilities as well as their weaknesses.

Things circulate in a midst of connections, cultural histories and symbolic values, but they themselves also compel activity. A well-known example from Latour (1991) is the hotel-room key. When the key has a large enough fob, it will change guests' activity from pocketing the key (and possibly misplacing it) to leaving it at reception. In a study of teachers' lives in public schools, Fenwick (1998) found that keys – ordinary keys to classrooms, teacher lounges, equipment lockers, etc. – exerted important effects on how people felt about their work, themselves and each other. One teacher told of the inconvenience, and even humiliation, of standing out in the hallway each morning waiting amidst her students for the school principal to come by and unlock her classroom door. This activity was compelled by the standardized classroom lock system. In another school, teachers narrated the antagonisms and subversions that unfolded when the head gym teacher tried keeping the gym locked to prevent accidents. Other teachers held gym activities in school hallways, jimmied the lock, and even retaliated by duplicating the key and then using it to lock the gym teacher out. A third teacher bemusedly recalled the discomfort of being compelled to control the key to the closet where the school's laminating machine was kept. As the 'keeper of the key', she wore it round her neck and was supposed to open, supervise and then lock this closet whenever any teacher or student wanted to laminate pictures or posters, which apparently was frequent. The material key literally tied her body to the door barrier, which not only interrupted her own activity throughout the day but also created rifts between herself and her colleagues. In each of these cases, there are other networks being mobilized to perform territory, security, classroom displays, resource control, and so on. However, these issues are shaped differently through the specific material of the key and the behaviours the key helps to produce, than they would be through other material enforcements of spatial boundaries, such as a written policy or a keypad code.

Things matter. It is this materiality in the associational work of networking that is often overlooked. Sørensen (2009: 2) complains about 'the blindness toward the question of how educational practice is affected by materials', and argues that its consequence is to treat materials as mere instruments to advance educational performance. In her book-length study of the materiality of learning, she shows how forms of knowledge and forms of presence – the dynamics of everyday 'performance' in education – are critically shaped through the material. Law and Hetherington (2003) categorize three kinds of materiality, or 'stuff'. Material things are only one kind, which besides tools and artefacts include, for example, classrooms and gymnasiums, installation of digital technologies, chemicals in science labs, parent meetings, hot lunch programmes, Ministry of Education offices, the production and effects of standardized tests, and teacher education colleges. A second kind of stuff is bodies, in particular how they are displayed and decorated, comported, manoeuvred, disciplined, gazed upon, impaired or amplified (with glasses, prostheses, illness). Textual things, those that embed language, are a third kind of stuff. While all objects carry some form of information, for textual stuff information – its expression, interpretation, management and regulation – is the primary purpose.

In education, textual objects proliferate in such things as curriculum documents, maps, educational journals, parent newsletters, student record systems, exams, text books, competency lists, newspaper editorials, training software and test instruments. While these are all cultural and discursive texts, they are also material. To focus only on the information and discourses they embed is to ignore the fact that activity changes if the materiality of the textual thing is paper, digital or plastic, heavy or delicate, mechanical or organic. Farrell (2006) argues that texts increasingly control, direct, monitor, document, make visible, shape, consolidate and inscribe what comes to be valued as knowledge. Texts, particularly technological texts, transport knowledge across distributed sites, and partially enact these sites. Indeed, the texts of new technologies are shifting and demanding new forms of engagement and exerting new forms of control. We will discuss these issues in greater depth in a later chapter.

The important point here is that ANT focuses not on what texts and other things mean, as in much qualitative research, but on what they do. What they do is always in connection with other human and non-human things. Some of these associations link together to form an identifiable entity or assemblage, which ANT refers to as an 'actor', that can exert force. 'Playground', for example, represents a continuous collaboration of bats and balls, swing installations, fences, grassy hills, sand pits, children's bodies and their capacities, game discourses, supervisory gazes, safety rules, and so on. This playground is both an assemblage or *network* of things that have become connected in a particular way, and an *actor* itself that can produce fears, policies, pedagogies, forms of play and resistances to them. Hence, the use of the term actor–network. There is no a priori agent or agency. The human subject is not agentic and intentional, but is itself an effect of a particular network of associations. The things that have become part of this actor–network are effects produced by particular interactions with one another.

In educational research, important questions are opened up when we consider how things work in and through complex human–non-human relations to enact social worlds, expertise, learning, pedagogy, policy and curriculum. We can examine how things enact conceptual categories and reconfigure relationships. We can trace how things like textbooks and unit descriptors move about to transmit knowledge and values across time and space. We can study how, in educational encounters, things of particular significance and apparent force, whether a standardized test or a key to the storeroom, come to emerge, how value becomes attached to them, what traces they leave, what energies they provoke in different spaces, and how and when they fade out of significance. Finally, we can examine messy things that refuse to hold their shape or that somehow maintain continuity through what appears to be disconnection and incoherence.

Translation – how things come to (dis)connect and change

An early formulation of ANT was as the 'sociology of translation'. Translation is the term used by Latour (1987) to describe what happens when entities, human and non-human, come together and connect, changing one another to form links: a teacher's body, with a key on a string, with a locked door, with a storeroom of supplies, with desires for those supplies, and so on. Entities that connect eventually form a chain or network of action and things, and these networks tend to become stable and durable. At each of these connections, one entity has worked upon another to *translate* or change it to become part of a collective or network of coordinated things and actions. ANT's unique contribution is first, to focus on the individual nodes holding these networks together, examining how these connections came about and what sustains them. These include negotiations, forces, resistances and exclusions, which are at play in these micro-interactions that eventually forge links. Second, as we have indicated, ANT accepts nothing as given, including 'humanity', 'the social', 'subjectivity', 'mind', 'the local', 'structures' and other categories common in educational analyses. What we usually take to be unitary objects with properties are better understood as assemblages, built of heterogeneous human and non-human things, connected and mobilized to act together through a great deal of ongoing work. Translation is 'the process ... which generates ordering effects such as devices, agents, institutions, or organizations' (Law 1992: 366).

The insistence upon treating human and non-human entities the same way, looking at their performances and linkages rather than distinguishing them according to some a priori essentialized features, forms the generalized symmetry that is characteristic of ANT. It is also one of the hardest things to keep hold of and operationalize, especially when the weight of history and culture is so great towards privileging human intention and agency, putting us at the centre of things rather than being a part of them. In a real sense, the very notion of actor–network itself inscribes this symmetrical approach; an actor is a network and vice versa.

Early ANT analyses also used a distinction between *actor* and *actant* to enact this approach. While the working entity is an actor with agency, that which goes into the network to enable this activity is the actant. When actants are translated to become a performing part of the network, they can behave with what appears to be particular intentions, morals, even consciousness and subjectivity, that is, as an actor with agency. Harman (2007: 36) argues that the enactment of symmetry produces a philosophy where 'a total democracy of objects replaces the long tyranny of human beings'. We agree that an ANT approach provides an important counter to educational practices derived from transcendent humanism that overlook the centrality of material things to human intention and agency. However, while the language of actants and actors will surface throughout this book, we find it neither particularly necessary nor helpful to distinguish between them. It is also noticeable that the 'actant' term is not much used in after-ANT analyses.

When translation has succeeded, the actor–network is mobilized to assume a particular role and perform knowledge in a particular way. Thus, from our earlier example, the key translates certain actions of the teacher to mobilize her into a role as bodyguard and gatekeeper of supplies. The key does not act by itself, but is also acted upon by other entities linked in the network. These might include the demand that exceeds funds for laminating plastic, the pedagogic activities that demand laminated pictures, the administrative policy to control these resources by locking them in one closet and the naturalized expectation that teachers have responsibility for creating plasticized classroom materials. Many of these entities are themselves networks in which a series of connections among material and immaterial things have settled into a particular routine, network of distribution, or technology. They can become durable, naturalized, taken for granted and black-boxed. The work that is necessary to sustain them becomes lost to critical intervention.

Translation is not deterministic, for what entities do when they come together is unpredictable. Keys break and get lost, locks are jimmied, locked doors become devices of sabotage, deals and thefts subvert the network. In other words, entities negotiate the connections when they come together, using persuasion, force, mechanical logic, seduction, resistance, pretence, and subterfuge, etc. Furthermore, the connections produced through translation are diverse. The connection between a lock and key is qualitatively different from that between the locked door and the laminating machine or between the machine and the plasticized picture it produces. Translations may be incremental, or delayed. Or they may be partial, producing weak connections or even disconnections. Entities may only peripherally allow themselves to be translated by the network, like posters that get laminated outside the school or pedagogic activities adopted by teachers that forego laminated materials. Tracing exactly how entities are not just effects of their interactions with others, but are also always acting on others shows that all are fragile and all are powerful, held in balance within their interactions. None is inherently strong or weak, but only becomes strong by assembling other allies.

The key point, as Harman (2009) points out, is that each element or actor is separate, cut off from one another. Nothing is reducible or irreducible to anything else, but must be connected together through the work of translation. This principle of irreducibility, claims Harman, is a central point of Latour's metaphysics:

> Actors are defined by their relations, but precisely for this reason they are cut off in their own relational microcosms, which endure for only an instant before the actor is replaced by a similar actor. The work of mediation must be done at every moment to restore or maintain the links between actors.
>
> (Harman 2009: 116)

Eventually, these dynamic attempts to translate one another can become stabilized. The network settles into a stable process or object that maintains itself. Like a black box it appears immutable and inevitable, while concealing all the negotiations that brought it into existence. Educational examples of this would be a mandated list of teaching competencies, or a so called evidence-based educational practice. Each entity also belongs to other networks in which it is called to act differently, taking on different shapes and capacities. A teaching contract, for example, is a technology that embeds knowledge, both from networks that produced it and networks that have established its use possibilities and constraints. In any employment arrangement, the contract can be ignored, manipulated in various ways, or ascribed different forms of power. Thus, no entity has an essential existence outside a given network. Nothing is given in the order of things, but all performs itself into existence. Finally, however stable and entrenched it may appear, no network is immutable. Continuous effort is required to hold it together, to bolster the breakages and counter the subterfuges. Counter-networks are constantly springing up that challenge existing networks. Laminated pictures and laminating machines, for example, are becoming rarer in schools in certain contexts as virtual graphics and smartboards gradually replace plasticized pictures.

A useful approach to understanding how translation works in networks is Latour's (2005b) distinction of mediators and intermediaries. These are things that circulate through a network and perform particular functions. In some early ANT analyses, they were referred to singularly as tokens. An intermediary simply transports another force or meaning, without acting on it to change it. The paintbrushes in a school's art classroom, the sign directing all visitors to check in to the office, the university's calendar of dates, all can be intermediaries helping the network to translate entities to perform particular roles. A mediator, on the other hand, also circulates through the network but can transform, distort and modify the meaning in the elements it is to conduct. A particular pedagogical practice, a professional's learning plan, a blog, a cell phone, an achievement award or anything that creates possibilities and occurrences for connections can be a mediator. Latour notes that there are endless numbers of mediators at work in any network and that each can become complex, leading in multiple directions which will modify the contradictory accounts attributed to its role. Sometimes a mediator turns into an intermediary that then must be accounted for by more work, usually by mobilizing more mediators. An example would be any process or piece of equipment that becomes institutionalized and black-boxed in ways that prevent tinkering and experimentation. Similarly, an intermediary can break down and become a complex mediator, as when the paintbrushes create graffiti on the school wall or the 'visitors only' sign is challenged to become a focal point symbolizing elitist exclusion. As Latour suggests, it is this constant uncertainty over the intimate nature of entities that refuses complete stabilization or reified representation of a network. Things that appear durable are not. It is only through the effectiveness of translation practices that they can become so, at least, temporarily.

In summary, ANT's notion of translation helps to unpick practices, processes and precepts to trace how things come to be. Translation focuses on what actually happened/is happening at each of the micro-connections among heterogeneous things that are holding together to form what sometimes appears to be an immutable pattern, or an object with properties. It is for this reason that in early ANT analyses translation was enacted as a form of heterogeneous engineering. In education, translation provides a new language and a richly materialized conception to intervene more precisely, more honestly, within the messiness and multiplicity that make up those processes that we refer to as learning and teaching, curriculum and pedagogy, educational implementation, reform and evaluation. We shall have more to write about some of the different elements of translation in later chapters.

Networks – how they grow and what they are not

In ANT-ish terms, a network is an assemblage of materials brought together and linked through processes of translation that perform a particular function. A network can continue to extend itself as more entities become connected to it. It often stabilizes dynamic events and negotiations into a black box that becomes durable. A textbook or an educational article, for example, each bring together, frame, select and freeze in one form a whole series of meetings, voices, explorations, conflicts, possibilities explored and discarded. Both are in a form that appears seamless and given, concealing the many negotiations of the network that produced it. A textbook or article can circulate also across vast spaces, gathering allies, shaping thoughts and actions and thus creating new networks, as we hope will be the case with this book. The more allies and connections, the stronger the network becomes. Law (1999: 7) explains that in a network 'elements retain their spatial integrity by virtue of their position in a set of links or relations. Object integrity, then is not about a volume within a large Euclidean volume. It is rather about holding patterns of links stable'.

This network ontology is particularly useful for enabling rich analyses of contexts, which have become increasingly important in educational studies of learning, pedagogy and curriculum. 'Formal' learning is still differentiated from 'informal' learning in terms of the institutional setting. Professional learning is understood to be embedded in particular situated environments and practices. Children's learning is understood to vary according to the class size, community expectations, resources, youth subcultures, and so on. However, contexts are not made up of fixed places and distances as though spaces were essentialized containers in which humans move about (Edwards *et al.* 2009a). Instead, contexts such as schools, lecture halls and workplaces are performed and continually shaped through the folds and overlaps of material practices. These folds and overlaps are very much about network relations. Indeed, human geographers have long worked with ANT concepts to understand space as a multiplicity of entities and the fluid, simultaneous, multiple networks of relations among them. Notions from ANT have led geographers to explore the effects produced by different fluid spatial assemblages, including the ways that even taken for granted contextual categories like 'nature', from garden plants to wildlife animals, are actually produced through intricate relations among humans and things (Whatmore 2002, Hitchings 2003, Murdoch 2006). In the process, they have helped to critique and extend – to transgress – the concepts upon which they have drawn. Thus, Ingold (2007), an anthropologist, has argued for the concept of meshwork, as an alternative to that of network, where threads and traces are more significant than nodes and connectors. There is a sense, therefore, of the possible limitations of the network metaphor in ANT, to which we need to be alert.

Power is central to any understanding of space and context translated through networks. Bosco (2006) credits ANT for drawing attention to how highly diverse different entities emerge and become positioned through these relations, and how they come to enact different forms of power. ANT can also trace how assemblages may solidify certain relations of power in ways that continue to affect movements and identities. The sedimentation of power relations in educational spaces and their continuing effects are ubiquitous. One only has to consider the university lecture hall with its large front stage, giant screen, windowless semi-darkness, wheelchair access limited to designated spaces and fixed seats facing the front to see how particular forms of knowledge, learning practices and identity are produced. But how was the lecture hall produced? It is not natural. It was made through a series of practices that sedimented over time, extending from medieval universities and continually modified as new technologies afford novel ways to transmit and amplify information. And yet, a lecture hall filled with students is a mass of shifting humanity, dropping books, crackling wrappers, dozing off, texting messages, nodding rhythmically to iPod tunes. There are dozens of translations which recreate the space and the power relations that constitute it. Nespor's (1994) study of the differences in behaviour and curricula between physics and business students at a university, described in Chapter 3, examines the ways that architecture interacts with particular codified knowledge to order flows of action, people and things, constituting space in fundamentally different ways.

How does a network actually grow? One suggestion offered in ANT's early years by Callon (1986), in a much cited and critiqued conception, framed networks assembling and extending themselves through 'moments' of translation. These moments are not sequential, although they lend themselves to be taken up in this manner. Callon proposed that a network, or at least some types of networks, entails *problematization*. Here, something tries to establish itself as an 'obligatory passage point' that frames an idea, intermediary or problem and related entities in particular ways. Other entities are attracted or invited to this framing, detach themselves from their existing networks and negotiate their connection and role in the emerging new network. Callon referred to this as the moment of *interessement*, which not only selects those entities to be included but also, importantly, those to be excluded. Interessment 'confirms (more or less completely) the validity of the problematization and the alliances it implies' (Callon 1986: 209–10). Those entities to be included experience enrolment in the network relations, the process whereby they become engaged in new identities and behaviours. Enrolment:

> designates the device by which a set of interrelated roles is defined and attributed to actors who accept them ... To describe enrolment is thus to describe the group of multilateral negotiations, trials of strength and tricks that accompany the interessements and enable them to succeed.
>
> (Callon 1986: 211)

The moment of *mobilization* is when the network becomes sufficiently durable that its translations are extended to other locations and domains. Two examples of educational research working with these moments of translation include Luck's (2008) tracing of technological implementation that wrought massive pedagogical change across a multi-campus Australian university, and Clarke's (2002) analysis of the mobilization of a UK literacy policy across disparate disciplinary fields and communities. We will discuss both in greater detail in Chapters 5 and 7.

Critiques of the moments of translation have centred on problematic applications of Callon's ideas as a fixed model which tends to freeze and distort the complexity it was intended to liberate. Rather than being used to tease out the multiple forms of negotiation in the translation of a network, the moments are used somewhat mechanistically as a pre-given heuristic framework. This is undoubtedly as true in educational research as it has been in other fields of social science. However, as we will come to later in the book, there also exist educational studies showing the utility of Callon's moments of translation in illuminating how some networks become so durable and apparently powerful in education, exerting influence across far-flung geographic spaces and time periods.

One problem with this network conception is what and where one should focus in conducting educational research. Much has been made of the invocation to follow the actors in conducting research with ANT. Indeed, many of the studies draw upon ethnography and ethnomethodology to provide rich empirical case studies (for example, Law 1994, Latour 1996). However, if all things in a given network are simultaneously linked to multiple networks and have been created through other networks that brought them into presence, which themselves constitute layers and layers of networks, there is no immediately identifiable or justifiable object of inquiry. Miettinen (1999) makes this point in his critique of ANT, arguing that the network ontology is infinite and therefore unworkable for researchers. However, for Strathern (1996) and others, this is simply a question of where to 'cut the network'. The critical issue is that wherever one puts boundaries around a particular phenomenon to trace its network relations, there is a danger of both privileging that network and rendering invisible its multiple supports and enactments.

Critiques of certain ANT studies have noted, for example, a predilection to focus on the most powerful or most visible networks, or to simply reproduce network participants' views of their reality (Lee and Brown 1994, Hassard *et al.* 1999). A related danger is that representations of networks are themselves concrete, implying the realities to be far more stable and durable than shifting socio-material relations ever can be. And the familiar issues of reflexivity are no less problematic in ANT accounts. They can themselves objectify networks as something produced solely in the eye of the researcher, and simultaneously forget to paint the researcher's representations into the portrayal of network translations, leaving the entire analysis in control of the researchers. In other words, ANT performs ANT as a network effect through its own practices and translations. This not only turns a supposedly heterogeneous, symmetrical perspective into a decidedly human centred one, but also pretends to be capturing uncertainty and complex messiness in what is in effect a predetermined account. McLean and Hassard (2004) raise a number of issues of representation, including ethnocentricity in ANT's attempts to represent other times and places, indeed other non-humans, using only the tools of the present. So, in cutting the network to choose a focus for study, ANT researchers confront McLean and Hassard's (2004: 516) challenge:

> to produce accounts that are sophisticated yet robust enough to negate the twin charges of symmetrical absence or symmetrical absurdity ... to understand the paradoxical situations in which ANT researchers find themselves in conducting field studies and producing accounts, notably in respect of notions of power, orderings and distributions.

In ANT's early years, the term network was employed to suggest both flow and clear points of connection among the heterogeneous entities that became assembled to perform particular practices and processes (Latour and Woolgar 1987, Latour and Woolgar 1979). However, with the proliferation of technological network systems, to say nothing of the concomitant ubiquity of the network metaphor to represent globalization and social capital, the term itself has become problematic. The notion of a network has the potential, for

example, to suggest fixed points, flat linear chains, enclosed pipelines and ossi-
fied tracks. As Frankham (2006) points out, educators have particular reason
for caution when networks are often invoked to represent idealized learning
communities that are homogenous, apolitical and closed in ways that prohibit
dissension, discontinuity and difference.

Writings associated with ANT (Mol and Law 1994) have, therefore, explored
alternate metaphors of regions and fluid spaces to supplement that of networks
to approach the complexity of socio-material events and avoid imposing a linear network model on the ineffable and imminent. Some have explored ways
of retaining notions of network by refusing pipeline associations and showing
diverse shapes and forms that a network can assume. Indeed, Latour (1999a:
16) originally intended 'network' to mean 'a series of transformations – translations, transductions'. Networks are simply webs that grow through connections,
and can be envisioned as ephemeral and rhizomatic in nature. The connections
which have lots of spaces between them can be thick and thin, rigid and limp,
close and distant, dyadic and multiple, material and immaterial. Czarniawska and
Hernes (2005) propose that we talk of action nets rather than networks to avoid
the sense of inevitability and lockdown that 'network' seems to imply for some.
Murdoch (1998), for example, argues that in some networks the actors and
intermediaries are provisional and divergent, the norms are hard to establish, the
network standards are frequently compromised, and various components of the
network continue to negotiate variable coalitions that cause it to appear in ever-
changing shapes. However, there are also tightly ordered, stable and prescriptive
networks where translations are perfectly accomplished, entities are effectively
aligned and one speaks for the entire whole despite the heterogeneous character
of the participant entities. In education, Nespor (1994) points out that this is
especially true. Conventions of classroom life, teaching practices and processes of
curriculum implementation and testing circulate in deep trenches in often highly
prescriptive networks. The inequities and exclusions characterizing these conventions have proven notoriously difficult to interrupt and reconfigure.

For all of these reasons, we wish to retain, and perhaps even reclaim, the
term network in exploring the socio-material complexities of educational life.
This does not necessitate imposing a linear network ontology on the ceaseless
dynamic immanence of pedagogy and curriculum, teaching and learning and
knowledge generation that always exceeds and escapes representation. Perhaps it
is helpful to think of working with network readings, understanding networks as
diverse in shape, strength and substance. Here, network signifies fluid complex
associations with distinct internal points of connection achieved through processes of translation. These can be complete, partial, ongoing, conflicted, delayed
or imminent. In this way, we hope to show, during the course of this book, that
ANT's network readings can help researchers to respond to important questions
in education in different ways, to ask different forms of question and engage in
different types of questioning.

Network effects – agency, power, identity and knowledge

An overriding insight of ANT-ish interventions, whether one accepts network metaphors and translation activities or not, is that all things, as well as all persons, knowledge and locations, are relational *effects*. A teacher, for example, is not a distinct entity that pre-exists her activities in a particular school, gathering children in a reading circle, collecting field trip money and downloading notes on the industrial revolution for tomorrow's class. Her 'teacheriness' is not given in the order of things but is produced in the materially heterogeneous relations of these activities. The teacher is an effect of the timetable that places her in a particular room with particular students, in a class designated as Social Studies 6, amongst textbooks and class plans and bulletin boards and stacks of graded papers with which she interacts, teaching ideas and readings she has accumulated, and particular relationships that have emerged with this year's class of children. In the pedagogical practices of her work, she is a 'knowing location'. In one example, McGregor (2004: 366) traces how the teacher as a knowing location is produced in science classrooms, through:

> the laboratory, with its electricity points, water and gas lines. The Bunsen burners and flasks set up by the technicians, who have also ordered and prepared the necessary chemicals according to the requisition sheet, the textbooks and worksheets that the students are using. Mobilized also are the teacher's experience and education.

This knowing location is also affected by the networks of activity that composed and timetabled the student group in a particular way and allocated the teaching assistants to the class. To enact students and teachers as knowing locations rather than as individual subjects begins to reframe how we intervene in educational issues.

This knowing effect is acted upon not just by material objects and intentions imminently present, but also by things at a distance. From the central office, the school buzzer controls when the class starts and ends, and frequent announcements over the PA system interrupt the students' conversations. On the teacher's desk is her plan for this class, prepared that morning as she checked the prescribed curriculum guide to see what objectives she could work into the day's activities. The computer screen on her desk presents the database on which she must enter names of absent students, daily assignment grades and anecdotal notes about student behaviour. This database was constructed with such categories in the school district office, where the information that she enters will be aggregated and assessed in ways that link her as teacher–surveillor into part of a much larger network. The textbooks in the classroom are enactments of knowledge that came into presence in a location and set of network relations far removed from this particular teacher gathering her students. These networks of knowledge bound into a book have travelled here and are now circulating in this classroom. The book acts materially as a thing that must be distributed, collected, stored and hopefully saved from graffiti, pedagogically as a sequence of content that stimulates particular learning activities from teacher and students, and epistemologically as an object of knowledge holding together a set of perspectives, assumptions and relations among pieces of information.

These things that act at a distance – buzzer, database, textbooks – are what Latour (1987) originally called *immutable mobiles.* Immutable mobiles are only visible within a particular network of relations. They can be silent, ignored, or overridden by other active objects. However, they have developed enough solidity to be able to move about and still hold their relations in place. In effect, they function as the delegates of these other networks, extending the power of these networks by moving into new spaces and working to translate entities to behave in particular ways. Law and Singleton (2005) explain that whether an object is more or less abstract (a pedagogical idea compared to an instrument) is not the point. The key feature is that it is identified, has reality, in particular networks of historical, cultural, behavioural relations that make it visible. However, immutable mobiles often are not terribly immutable, but require a good deal of effort to hold them together. The teacher's database, a massive set of records that computes, measures and directs the students' bodies throughout the district, also directs the teacher's practice, compelling her to count students and related objects (homework assignments, lunch money) at the class beginning. However, the computer often freezes when she is hurrying back and forth to it while settling kids into the class and sorting out their myriad problems and jostlings, so she may jot down the information and try to enter it later, or not.

Some immutable mobiles become what Latour (1987) has called *obligatory points of passage.* These are central assemblages through which all relations in the network must flow at some time. The teacher's curriculum guide functions as an obligatory point of passage. Her lesson plans, her choice of texts and assignments all must at least appear to be aligned with it, and are at least partially translated by its prescriptions. Thus, this teacher's knowledge and activity, along with all the other Social Studies 6 teachers and classes, the consultants that assist them, the administrators that supervise them and perhaps the textbook publishers preparing materials for them, must pass through this obligatory point, this curriculum guide, to form their own networks. The curriculum guide itself is an effect, of course, not only of the materially heterogeneous networks of people and things that worked to bring it into existence but also the historical and political networks that produced the conceptual content it draws on, the public interests it tries to satisfy, and the professional practices that call for something called a curriculum guide.

The network effects that produce these immutable mobiles and in particular, things and locations that become obligatory points of passage, are important dynamics in the power relations circumscribing education. The circulation and effects of these things can assemble powerful centres that accumulate increasingly wider reaches of networks to hold them in place. *Delegation,* the ability to act at a distance through things, is one way that power circulates through a network. How fast these immutable mobiles move, their fidelity or how immutable they really are as they move through diverse networks, and what barriers they encounter or damage they sustain to their internal network relations, are questions worthy of exploration in different educational interests. *Scale* is another important area for consideration. In fact, as Law and Hetherington (2003) note, if space is performed, if it is an effect of heterogeneous material relations, just as things are, people and obligatory point of passages, then distance is also performed. What makes near and far, here or there, is not a static separation between two points that is travelled by something. Instead, these concepts of distance are created by relations that are always changing, as the introduction of the internet into daily life has made abundantly clear. When multiple points are linked together through actor–networks, the concepts of micro and macro thus do not hold. The teacher planning her morning class and the final meeting of the curriculum guide developers simply represent different parts of a network that have become extended though space as well as time. There do not exist separated spaces of 'local' and 'global', as though these are identifiable and distinct regions. Instead, these are scale effects produced through network relations. A series of intricate links runs among the different enactments of, for example, an educational policy whether visible in OECD documents, school district-wide databases, parent discussions, or a teacher's correction of a student. ANT analyses upend and play with notions of scale, eschewing scale as ontologically distinct layers or regions, in ways that help to penetrate some of the more nuanced and multi-faceted circulations of power in educational practice and knowledge.

For some this is a weakness of ANT. Macro notions of social structure are not comprehensible in ANT logic. When anyone speaks of a system or structure, ANT asks: How has it been compiled? Where is it? Where can I find it? What is holding it together? Soon one sees a number of sites and conduits, and the connections among them. While some have criticized ANT for supposedly failing to address broader social structures of capitalism, racism and class–gender relations in a preoccupation with the local and contingent, ANT commentators reject the dualism of micro and macro locations. There are no supra-structural entities, explains Latour (1999a: 18), because 'big does not mean "really" big or "overall" or "overarching", but connected, blind, local, mediated, related'. These connections among entities can be explained in the same way regardless of what points of the network one chooses to examine. A focus on immediate action, on following the entities and actors and what they do, reveals the extended network forces embedded in and acting upon the everyday. This focus also traces the circulations of entities that continue to alter one another and the networks they act within, as well as the empty spaces between networks.

As much as network relations are useful to trace in these dynamics of delegation, the temptation to collapse all interactions and connections into networks needs to be avoided. While most entities and forces are usefully viewed as effects within an ANT-ish gaze, not all relations that contribute to producing these effects will be networks. There are other types of regions, other kinds of connections, other forms of space and foldings of space that work alongside and through networks (Hetherington and Law 2000). A tendency in educational research is often to focus on relations, as though seeking lines of coherence, causality and connection rather than to acknowledge the incoherence, disparateness and odd alignments of disjuncture. Indeed, as Singleton (1998) argued in her study of a cervical screening programme, the relative stability of certain networks occurs not through their coherences but through their incoherences and ambivalences. An overly narrow preoccupation with network relations speaks to a bias that will inevitable banish from sight some of the more interesting or puzzling messiness of educational phenomena. This is not to downplay the importance of understanding entities and forces as effects; it is to encourage more open and richer explorations of the multiple forms, lines, and textures of materials that come together in different ways, in connections, disconnections, partial connections and non-connections, to produce these effects.

Harman (2009), in the spirit of celebrating and strengthening Latour's 'metaphysics', raises two major critical concerns about Latour's networked relationality. First, that if all things are effects of their present alliances, we cannot explain how change is actually introduced. The future of an actor, argues Harman, cannot be explained by examining only the links causing its enactment in the present. Second, the full present of an actor cannot be explained if we are limited to the alliances trying to articulate it: 'an actor is not identical with whatever it modifies, transforms, perturbs, or creates – but always remains underdetermined by those effects. The effects cannot occur without the object, but the object might well exist without those effects, or perhaps even without *any* effects' (Harman 2009: 186–7). In extending Latour's views towards what he calls an object-oriented philosophy, Harman distinguishes between 'intentional' and real objects, and focuses attention on the nature of relations: what links objects if not more objects?

In educational research, Sørensen (2007) also focuses critical attention on the types of relations that link objects. Her concern, however, is not to reconcile Latour with metaphysics but to theorize materiality, which she maintains is not adequately explained in ANT's relational views. She works with ANT to examine three educational occasions, showing how the pattern of material relations in each varies according to the temporality of each. A blackboard in a classroom activity, for instance, exercises a 'regional materiality' that is atemporal. In contrast, a distinct temporal horizon enacts a 'networked materiality' in her example of a school celebration of a bed-loft built in the classroom. The celebration brings together parents and headmaster with children, snacks and a song in one event, which is also networked with the substances and activities constructing the bed-loft and the children's activities on the loft following the celebration. The materiality is networked, claims Sørensen, but with temporality linked to the lifetime of the bed-loft (as long as no representations of it circulate beyond this materiality, which would constitute a different pattern of material relations). In her third example, learning activities within an online virtual environment have a 'fluid materiality', mediated by ongoing transformation in a temporality that was extended and continuous.

Returning to the teacher as a network effect, as a knowing location, what of her agency and subjectivity? She is planning lessons, choosing particular pedagogical approaches, deciding whether to solve the myriad classroom problems that emerge in this way or that. How does ANT avoid casting her as determined and recognize her own force exercised through her pedagogical participation? How does ANT understand the sources and effects of her intentions, her desires, and the meanings she makes of her pedagogical encounters with students? Certain critiques of ANT have accused it of failing to appreciate what is fundamentally human and subjective in flows of action. This suggests that perhaps ANT ought to modify its stance of radical symmetry to admit that humans are different because they make symbolic meaning of events and exert intentional action (Murdoch 1998). However, ANT's ontology of folding and unfolding networks is incommensurate with any agency/structure dualism. ANT does not conceptualize agency as an individuated source of empowerment rooted in conscious intentions that mobilize action. Instead, ANT focuses on the circulating forces that get things done through a network of elements acting upon one another.

> Action is not done under the full control of consciousness; action should rather be felt as a node, a knot, and a conglomerate of many surprising sets of agencies that have to be slowly disentangled. It is this venerable source of uncertainty that we wish to render vivid again in the odd expression of actor–network.
>
> (Latour 2005b: 44)

In this way, ANT understandings are reminiscent of certain post-structuralist views of subjectivity which understand the subject to be entangled in a web of relationships and practices, and agency to be a flow of forces in which the subject is continuously performed and performative. As Butler (1992: 13) writes, the 'subject is neither a ground nor a product, but the permanent possibility of a certain resignifying process', a process in which a subject participates by recognizing how it is being constituted. From an ANT perspective, what appears to be the teacher's agency is an effect of different forces, including actions, desires, capacities and connections that move through her, as well as the forces exerted by the texts and technologies in all educational encounters. Yet, while networks and other flows circulate through the teacher's practices, her own actions, desires, and so on are not determined by the network, but emerge through the myriad translations that are negotiated among all the movements, talk, materials, emotions and discourses making up the classroom's everyday encounters. Agency is directly related to the heterogeneity of actors in networked relations. McGregor (2004: 367) concludes from her study of teachers in Science education, 'knowing is a relational effect where pedagogy is a collective accomplishment and learning a situated activity'. Within such a view, it no longer makes sense to focus educational reform upon (re)training the individual teacher and her practices alone. Instead, researchers can attempt to disentangle the network(s) of connections and other relations that together produce particular effects in classroom activity or children's engagement and learning.

Similarly, learning in ANT-ish interventions is not a matter of mental calculation or changes in consciousness. Instead, any changes we might describe as learning – new ideas, innovations, changes in behaviour, transformation – emerge through the effects of relational interactions, in various kinds of networks that are entangled with one another, that may be messy and incoherent, and that are spread across time and space. As Fox (2005) explains in analysing learning processes in higher education, competence or knowledge from an ANT perspective is not a latent attribute of any one element or individual, but a property of some actions rather than others as a network becomes enacted into being. The process of enactment, this interplay of force relations among technology, things and changes in knowledge at every point in the network, is a continuing struggle. This struggle is learning. This conceptualization offers a way to think about education that steps outside of the enculturation projects that typify pedagogies ranging from the emancipatory to the transmissive. Regardless of ideological persuasion or educative purpose, these projects impose some future ideal on present human subjects and activities, with the objective of developing learners' potential to become knowledgeable, civic-minded, self-aware, and so forth. However, as ANT enacts all things as emerging through their interconnections in networks, where their nature and behaviours are never inherent but are produced through continuous interactions and negotiations as they work upon one another, there can be no conception of 'future potential'. This is a powerful counter-narrative to the conventional view of developmentalism that dominates the pedagogical gaze, positioning learners in continual deficit and learning activities as preparation for some imagined ideal. ANT's ontology forces attention on all the material work that is too easily swept away by such neat developmental teleologies.

> We cannot say that an oak tree is contained potentially in the acorn, since this would spare us the labour of following the series of risky transformations by which the acorn and each of its analogous successors seek their respective fortunes.
>
> (Harman 2007: 40)

In its insistence on attending to these minute interactions, ANT analyses challenge many assumptions underpinning certain educational conceptions of development, learning, agency, identity, knowledge and teaching. They make visible the rich assortments of things at play in educational events and how they are connected. ANT's examination of the different processes and moments at work in translation, in particular, extends beyond a simple recognition that artefacts and humans are connected in social and cognitive activity. ANT's main contribution is to 'transform the social from what was a surface, a territory, a province of reality, into a circulation' (Latour 1999a: 17), where time and space are understood to result from particular interactions of things. The conception of symmetry unlocks a preoccupation with the human, the intersubjective and meaning, and refuses a rigid separation between material and immaterial, human and non-human objects. In tracing what things do and how they came to be, ANT offers a method for picking apart a priori categories and structures in education, some of which appear to exert power across far-flung distances and temporal periods. ANT's notions of immutable mobiles, how they are enacted, held together, and work to disguise their precarious mutability, offer an approach to understand and challenge the strategies of powerful networks in education that work to authorize, control, compel and measure practices and knowledge. For analysing politics and policy in educational research, Nespor (2002: 376) argues that ANT raises important questions about 'how and in what forms people, representations and artefacts move, how they are combined, where they get accumulated, and what happens when they are hooked up with other networks already in motion'. ANT analyses can reveal not only the shifting locus of power, how different actors are dominant at different times within different networks (Hitchings 2003), but also shows the nuances and ambivalences within this performance of power. Perhaps, as Neyland (2006: 45) puts it, ANT's most important contribution to education is providing an entry point to better understand:

> mundane masses (the everyday and the humdrum that are frequently overlooked), assemblages (description of things holding together), materiality (that which does or does not endure), heterogeneity (achieved diversity within an assemblage), and flows/fluidity (movement without necessary stability).

It is to an exploration of the mundane masses, assemblages, materiality, heterogeneity and fluidity that the rest of this book is dedicated.

Chapter 2

Knowledge, innovation and knowing in practice

At the heart of educational concerns – in schools, training centres, universities, community agencies, colleges, laboratories, policy boardrooms and work organizations alike – are knowledge practices. ANT joins the many contemporary perspectives of knowledge and knowledge production that treat knowing as situated, embodied and distributed. ANT approaches challenge any simple notion of knowledge as a codified, identifiable commodity, as a 'body of knowledge', as 'evidence'. Indeed, one strand of ANT emerged through the study of the ways in which the messiness of laboratory work was translated through inscription in texts into representations of neatly bounded experiments with clear methods, where the activities necessary to produce such texts were completely excised from their content (Latour 1987, Latour and Woolgar 1979). Knowledge is not universal or stable; nor can it be restricted to conceptual cognition, or limited to subjective constructions through meaning-centred interpretations of the world, as is the case with much interpretative research.

In ANT analyses, there is no 'out-there' reality separated from an 'in-my-head' interpretation of this reality and an 'in-the-book' scientific coding of this reality. For ANT writings, knowing is enactment, brought forth and made visible through circulations and connections among things. An object of knowledge – whether it is a mathematical concept to be taught to sixth graders, a new evidence-based medical protocol to be implemented through continuing education, or an academic monograph – is held together by a network of connections that must be continually performed to make the knowledge visible and alive. Knowing does not arise simply from certain institutionalized practices of education or the cognitive activities of individuals. In this chapter, we will explore the ways in which these ideas are played out in various studies of knowing practices conducted in schools and post-secondary institutions as well as in professional contexts and workplaces more broadly.

Such understandings of knowledge are particularly useful at a time when continuous and lifelong learning are promoted in all sectors, increased production of knowledge for the global economy is a naturalized pursuit in policy, and knowledge exchange in a web-linked social order has opened difficult tensions around knowledge authority, use, convergence and ownership. Questions about what is knowledge, who produces it, how one can have ownership of it, and how it becomes generated and circulated are hotly contested. For educational research, ANT-ish appreciations for things and enactments in the generation and circulation of knowing afford useful questions about learning processes, expertise, competency, creativity and innovation. Classroom learning activities, for example, can be traced to appreciate the knowing practices that emerge through heterogeneous combinations of discursive and material things with various relations and joint actions. These knowing practices include the mundane and the weird and involve lumpy conflicts. These are the bits that Mol and Law (2002) describe as ironed smooth or made invisible altogether in strictly sociological or psychological accounts of learning that focus on meanings. The inscriptions reduce, simplify and smooth, denying the work that goes into enacting them precisely as such. In the process, they intervene to produce the very 'out-thereness' they set themselves as representing. In other words, they enact what they take to be natural. If the world is messy, how are accounts of the world in research tidy? With an ANT sensibility, expertise is challenged to recognize its own mechanics, the inclusions and exclusions wrought by material networks of action that produce certain competencies and ignore other knowing enactments.

In its conceptions of knowledge and its approaches to unpeeling the ways knowledge, knowledge objects, innovation and related identities are enacted and held together, ANT opens important new possibilities for educational research. Woolgar *et al.* (2009: 19–21) summarize these contributions within the context of science and technology studies (STS):

> (1) a propensity to cause trouble, provoke, be awkward; (2) a tendency to work through difficult conceptual issues in relation to specific empirical cases, deflating grandiose theoretical concepts and claims (and even some ordinary ones); (3) an emphasis on the local, specific and contingent in relation to the genesis and use of science and technology; (4) caution about the unreflexive adoption and deployment of standard social science lexicons (e.g. power, culture, meaning, value); (5) reflexive attention to the (frequently unexplicated) notions of our audiences, value and utility ... Consistent with the premise that users are performed, enacted, and configured ... for a whole range of cultural artefacts, this style of STS maintains an active interest in the transposition of social science research across sometimes challenging social-organizational boundaries. This we construe as a radical intellectual challenge, not merely a political preference or a practical obligation.

However, similar observations can be made of ANT. The studies highlighted in this chapter show the fundamental importance of the shift to viewing knowledge as enactment, and tracing the different knowledges that jostle together in the enactment of a concept, an identity or a practice.

Knowledge in the everyday – the importance of the mundane

In everyday practice, within the practices of learning enacted by children in a classroom or the practices of workers in contexts ranging from a construction site to a surgical theatre, forms of knowledge are circulating and being enacted. In some ways then, the everyday is pedagogical, even if not always educational. Some call this competence. However, the danger is to assume that competence resides in the individual or group of human subjects who are participating together in an occasion. This assumption overlooks the important types of connection among them. A particularly interesting examination of what everyday knowledge looks like and how it comes to be performed was offered in a study of safety competence in the workplace by Gherardi and Nicolini (2000). They studied how cement laying workers learn and practice safety skills, using ANT to follow how knowledge was translated at every point as it moved through a network. Safety knowledge was embedded in safety manuals, protective equipment that workers were required to wear and use, signs reinforcing safety rules, and inspectors with lists of specific safety practices.

However, within this network, safety knowledge was continually being modified or even transgressed. For example, one worker would show another how to adapt a new safety procedure to make a task easier, or two together would adapt a particular tool to solve a problem, depending on who was watching. The inspection is a negotiation of both the visible objects ('making the site look in order' so as not to attract the critical attention of the inspector, but leaving certain minimal details so that the inspector may have something to write about) and the meanings of what is visible ('Inspector: This parapet is out of order ... it's too low. Site foreman: You must be joking ... Aw come on, its five centimetres' (Gherardi and Nicolini 2000: 342)). Deadlines and weather conditions caused different safety knowledge and different standards of evaluation to be performed. The equipment itself and the crew's culture embedded or 'grounded' a history of use possibilities and constraints that influenced the safety skills performed by those who interacted with the equipment. No skill or knowledge had a recognizable existence outside its use within the network. Every transaction was enacted within an overall bureaucratic discourse of safety control and accountability, where prescribed knowledge (such as rules and mandated protective equipment) was continually reproduced and renegotiated, and where accidents were construed as individual disobedience.

The role of things in this circulation of knowledge is particularly important. For example, in a safety inspired design improvement for a cement mixer, a disk was attached over the spokes of the mixer's steering wheel to avoid the worker's arm becoming caught should it spin (Gherardi and Nicolini 2000). This required modification in practices of using the wheel, as well as changes in the safety manuals and instruction provided. The new disk, as well as the mixer to which it was attached, represented networks of experimentation – innovative knowledge production, testing, prototyping, marketing, etc. – that had become solidified in the instrument. We could think of the mixer and disk as an immutable mobile that would now travel to different construction sites and change practice. However, implementation of this wheel required compliance from the industry to purchase it and the workers to use it, which may or may not occur. Workers could remove the attachment and, in fact, some more experienced workers did this while others altered their practice to adapt to the new safer mixer. The processes of innovation were translated as they entered the network, something we can imagine happening in education institutions as, for instance, new curricula or technologies are introduced.

The practice of the 'work-around' may also offer a mundane example of such spaces in which knowing is enacted. A work-around occurs when a worker is confronted by a technology that is constraining in some form, and finds a way to work around it by exercising some form of discretion or resistance to subvert or redeploy it. Pollock (2005) argues that if we understand user and technology to be each well bounded, the user role is sometimes tightly defined as if scripted, and users will tend to work against it. Increasingly, technologies are designed to be flexible, with the anticipation of work-arounds. Pollack offers an ANT reading of how workers shape and customize the final design for a computer system. This process may be inventive, but creates ambiguities in user–producer relations as technological difficulties require local resolution. The result is both multiple contrasting modes of use, sometimes conflictual, as well as new inter-reliances and needs for local resources as people create and share technical solutions. For Pollack, in these blurred and potentially inventive spaces, technologies are enacted through practices of designing and using that are not necessarily designated to particular groups and individuals. The result is increasingly confused networks filled with tensions and issues about who has responsibility for what.

In ANT readings, competence is 'not a latent intrinsic capability or potentiality belonging to an entity, but a property of some actions rather than others, as judged by knowledgeable witnesses' (Fox 2000: 861). Competence is an effect, not the driving force for making things happen. It is a knowing-in-practice produced by a particular mix of action with things. Elements that interact in the network of knowledge circulation to produce an effect of competence are not distinguished according to which is active and which passive, but by how things react and resist one another. Anything that appears to be passive, like the wheel disk, is in fact a package of sedimented knowledge, and a force in its own right. It was produced through histories of innovation (research, design, development), prompted by other networks such as safety discourses focused on reducing accidents and market conditions promoting competitive new products. The disk affords a series of tangible, material possibilities. Individuals encountering the disk act upon themselves to accommodate the action required to operate the wheel, comply with a supervisor's or fellow worker's gaze, or perhaps to avoid the threat of accident. In this way, 'learning ... is seen as the outcome of a process of local struggle and that struggle is many faceted involving the self acting upon itself, as well as upon others and upon the material world' (Fox 2000: 860).

Knowledge is produced and circulated through minute translations at the most mundane levels of everyday activity, even though we tend to focus most on the spectacular or exotic levels: the puzzle solved, the concept understood, the innovation realized, the major decision achieved, the major problem articulated, the most interesting novelty or deviation brought to story. ANT takes us back to the mundane and illuminates how knowledge-making occurs through multiple negotiations and performances that often slip by the researcher's and the educator's gaze. Positioning research to focus on the mundane practices of education may not seem very exotic, but working this through ANT certainly makes the familiar strange.

For example, Latour (1999b) studied a botanist, geographer and pedologist, who were analysing the soil of the Boa Vista in the Amazon, tracing the practical everyday work of scientists. He showed how most of it consisted in the most tedious details of gathering samples, counting and labelling them, comparing, boxing, storing, transporting and recording them, observing and interpreting these details and eventually producing a report. Furthermore, much of this work was woven with puzzling or frustrating incidents, periods of waiting and boredom, errors and spoilage that had to be managed, backtracking, tentative deviations and dead ends. Latour was showing not only how scientists' knowledge production is grounded in the mundane of practical activity, but also how this activity is ordered through a sequence of tasks, each with particular methods and apparatuses. The technical knowledge embedded in these methods and instruments directed not only particular actions, but also particular chains of action. These chains produced new knowledge in ways that are already partly circumscribed by things. Further, the new knowledge became stabilized in rather humble objects: the inscription in a logbook comparing a soil sample to a Munsell code chart, a labelled photograph intended to demonstrate a phenomenon, or a published scientific article. These mundane objects of knowledge can be shared, mobilized, and basically stretched out across many associations to take on the power of exotic scientific knowledge.

Studying mundane things and how they are used is not easy, as admitted by Laurier and Philo (2003) in their ANT-inspired research on how workers used cardboard boxes. There are the difficulties of the researchers' own boredom. Selecting a focus among the overwhelming myriad mundane things circulating in any given site is also a challenge.

> Part of our tactic when looking in detail at the activities that happen with really rather dull anonymous cardboard boxes was to wait to see what it would give us of interest, rather than, as Sacks notes, exploiting a kind of thing that might be taken to be interesting already, like a 'big decision' at headquarters.
>
> (Laurier and Philo 2003: 102)

The researchers followed a worker who travelled through her company's differ-ent regional sites to promote branded products. An important part of her job was packing the items into her vehicle each day, which involved warehouse visits to identify, select and sequence boxes of products, then load, select, locate and unload from her vehicle to her visitors. What is particularly interesting about the study is the detailed way in which the worker is followed through all of these transactions with things: boxes that are placed or left open or colour coded in ways to signal next actions; trolleys, lists, packing and unpacking and searching and repacking, dirty hands, the car as a mobile office, the constrictions of the car's storage space, parking meters, and so on. The things themselves, or more particularly, the ways in which the things are laid out, formulate the space as well as the knowledge that emerges in the different spaces through which the worker moves. The worker is continually solving mundane problems of the everyday, working with the action directed by the things as well as the problems they pose. These solutions are the ongoing generation of knowledge that is so often missed in studies of learning.

Further, Laurier and Philo (2003) draw attention to the way the sequence of actions directed by the things, just as in the case of Latour's scientists, focuses the human participant on 'what's next'. Each task proceeded in a particular sequenced arrangement that did not permit a permanent and stable overview. The researchers conclude by showing 'unpacking' as a method for understanding what is embedded in everyday things, untangling a collection not just to make visible what it contains but also what has been left behind. How often, in the study of education, do we detail the mundane things and practices that govern our day-to-day interventions in the world? Education tends to be studied as an exotic practice; its enlightenment translations result in it being enacted as exotic rather than mundane.

In relation to schools and classrooms, Roth (1996: 180) conducted a simi-lar sort of examination to unpack knowledge production and circulation in an elementary science class through the role played by things:

> Science classroom communities are characterized by their knowledge, that is, (a) the material, social, and conceptual resources available to the activities of individual members working alone or collaboratively; and (b) the com-mon, embodied laboratory and discourse practices. By investigating how these different types of knowledge (simple facts, tool-related practices, and intellectual practices) diffuse throughout a classroom and come to be rec-ognized as shared by the students, one can, through this examination of Grade 4–5 children studying an engineering unit, provide empirical evidence for understanding the distributed and situated nature of knowing and learn-ing in school settings.

Roth's study is particularly complex in illustrating at least three levels of knowl-edge-making that are occurring. There is the ongoing knowledge-in-use of everyday classroom practice, alongside the knowledge generation that each child is being encouraged to develop as an outcome of participation in the pedagogic activities of the classroom network. There is also the researcher's knowledge generation produced from interaction with these networks. Roth discusses the everyday challenges of studying a classroom with a commitment to including all actors and nodes being translated in the various networks, as well as their simultaneous membership within multiple networks. All this, while remaining alert to the networks and invisibilities imposed by the researcher's presence and ordering activities of noticing and observation. None of these knowledges emerging and circulating to constitute that setting and its subjects is more mundane than any other.

Roth's team used video to record the children's activities. Directing the focus of those cameras was a careful consideration made each day of who, what, where, when and how to videotape:

> I wanted to collect data that (a) documented practices (e.g., discourse, tool use, problem solving) and resources (e.g., tools, products of children's work, concepts implemented); (b) showed the same students over longer periods of time; (c) represented a broad range of student abilities, interests, and attitudes; and (d) refuted or supported emerging hypotheses about shared resources and practices in an elementary science classroom.
>
> (Roth 1996: 192)

The class was learning triangle principles of engineering by creating structures. Among the many materials being employed, Roth became interested in how glue guns began to focus the activity. At first, there was only one glue gun and one student who knew how to use it – who monopolized it while the other students used different means to fix joints in their structures – and did the gluing for those who wanted to glue their joints. It was four weeks before another student brought a glue gun, despite the evidence that the glued joints were more stable and durable than joints held with pins or tape. Quickly following that, glue guns began to appear as more students brought them, and decided to learn gluing practices. The proliferation of glue guns necessitated reorganizing of the classroom space to accommodate new groupings of students, the need for electric plugs, safety measures and containment of glue mess. In fact, a range of gluing practices developed as the students solved new problems. Hot glue began to circumscribe the projects as it became ubiquitous, to the point where students were unsuccessfully trying to use it on materials like spaghetti, or solving structural problems by simply using glue on available materials rather than the triangle formulas that the activity was supposed to teach in the first place.

Overall, Roth's examination showed that the knowledge emergence – in this case, technological invention and new cultural norms learned and further developed by the children – occurred through a series of mundane translations with things. The network was created because it could sustain and propagate accomplishments that were desired by all the participants. The glue gun became the dominant technology because it was flexible enough to satisfy students' various needs (for strong joints, faster assembly, or more aesthetic product) and could bring together all other necessary entities (glue sticks, power outlets, pedagogy, etc.).

Gough (2004: 258) is another researcher who urges educators to look more closely at the 'banal structures and simplistic textual practices' of education. As a science educator, his interest is in the interpenetration of humans and things in the everyday. He suggests that we should begin by unpacking mundane everyday tasks to trace the seemingly infinite interconnectivities among things and people that hold together any action in a particular place and moment. Making a cup of coffee, for example, connects simple human actions with water from a tap connected to a reservoir by miles of piping, to an electric kettle plugged into a plastic plate on a tiled wall into a complex grid and flow of electric power, poured into a coffee pot holding together bits of plastic, glass, screws, then to an aluminium mug with Starbucks stamped on it, attached to an arm then lifted to a mouth containing a new dental crown … and so on. Gough draws upon Angus *et al.* (2001: 195) who suggested the need for a 'cyborg pedagogy', engaging students in mapping such myriad details 'between heres and theres, between humans, between humans and non-humans, between non-humans and non-humans'. However, he considers that, while useful, this approach may problematically stop at *tracing* the networks of the 'real', which may only reinforce and entrench our routine interconnections with objects. In other words, it will provide a representation of networks of practice, a learning *about* something, rather than a learning *of* something.

Taking a more direct ANT approach, Gough suggests that pedagogies which invent or imagine new ways to *experiment* with the real and make it move are necessary, where knowledge and practices are to intervene and not simply to represent. Gough begins with the assumption that humans and things are infused with one another in various combinations, an awareness which is important for both educators and students. However, there are always possibilities to open spaces of ambiguity and undecidability, spaces in which new associations and gatherings of technologies, people and materials can be invented or imagined. Gough's encouragement to educators is to begin by enacting stories that propose new fabulations of 'becoming-cyborg' which can subvert fixed knowledge like science texts and open such spaces. Here, knowing becomes more a form of intervening and experimenting than a (re)presenting of facts, and we witness how ANT itself may appear to be exotic but actually has mundane, if important, implications for educational practice and policy. We will develop this further in Chapters 4 and 9.

One world, different perspectives or multiple worlds

It is a commonplace, one repeated by Law and Singleton (2005), that the epistemological issues to do with knowing or knowing well are bound up with the ontological question of what exists. What is, as well as the knowledge of what is, are produced together. Yet, in education there is much emphasis on learning as knowing through (re)presentation. In conventional enactments, it is often suggested by realists and social constructionists that there is one world about which humans can have diverse perspectives. This assumption underpins a certain common form for education, and in so doing enacts what it assumes.

Certain strands of ANT, in particular after-ANT, suggest that while we do have multiple perspectives, we are actually part of multiple worlds within which we dwell. An oft-cited example, discussed further in Chapter 10, is a study conducted by Mol (2002) exploring health professionals' diagnoses of lower limb atherosclerosis. She found that the actual condition, the thing known as artherosclerosis, was performed quite differently in different medical departments within the hospital she studied. Artherosclerosis was not just perceived differently in these environments; it was enacted as different things. How can one transcendent medical concept provide valid unity to these different things? Even the concept as it is represented in a canon of medical knowledge is yet another enactment, another different thing. Mol (2002) argues that these examples illustrate multiple (co-existing) ontologies, and suggests that the practical problem is patching together the different things to achieve some coherence so that a medical intervention can be determined. This coherence of knowledge is also, she points out, an enactment, a make do.

In their study of alcoholic liver disease (ALD), Law and Singleton (2005) also found that this apparently singular thing was conceived, treated and performed differently. They followed the same patient in acute care wards, in community treatment centres, and in private physicians' clinics. They, like Mol, found that this was a case not just of different interpretations, meanings or perceptions. It was a case of different enactments, different *things*, all insisting they were the same thing: more than one and less than many. Furthermore, they found slippage between what was described by the medical professionals and what was enacted as knowledge. For example, all claimed that only strict abstinence would produce recovery from ALD, while all acted as though any reduction in alcohol consumption was better than nothing. Thus, different objects of knowledge (solutions) existed simultaneously.

The educational implications of this are interesting to explore in an era where both problem-based, experiential and inter-professional approaches to professional learning are being encouraged. It becomes a question of the fragile enrolments of multiple ontologies, rather than the stable transcendence into a single ontology. This concept of multiple ontologies is a challenge to much that is familiar in liberal education. The problem of difference in knowledges of the same thing across different regions is not particularly new. However, the dynamics of this difference, its problems and its enactments, become increasingly important to understand as globalizing production processes distribute and attempt to enforce particular standards of knowledge (definitions, competencies, practices, league tables) among vastly different associations. In these assoiacions, knowledge standards are performed alongside competing local knowledges enacting the same thing. Associations can be separated by distance, status (e.g. patients or children, families, bureaucrats, professionals), culture and language (e.g. indigenous and scientific knowledges, or even different professional department cultures). In the field of inter-professional education and practice, the problem of knowledge difference has long been identified. ANT-oriented approaches can help make visible the processes and complexities of these different simultaneous ontologies and the potential of network relations enacted within them.

Multiple ontologies are not equally powerful and they are themselves network effects. What happens when a network of dominant knowledge attempts to control a weaker knowledge that lacks the recognition, resources and supporting networks to negotiate can be referred to as an 'interstanding'. Interstanding points to the possibility, at least for negotiated enactments, of knowledge between ontologies. In an example of knowledge-making about genes and their link to heart disease, Hall (2004) followed multiple, competing strands of knowledge produced from various locations. In this study, a dominant knowledge was enacted by the cardiology consultants and cardiac rehabilitation nurses that heart disease was caused solely by individual behaviour. The lay patients and their families, who were assumed to be unknowledgeable by the professionals, demonstrated very different understandings. Through their words, actions and embodied experiences of the unpredictability of the disease they enacted a heart disease as a genetic disorder. Hall (2004: 317) found that, even when powerful actors, such as a network of health professionals, used every resource at their disposal and attempted translations, they could only ever achieve 'a precarious and temporary outcome of heart disease as non-genetic' in the face of the complexity continually presented by the patients' competing knowledge.

ANT analyses have proven useful in tracing the micro-encounters of public or experiential knowledge with scientific knowledge as sets of practices. In a study of agricultural extension, traditionally an important area of adult education, Coughenour (2003) examined the introduction of no-tillage practices among US farmers. Such development is often approached through a model of external agencies imposing innovative technological knowledge on farmers. In this case, Coughenour (2003) traced the contestations among the knowledge networks of local indigenous farmers, farm advisors, agricultural scientists and farm supply representatives. The process was lengthy and potentially fragile, a case of coalitions gradually forming through the discovery of certain common goals as well as some congruence in the technological developments of the separate innovation networks. The process was also enhanced by extending the local network through extra local linkages that enrolled actors and mobilized networks well beyond those in the same region, while maintaining the power of the immediate networks and the importance of individual participants as innovators. Network participants – not just farmers, but scientists and everyone else involved – eventually had to allow themselves to become translated into new relationships between farming and soils. These new relations also translated their former roles and reputations as farmers or professionals. In these ways, the new no-till cropping practices developed through reconstruction of both indigenous and professional knowledges. This entailed neither a blending of the two, nor a colonialist attempt by one to dominate the other, but a dwelling in different ontologies.

The different locations or associations in which different knowledges of the same thing are performed are perhaps most easily interlinked by information and communication technologies (ICTs). In a fascinating study of the new remote consultation practices that link cardiac specialists through ICTs, researchers adopted ANT approaches to trace what they call a 'system of fragmented knowledge' (SFK) (Bruni *et al.* 2007). The heterogeneous things of this system had to be brought together and aligned to support an interpretation of the patient's condition. These things, which were also places of knowledge, included patients and professionals, as well as the electrocardiograph and the language codes needed to mobilize it, rules, medical protocols, telephones/computers for communication, artefacts such as patient file cards, and a call centre delivering the service. Many of these repositories of knowledge remain silent and invisible, such as the technological infrastructure, organizational habits and the call operators' work, unless they are performed through alignment work. The researchers were interested in how participants learned to mobilize knowledge from these different locations:

> If all these interdependent elements, whose reciprocal relations constitute an SFK, are to become recognizable expertise (and if the cardiologist is to attribute meaning to the ECG on his/her computer screen and be able to say that she/he has mastered a new practice – remote cardiological consultation), they must be aligned and held together: That is, performed within the SFK. This requires that all the heterogeneous elements that make up the system and embody fragments of the necessary knowledge must be mobilized and transformed from 'known' into 'knowing'. This activity does not require conscious and intentional production; rather, it arises from emergent co-construction that aligns the heterogeneous elements of the SFK by means of situated material-discursive practices.
>
> (Bruni *et al.* 2007: 98–9)

Bruni *et al.* (2007) observed workers developing particular discursive practices to mobilize 'fragmented knowledge', skills which the researchers suggest may be necessary for working at a distance. For example, 'framing' generates a space of signification for a subsequent action, and 'post-scripting' commands what is already done. 'Footing' enables people to align themselves with, and then later disturb, a predetermined frame. 'Delegation' is a practice of treating non-human systems as subjects to which clinical practices can be delegated. What is interesting here is how professional workers, in particular, workers such as cardiologists trained in the 'acquire-and-apply' model of disciplinary knowledge, adapt to distributed circumstances of practice, inventing alternate modes of connecting knowledge. The separations of distance simply help to highlight the pragmatic problem in any practice of aligning various human and non-human elements that embody knowledge, and mobilizing them to enact it.

Clearly, as ANT explorations have shown, knowledge cannot be viewed as coherent, transcendent, generalizable and unproblematic. These various studies also show that knowledge and the real emerge together. The thing is not separate from the knowing that establishes it as a thing. Furthermore, a thing can be enacted through multiple knowings or ontologies that co-exist, in a contentious and discontinuous dynamic. This has implications for education and educational research. Researching schooling, Fountain (1999) urges educators to adopt an ANT approach to knowledge. She challenges conventional science education that:

> privileges detached, scientific reasoning [and] will fail to recognize the complex interpenetration of the various factors which make up these issues. It will also mean taking a political position which often denies the involvement, interests, and complicity of science in the issue in question.
>
> Fountain (1999: 355)

Fountain suggests a range of instructional approaches integrating ANT, such as asking children to map the associations that are employed to produce and to represent a particular scientific explanation, and then to examine what associations in an educational context enable or constrain particular points of view. Learners can trace what and who have been rallied and mobilized to enact and uphold particular concepts, but also – perhaps more importantly – the associations that do not appear, the things that are not mentioned or are discredited, the things that are not yet imagined but that may be at work. In both science education in particular and curriculum theory in general, Fountain (1999: 339) contends that ANT moves education 'from a rhetoric of conclusions towards a rhetoric of contentions'. This is in line with the argument above that education could be about experimenting and intervening rather than simply the (re)presenting of facts.

Knowing locations – objects and subjects of knowledge

In ANT analyses, we often see reference to humans and non-humans as though there is a distinct boundary separating them, a boundary that, incidentally, privileges humans in an a priori way. However, the distinction is far less clear. A human being is not an autonomous clump of emotions, intentions, memories and acquired skills in one isolated sack of skin, because these elements are each shaped and inscribed by non-human things. Humans also integrate material prostheses and technological tools, such as spectacles, implants and earphones. Animals and other sentient non-human beings are different in kind to rocks, but all natural objects perform in particular ways according to the networks in which they become mobilized. Natural objects are different to tools designed by humans and material representational texts that encode social and cultural information; and things manipulated in virtual immersive worlds are neither human nor non-human. To write of the human and non-human is itself a simplification.

Jöns (2006) has suggested a vocabulary for ANT and other network analysis that extends the human/non-human referents, built around what he calls 'dynamic hybrids'. This is in line with Latour's (1993) argument that we have never been modern, as the modern entails a purification or separation out of things into distinct objects with properties. For Latour, this is not achievable and all is hybrid. For Jöns, all objects, including those with human characteristics could be considered to embed some combination of three elements: materialities, immaterialities and dynamic mediators. Dynamic mediators are connections between material and immaterial (as well as hybrid material–immaterial) elements of an object that provide a continuous circulation.

> Materialities, which always incorporate some kind of information ... represent the world of matter, things and nondynamic (socio)materialities. Immaterialities, which in turn are always embodied in some kind of physical vehicle ..., incorporate the world of thoughts, imaginations, memories, feelings, (shared) meaning(s), concepts, social conventions, ideologies, instincts and the virtual reality.
>
> (Jöns 2006: 573)

One study of nursing knowledge enacted in an intensive care unit shows the usefulness of this vocabulary in examining objects of knowledge and how they become distinct or purified in practice. Mullen (2002) explored how nurses and technology interact in the work of knowing the patient and providing individualized care. She found that technologies, such as the cardiac monitor, were not separated from the nurse and her actions, as though they were distinct objects that shaped one another. Instead, the technology and the nurse were infused, part of one another. Further, the patient was also part of this object. Mullens began referring to the dynamic hybrid of 'nursetechnologypatient', which was involved with and further guided by the process of information management. This formed the basis for the nurse's knowledge about the patient. We may identify objects of knowledge as distinct from humans, but ANT points to the 'bringing togethers', the hybrids and networks that make this separation possible. This might seem paradoxical at first, but we will have more to write on this in Chapter 3.

ANT analyses upend any clear boundaries delineating this thing from that thing or that person. They show that what appear to be separate entities – materials, people, numbering systems, standardized tests, etc. – are linked together in ways that are far from distinct, stable and identifiable. The ties binding them are not neutral, linear tunnels. A portfolio or learning plan, for example, exerts significant force but behaves in multiple forms. Law and Singleton (2005) suggest that what passes for knowledge are boxes that each contain a network of ideas and histories that have been performed into place. While some networks are not successful, others manage to stitch together objects (e.g. children, glue guns, triangle shapes, Grade 5 science curriculum objectives) that become acceptable as knowledge. Further, an object that is taken to be singular is, in fact, often performed in different ways. Things get added to it and modify it; conflicting knowledges are performed *simultaneously*, and any sense of coherence among these different performances of a single object of knowledge is also performed. Thus, the futility of trying to design teacher and student proof online learning objects that can be 'delivered' uniformly across multiple settings. All of these enactments perform not only a thing – something known – but also a subject who is doing the knowing. They enact a knowing location with particular subjectivities. Particular kinds of science teachers are enacted by particular alignments of things. Particular subjectivities of learners come into being with knowledges that may be racialized or gendered in particular ways. Even particular kinds of worker subjectivities become enrolled with organizational positionings through strategic constitution of (knowledge-embedded) things (Suchman 2005). Knowing locations are therefore about the enactment of subject and object together.

What, then, becomes visible and *distinct* as an object of knowledge? To whom is it visible, and under what circumstances? This is one issue that occupies ANT-informed research, and holds critical importance for education. The question of the recognition and valuing of knowledge, what and whose knowledge counts and what is rendered invisible, illuminates the practices that become manifested in educational privilege and exclusion. What dynamics, what elements, enable some enactments of particular objects of knowledge and constrain others? If *different* knowledge enactments bound together are each performing the same thing, what is its nature? Is there a way to discern different kinds of knowledge objects, and perhaps even to link them with different regions, constraints, desires, representations, identities, affiliations, and so forth? This is an important issue for considerations of pedagogy as well as educational policy which aspire to foster learning – the becomings and enactings of subjects as well as objects, the coming into existence of human beings, understandings, and ways of being. For education, this question is important also in considering subjectivities, how certain identities are constrained by educative practices and approaches to knowledge and other possibilities enabled. It is also critical to better understand the enactment of knowledge in pedagogy and curriculum, as well as knowledge *about* and *for* educative practice, as in situations of implementing new innovations of practice.

These issues surface in a study of knowledge objects and their enactments conducted by Harrisson and Laberge (2002). The situation was an innovation implementation project in a multinational manufacturer of electronic components, and the research was intended to examine the organizational learning involved. The innovation process was conceived by managers in rather conventional terms as implementing innovative knowledge (a new production system) that had been designed by engineers and was supposed to be diffused throughout the workforce. The new knowledge consisted of two parts: information technology that remodelled production, and teamwork technology that reorganized work relations. In tracing what happened over three years, the researchers concluded that even though implementation of the innovation was considered to be complete and worker 'resistance' overcome by management, the 'real innovation' existed in multiple forms that were very different to the initial blueprint drawn up by the core group.

Some workers, motivated by a sense of the economic precariousness of the organization and poor product quality, formed inter-organizational alliances and began to experiment with forms of the technology early in the project. Thus, a network began to form, strengthened by its links across groups, which enacted an inventive, dynamic form of knowledge that escaped the confines of the original design. Other workers resisted the identities inscribed within the new teamwork and ICT knowledges. They appropriated and shared the technology in unexpected ways, and invented new intermediaries that brought together groups that interrupted the planned sequence of implementation (informal committees, agreements). Ultimately, they enacted different forms of what comprised a team and how it used the technology. The union was also interested in mobilizing and reframing the new teamwork knowledge practices for greater workplace democracy. This reconfigured the ways that relations of power and influence were performed between management and labour. The study findings showed both the different simultaneous enactments of the same innovation and the fragility of the different networks that were created, which shifted identities of both workers and what became recognized as knowledge. These networks enacting different knowledges were related to the existing associations of individuals, groups and technologies, and their particular interests. They were also related to different affinities that individuals and groups formed in the enactment of the innovation.

In a similar analysis of an implementation of new technology, 'BPC', across a major telecommunications company (3,500 employees), researchers also found that what was originally considered to be the new object of knowledge in fact became enacted differently in different regions of the organization (Sarker *et al.* 2006). Top management executives, the implementation team members and other employees used different definitions of BPC, different techniques and principles. In effect, they created different BPCs. Furthermore, these different objects – all called BPC – were emergent, varying temporally according to different combinations of human and non-human elements that became mobilized in enacting BPC. Despite conventional wisdom that implementation involves creating alignment between participants' interests and the new object, the researchers found that the interests of different actors also were emergent effects of the sociotechnical processes of translation. Human interests, in other words, are not stable or pre-existing empirical realities.

We will explore many of the issues above in greater detail in later chapters, each of which seeks to both extend understanding of ANT in the context of educational practices and issues more specifically. Some of what we have explored in these first two chapters points to the interruptions and unfamiliar dynamics that can be traced in the micro-connections that form among human actions and different objects embedding knowledge (Roth 1996, Gough 2004, Bruni *et al.* 2007). Fountain (1999) contends that ANT disrupts the knowledge-making that drives curriculum processes, turning education from a rhetoric of predeterminations to a rhetoric of contentions. Woolgar *et al.* (2009) emphasize that these understandings of knowledge are particularly important for opening new approaches to analyse policy-making processes. For educators and educational researchers examining knowledge generation and learning, whether in encounters of policy making and its uptakes, curriculum and pedagogy, professional practice, innovation, or workplace/organizational learning, ANT approaches do not afford tidy accounts or generalizable conclusions. Instead, ANT patiently traces the actual enactments of knowledge(s) and practice(s), discerning the micro-politics at stake and the mess. ANT analyses make visible its ambivalences and contradictions as well as the multiple associations and (dis)continuities that form among material and immaterial elements to constitute what passes for knowledge. This is why we maintain that ANT is important for educational research.

Chapter 3

(De)naturalizing teaching and learning

Having explored some of the key concepts in ANT in the first two chapters, we now move on to focus on particular educational issues and how they have been explored through ANT. At the heart of discussions of education is the question of pedagogy – those educative practices through which people teach and learn. How does ANT help us to understand pedagogy? What particular insights does it provide us with? These are the questions to be addressed in this chapter. What could be more taken for granted than that education is about teaching and learning? Yet, at the very start of the chapter, we need to note again the importance of what we take to be a priori in our representations of, and enactments in, the world, for we have already introduced three different categorizations upon which we could build this chapter. 'Teaching and learning', 'pedagogy' and 'educative practices' are not necessarily equivalent, and indeed specific work is necessary to enact an equivalence between them. Thus, in writing about teaching and learning, we are not only interested in the practices enacted through this particular categorization and the black-boxing it attempts, but also the ways this categorization is itself enacted.

In education, there is no shortage of discussion of teaching and learning, or, as is the case in many discourses, learning and teaching. There is also no shortage of theories attempting to understand and explain these practices. Behaviourism, cognitivism, constructionism, etc. have all been deployed to explain the ways in which changes in human doing, knowing and feeling are possible. Here, we need to contrast the concern with knowledge practices in studies of organizations and workplace learning that we explored in the previous chapter with the more specific focus on the teaching of individuals and subjects and the learning of individuals in the study of education. This marks a distinction between educational and organizational studies, a boundary we wish to trouble through our uptake of ANT in this book.

In recent years, many have drawn upon Sfard's (1998) discussion of two overgeneralized metaphors of learning as a way of providing umbrellas for a wide range of learning theories. The metaphor of acquisition is used to embrace those understandings of learning, which are about *having*, such as gaining knowledge and understanding. These tend to be individualist theories. By contrast, the metaphor of participation embraces theories which are identified as more social in focus, based upon *doing*. Each of these metaphors continues to enact an anterior distinction between the social and the individual, which, as we have outlined, is an effect from an ANT analysis. The material is often invisible in such theories. For example, situated and practice-based learning theory, communities of practice, cultural historical activity theory and ANT can all be positioned as primarily about participation, although how that is understood varies significantly. However, ANT is not a theory of learning as such, but an attempt to explore how the social is enacted. There has been a tendency to see the metaphors of acquisition and participation as contrasting and distinct, when one can of course also accept and explore their interrelationship. Does one acquire learning through doing? Is what one does based upon what one has? These diverse theories have been utilized and technologized as pedagogic practices in different ways in the disciplining technologies that we call schools, colleges and universities. The institutionalizing of such practices has been extended also through the discourses of lifelong learning to include workplaces, community venues and the home. Here, living and learning become positioned as almost inseparable. All of this takes work, for how else can life be enrolled to learning. It is such work that ANT can be used to trace.

Most of the discourses surrounding teaching and learning have tended to focus on changes in humans and human–human interactions. However, this has shifted with the rise in interest in more social and practice focused theories of learning. While having very different genealogies – situated learning theory in symbolic interactionism and anthropology, activity theory in Marxist-informed psychology – both have given more attention to the material artefacts in the learning process. However, they still also situate learning, intention and action primarily within the human domain.

As we have written, ANT has developed as an alternative view of enacting practices. However, because of the principle of symmetry, things are not second-ary to the human, but it is through their being together that actions, including those identified *as* learning, become possible. Learning is, therefore, an effect of the networks of humans and non-humans that identify certain practices as learn-ing, which also entails a value judgement about learning something worthwhile. Thus, teaching is not simply about the relationships between humans, but is about the networks of humans and things through which teaching and learning are translated and enacted. Teaching and learning do not exist and cannot be identified as separate from the networks through which they are enacted. They are not independent entities or processes, but assemblages.

An early illustration of this was provided by Verran (1999, 2001), who drew upon ANT conceptions in her analysis of the multiple ways of knowing and being that were enacted in Nigerian students' engagement with science. Learning in school curriculum, Verran notes, is expected to unfold usually within a single metaphysical frame. In her work with Yoruba children she shows that, while these children worked from Yoruba metaphysical logic, they were expected in the school curricula to think in Western metaphysics. For instance, Western assumptions about what numbers represent and how they can be manipulated (in terms of measuring volume, quantities, distance, calculating changes in matter, and so forth) are very different to Yoruba approaches to generalizing matter. Yoruba understandings begin with the particular sort of matter, and generate a unit appropriate to quantify that matter in the here and now. What surprised Verran was finding that Yoruba children not only learned to work within these two noncoherent and profoundly different worlds of working and thinking with the same objects, but that they could work across both accounts of realness: choosing one or the other, or juggling both simultaneously. They were literally juggling different ontologies, a form of enactment that Verran (2007: 34–35) calls 'being-ontics':

> Recognizing and being open and explicit about the possibility and nature of interrupting and connecting at a level of cognition that very few people are aware of, we are working at the level of entities' existence or being-ontics. It is about learning to manage knowing along with doubt; weaning oneself from certainty that is allowed by working within just one metaphysical frame. It implies recognizing that reality can be done in this way or that, through this series of gestures, words, and material arrangements, or an alternative set.

Learning to interrupt the very structures of knowledge, to recognize multiple ways of enacting reality and to even manoeuvre among these different realities is one of the challenges for teaching and learning opened by ANT approaches. The leap is away from thinking about entities to understanding that, as Verran (2007: 38) describes it:

> All entities lie suspended between enactments of their possibilities. Entities lurk or loom in the interstices between the repetitions by which they are done. The relationalities through which they exist are external to their being 'clotted' entities. That is how all entities express relationalities; how entities (actors or actants) are networks; and how networks of relations are entities.

Educators have also found ANT useful in developing critical approaches to teaching and learning that move beyond normative assertions. In one project to articulate a critical sociology of numeracy for the teaching of mathematics, Yasukawa (2003) finds that ANT's approach helps to reveal the ways in which different goals and interests of people, as well as intended purposes of technologies, objects and claims, such as mathematical theorems, penetrate and transform one another. ANT helps trace the practices through which particular mathematical knowledge, such as probability theory, becomes inscribed and mobilized. This provides openings for transgressions to shift existing power relations in numeracy.

I offer a proposition that if we were to take a radical (or extremist?) view that being numerate means not just having a critical understanding of mathematics, but using that understanding for some form of social action; a framework such as ANT is a resource for numeracy. ANT allows us to focus on how existing interests are translated into something different as a result of interactions across a network of human and non-human actors, including mathematics.

(Yasukawa 2003: 29–30)

We will attempt to illustrate the particular contribution ANT can make to our enactments of teaching and learning in this chapter by drawing primarily upon two major studies. First, we will draw upon a significant early ANT study of university undergraduate education from the USA (Nespor 1994). This study aimed to use ANT as a way of critiquing early 'communities of practice' understandings of learning (Lave and Wenger 1991). The latter was a theory developed from ethnographic studies of how people learned in everyday situations. It was claimed that individuals enter a community of practice as legitimate peripheral participants, whether in clothing workshops or Alcoholics Anonymous groups. Over time they acquire the knowledge, skills and dispositions of experienced community members and gradually become full participants themselves. Nespor's empirical study suggested this was too linear a view of learning and also that people were parts of many communities of practice at any one time. He drew upon early ANT to provide a richer ethnographic representation of what was occurring in universities.

Second, we will draw upon a more recent study of literacies for learning in colleges in the UK (Ivanič *et al.* 2009, Edwards *et al.* 2009b). This project explored the literacies in which students engaged in their everyday lives and those that were required of them in their studies in college. The aim was to develop pedagogical interventions through which the students' practices from their everyday lives could be used as resources within their studies in order to enhance their learning and achievement. The project was initially framed through New Literacy Studies (Barton and Hamilton 1998), and people's literacy practices were taken to be situated and purposeful. The aim of transferring literacy practices from everyday situations into college situations raised questions about the nature and possibility of transfer. This is in line with discussions of informal, experiential and formal learning elsewhere in research. There was also the apparent paradox that, if literacy practices are situated, how they could be mobilized from one context to another? In the course of this project, ANT was introduced as a way of enacting the complexity within the data.

These two large-scale studies will provide the primary focus for this chapter. In addition, we will touch upon the ways in which ANT troubles any enactment of teaching and learning as simply sitting within a bounded context, for example the school, college, university. We will indicate that education institutions cannot be spaces of enclosure, as they are sometimes positioned, but are particular assemblages. We will also step back a little and consider some of the ways in which practices are enacted as teaching and learning in the first place and with what effects.

Assembling undergraduates

Nespor (1994) argues that, in education, ANT analyses tend to focus on powerful central actors. This does not particularly improve understandings of those at the margins, most obviously and importantly, students, whose subjectivities and actions are being mobilized. Furthermore, if ANT readings focus on a network's centre, the observer might be captured by the appearance of flow from every direction which misses the entrenchments and stable divisions that are more visible 'from a distance'. In education, these 'deeply worn channels' (Nespor 1994: 15) formed by particularly durable networks such as racism and colonialism – not to be confused with an a priori conceptualization of 'social structures' – are critically important to analysis. Far from abandoning ANT for education, Nespor (1994: 23) concludes that its frames help illuminate the 'structure of networks, the ties that bind them, and the nature of whatever it is that flows through them'. Furthermore, ANT readings can show precisely how educational practices order space and time as well as forms of participation in networks of power. That is, ANT penetrates the different socio-material negotiations occurring in the evolution, extension and sedimentation of these networks that appear to discipline people and knowledge as well as technology and the natural world so effectively.

In his exploration of teaching, learning and curriculum in undergraduate studies in physics and management in an American university, Nespor (1994) draws upon early ANT to examine the ways in which students are organized in space and time, and the implications of this both for knowledge and knowledge-building practices and also for subjectivity. In particular, he draws upon the moments of translation, illustrating that the different practices associated with the two subject areas result in different subjectivities, networks and representational practices. In other words, learning entails ways of being, ways of acting, ways of feeling, ways of interacting, ways of representing, as well as ways of knowing. For Nespor, these emerge through the networks and networking practices in which people enrol and the translations to which they are subject. These are network effects, which he traces in great detail.

The physics students he studied followed a traditional cohort-based, linear set curriculum. For them, space and time were compressed, as they spent all their time together working in groups long into the night. By contrast, the management students had a more disaggregated experience, because of their modular programme, which resulted in a churning of the relationships in which they participated. This points to the ways in which teaching and learning are organized and the socio-material networks that shape them, enacting different relationships, subjectivities and learning. The space–time compression resulted in students with a very firm disciplinary identity and tightly knit networks within the physics community. However, the management students belonged to a far more diverse set of networks. These networks were within management, but also outside it and indeed outside the university. This was because the business school, of which the students were part, had strong links with employers for both teaching and employment purposes. The management students' subjectivities, therefore, were enacted not simply in relation to the subject discipline, as was more strongly the case with the physics students.

The interessement and enrolment of the physics students may, therefore, be said to be more complete than the management students, if one accepts that the discipline network is that which is to be mobilized in teaching and learning in universities. It is certainly the case that many bemoan modularization and the decline of single subject degree study results in a lack of 'depth' to learning. However, others point to the benefits of greater breadth of study associated with modularization, not least in relation to the development of employability dispositions. In this sense, we note how two enactments of universities are at play here. One enacts universities as reproducing themselves through the disciplines, creating institutions as immutable mobiles. The second enacts universities within the network of the economy and the forms of knowledge and subjectivity required therein. It may be no historical accident that the latter has grown in significance as a greater range of professional education has entered the university, thereby reframing its external relations with professional groups, employers, etc. and the internal relations with its weakly framed disciplinary knowledge base. It is also indicative of the increased competitiveness associated with economic globalization, suggestive of the different networks that have been attempting to enrol university education with specific effects.

For the physics students in this study, their network was a site for forming ongoing friendships, with academic and social life merging. They spent almost all their time relating to each other. Nespor (1994) argues that this was precisely because they had to take required courses in a specified sequence. By contrast, the management students had far more electives in their course. Thus, the fact that there was more student choice in the organization of programmes resulted in a reordering of space–time and, with that, the range of networks to which students were connected. In others words, 'choice' was mobilized as a capacity for management students to develop in a way in which was not the case for the physics students.

Interestingly, this choice was itself mediated through student organized advice networks, even though the business school provided a formal advice service for students. Thus, even within the management students' experience, there were different networks attempting to enrol them. The informal student advice network was able to problematize and enrol more successfully than the formal advice service. Thus, 'instead of having their spatial and temporal trajectories shaped by programme requirements, students organized the space–time relations among their courses. Schedules were composed for reasons unconnected with the substance of the courses' (Nespor 1994: 89), which enrolled and mobilized specific knowledge-enacting networks and forms of subjectivity.

There is a tension in Nespor's argument here. His analysis suggests that there is a set of particular temporal and spatial framings for students varied by the degree of choice available to them in their programmes. As we have outlined above, this is certainly significant. At one level, this is the case and choice is important for differentiating the different forms of networking in which the students are translated. However, both sets of students, nonetheless, also remain governed by the timetable of the institution. Teaching and learning is coordinated across time and space in the same way airlines and trains are coordinated and ordered by schedules (Suchman 2007). Without the timetable, some of the expected enactments of teaching and learning – the coordination of people, things and spaces – would fall apart. Individuals, spaces and things are translated by and into teaching and learning by the timetable. Yet, the role of the timetable in educational institutions is often seen as simply organizational, rather than a major actor in teaching and learning. For the management students there may be some mediated choices in terms of the modules they chose, but this does not undermine the power of the timetable, not least in its capacity to help shape those choices. We see here, then, the potential play of interessement and enrolment in choice and the timetable within the networks of the two sets of students. Choice and the timetable have the potential to provide the in-between space of interessement for the students.

While there are limitations to Nespor's study with its focus on institutionalised forms of learning, the two contrasting examples in some ways symbolize two different enactments for the types of graduates expected from universities. The physics students, with their compressed spatio–temporal relationships and dense networks, are associated with one of the more traditional disciplines and its associated practices of disciplinary subjectivity. By contrast, the management students have more of the characteristics of employability, and it may not be accidental that their looser and wider networking is fashioned in a newer subject area, where course structure is mediated more by student choice. The actor–network of academic physics is more tightly bound than that of management and the mobilizations of time and space in some ways more restricted.

A strong disciplinary subjectivity is mobilized for and by the physics students, but it would seem to be somewhat insular and introverted. They primarily relate to each other as a cohort. By contrast, the looser organization of space and time associated with the modular management programme and the extensive network-ing beyond the university can be seen to mobilize a student who is more active and enterprising. This is the type of active subject central to conceptions of con-temporary advanced liberal governmentality (Dean 1999, Rose 1999). Indeed, for Nespor (1994) this represents something of a problem, as there is a lack of enrol-ment of the students in the academic side of the management programme. The students are more concerned with management practices in employment rather than the academic understanding of management; learning to be a manager is more important than learning *about* management. The very networks to which the university introduces the students, i.e. employers, therefore translates their inter-ests ambiguously, as there is then a tension within the network. This is a common tension in much teaching and learning, one that is often articulated as a tension between theory and practice – the university/college/school and the employers.

However, the situation may be somewhat more complex, as the overall organ-ization of space and time emphasizes the public performance of the management students, their presentational skills and dress – precisely the capabilities they require to mobilize themselves as managers in the employment market. Part of the teaching and learning of management, therefore, might be said to mobilize and translate enterprising more than those of the traditional discipline subjectivities. However, a certain caution is also necessary in suggesting a tidy categorization, as both sets of students are subject to aspects of traditional disciplinary practices through the normalizing practices of assessment and examination.

Nespor (1994) provides a detailed analysis of the participation within, and use of, space and time by the students he studied. This suggests the need for more extensive studies of the architecture and built environment of teaching and learning for the understanding of pedagogy. The material organization of spaces and times for teaching and/or learning can itself become an important focus for research. Nespor contrasts the isolated, almost bunker-like scientific spaces of the physics building with the newer, lighter, more open spaces of the business school, suggesting ways in which subjectivities are formed through the spaces to be utilized as well as the utilization of those spaces. 'Unlike the austere physics building, the business school wasn't geared solely to academic or scholarly activity ... [The] public interior space was organized in large part to simulate corporate spaces and function as a stage for the display of sociability' (Nespor 1994: 111). For Nespor, while the physics students learn to mobilize the physical world, management students learn to mobilize themselves.

When educative practices are articulated in network terms, each event arises within the connections made. Teaching and learning cannot, therefore, be identified as taking place in enclosed or contained spaces for they are themselves assemblages of the human and non-human and multiple in their enactments. Although somewhat human-centric in its uptake of ANT, in later work Nespor (2003: 94–5) provides an illustration which is helpful:

> Imagine, for example, a university student working in a dormitory room on a physic problem ... The space of the classroom is extended into the student's residence, and the student's out-of-school time is synchronized not just with the professor's pacing of course materials, but also to an institutional calendar, which organizes 'learning' into arbitrary units of time like semesters, and semesters into multi-year programmes of study. There are also links between the space-time of the problem-solving and anticipated evaluated events elsewhere in the future. At the same time, insofar as the problem solving is part of a 'course', there are connections to previous physics or math courses the student has taken where similar problem forms, tasks, and concepts were encountered. There are also connections to disciplinary sites where 'physics problems' are constructed and warranted ... and to physics courses around the world where the same or isomorphic problems are assigned ... The physics problem is not so much an 'articulated' moment as a moving articulation, the translation of a succession of place-makings, enrolments, decontextualization and recontextualization, temporally unfolding from secondary school onward.

Purification and translation in teaching and learning

The second empirical study of teaching and learning upon which we draw is the British-based *Literacies for Learning in Further Education* (hereafter, LfLFE) research project (Ivanič *et al.* 2009, Edwards *et al.* 2009b). The project involved collaboration between two universities and four colleges in England and Scotland. A central concern was to understand how the literacy practices required of college life and being a student relate to the wide range of students' literacy practices in their everyday lives. Literacy practices were initially viewed primarily as 'resources' for learning across the curriculum. The project explored different ways of mobilizing students' everyday literacy practices to enhance their learning in a number of curriculum areas. The intention was to achieve a critical under-standing of the movements and flows of literacy practices in people's lives: how literacy practices are ordered and re-ordered, mobilized across what were taken to be different domains (home–college, virtual–real, screen–book, reading–writing), and what things might mediate such mobilizations. Inevitably, this brought into focus questions of what counts as literacy and the differential values placed upon different literacy practices. In other words, it raised questions of difference and its affirmations and denials in assembling the educated subject. It also raised questions about the a priori status of the domains identified in the study.

New Literacy Studies, which was the starting point for the project, offers a socially constructed view of literacies as multiple, emergent and situated in particular social contexts (Barton *et al.* 2000). This meshes with the tradition of locating learning within socio-cultural practices of participation we have mentioned above (e.g. Lave and Wenger 1991). It is an approach that encourages us to talk differently about how texts are read and written as embedded in the everyday and often mundane purposes and activities of life, including education. In this view, literacy practices are situated within the diverse domains of their use. In this view, practices within education, however privileged, are only further examples of 'situated literacies'.

The focus of this project was on the multiple and multiplying semiotic land-scape, on differences in literacy practices in different networks, the forms of representation associated with them, and on the values, knowledge, expectations and subject positions which are inscribed in them. These different practices are shaped by hierarchies of value and taste of both those engaged in them and of others. First, there is a hierarchy between different literacy practices, for exam-ple, reading a novel and texting someone. Second, there is a valuing of what constitutes literacy and what does not, where, for instance, texting is not neces-sarily counted as literacy because it does not entail the standardized spelling and grammar associated with educational practices. Who has power to name these positions within hierarchies, and which are powerful in the realization of literacy and learning as practices and in enacting what is to count as literacy in specific domains, become important questions.

As certain 'educated' literacy practices are more dominant or influential, eve-ryday practices are often devalued within educational contexts. This is despite the many pedagogical attempts to enrol learning between networks, for example, simulations, the recognition of prior learning and work-based learning. Insofar as the everyday and the college were enacted as a priori separate domains, the project sought to identify the *border literacy practices* that support the *border crossing* of these practices from the everyday to the college. This is a common enactment in discussions of learning, especially in relation to adult or vocational learning. Such practice, once assembled, it is suggested, could become resources for learning and authorized in the teaching, learning and assessment associated with attainment in particular subject areas within colleges.

However, these a priori distinctions began to be too constraining of the messiness in the data arising from the project and ANT offered as alternative way of enacting this problem. The project therefore sought to examine literacy practices as multiple network effects arising from the processes associated with Latour (1993) – notions of purification, naturalization and translation. Edwards *et al.* (2009b) worked with Latour's argument that the practices of modernity aspire to separate things out, what he refers to as a process of purification. Latour suggests that we have never been modern, because all is mixed, hybrid, translated. In other words, nothing is something with properties. All is what he refers to as quasi-objects. This does not mean that there are no attempts to purify, merely that such purification is itself already an enactment of translation. Thus, while Latour does not use the moments of translation for his argument, he nonetheless continues that line of ANT associated with the sociology of translation. The LfLFE project drew upon these ideas to enact the alignments of humans and things in the naturalization of certain literacy practices as effects of purification, and the translations that contribute to and resist this effect. Humans cannot write without certain things that enable different forms of inscriptions and (re)presentation.

Edwards *et al.* (2009b) argue that in educational institutions, teaching and learning enact forms of selection and selection entails standards. However inclusive the practices are intended to be, education is the enactment of standards and, as such, exclusions are inevitable. In ANT terms, therefore, learning in educational institutions can be argued to entail purification and naturalization through the standards practiced. Purification refers to the way in which the educated subject is assembled upon the basis of the denial of the play of multiplicity and difference and the mobilizing of specific practices as more valuable than others. For example, essay writing is valued over texting, literature over popular magazines, books over television. Standards are mobilized to select and purify the what and how of literacy, and the people to be enrolled as literate. Purification, then, can be employed to refer to the ways in which learners and learning are bounded, classified and set apart, contained, based upon their capacity to communicate in specific ways. Purification entails the exclusion of that which is not valued. In terms of literacy practices, Edwards *et al.* (2009b) argue that purification is a process of excluding those practices which are not considered standard, that is, literacy practices which do not employ 'proper' grammar, spelling, genre, etc.

The setting of standards requires value judgments and enactment of what is to be included and excluded – purification – and once this work is achieved, its common sense existence is naturalized or black-boxed. 'Naturalization means stripping away the contingencies of an object's creation and its situated nature. A naturalized object has lost its anthropological strangeness' (Bowker and Star 1999: 299). Naturalization refers to the outcome of purification insofar as the thing becomes taken for granted rather than viewed as the result of contingent enactments. Thus, literacy may become seen as a unified thing mobilizing certain uses of vocabulary and grammar rather than as a multiple range of enactments mobilizing communication. The work of standards and standardization effectively becomes lost as certain forms of reading and writing are simply accepted as norms that all individuals need to acquire.

Alternative practices of naturalization based not upon purification alone, but upon a framing of standards within a logic of difference, embrace enactments of translation. Here translation 'creates mixtures between entirely new types of beings, hybrids of nature and culture' (Latour 1993: 10). Thus, the development of different forms of communication, for example, through the mixing of icons and written text, becomes something not to be decried as a falling away from literacy, but as a different possibility for communication. Such an enactment involves describing practices in terms of experimentation and desire as much as understanding and technique, something which is not necessarily comfortable to educators who are largely assembled within a culture of facts and rationality.

Central to the LfLFE project's uptake of ANT to understand the play of purification and translation in literacy practices was the concept of boundary objects. The notion of boundary objects has developed in ANT-related work (Star 1989), but has also been taken up by Wenger (1998) in his conceptualization of communities of practice. It is also to be found in activity theory. For Wenger (1998: 107) boundary objects work at the edges of communities of practice mediating their external relationships; 'they enable coordination, but they can do so without actually creating a bridge between the perspectives and the meanings of various communities'. However, Edwards *et al.* (2009b) caution against a simple uptake of Wenger's view of boundary objects, precisely because these sit at the edge of pre-existing communities, when, as they indicate, in ANT these objects can sit anywhere within a network, and boundaries both mark a separation *and* connection.

In ANT-related work, boundary objects are:

> plastic enough to adapt to local needs and the constraints of the several parties employing them, yet robust enough to maintain a common identity across sites [...] They have different meanings in different social worlds but their structure is common enough to more than one world to make them recognizable, a means of translation. The creation and maintenance of boundary objects is a key process in developing and maintaining coherence across intersecting social worlds.
>
> (Star and Griesemer 1989: 393)

'Like the blackboard, a boundary object "sits in the middle" of a group of actors with divergent viewpoints' (Star 1989: 46). Such objects are not merely material, they can be 'stuff and things, tools, artefacts and techniques, and ideas, stories and memories' (Bowker and Star 1999: 298). They are things which are neither contained nor containable by context, but can be enrolled in differing and multiple networks, dependent on the various affordances at play and the work entailed in naturalizing them differently within networks.

> Objects exist, with respect to a community, along a trajectory of naturalization. This trajectory has elements of both ambiguity and duration. It is not predetermined whether an object will become naturalized, or how long it will remain so, rather practice-activity is required to make it so and keep it so.
> (Bowker and Star 1999: 299)

This trajectory of naturalization entails a 'forgetting' of the conditions which gave rise to the object in the first place. Boundary objects do not sit between the borders of different contexts, at the edge, but express a relationship between, brought together through the enactments of purification *and* translation. These can be based upon pedagogic performances which seek to make certain connections rather than deny them, or simply because they are the tokens through which people relate their practices between one domain and another (Gaskell and Hepburn 1998). They do not pre-exist practices, but rely on those practices to make them into boundary objects.

As boundary objects are understood as not merely material objects, but can be 'stuff and things', there is the possibility for quite refined understandings of changes in practice that can alter the possibilities for purification and translation. Edwards *et al.* (2009b) use the spatial metaphor of folding to conceptualize the work of purification and translation, where pedagogic practice entails enactments to naturalize the hybrid, in which both essays and magazines have pedagogic possibilities and value. This challenges the spatial metaphors of boundaries and border crossing in certain enactments of teaching and learning, implying that any observation about learning something needs to be accompanied by observations regarding what has been naturalized and under what regime, the semiotic practices associated with the learning, and consequences for the subjectivity of participants. Edwards *et al.* suggest that this is not supportable by concepts of activity systems or communities of practice, each of which can be read as a series of containers, between which people, objects, practices and meanings move. Here, folding entails work and can take multiple different forms, signifying the play of purity and multiplicity in naturalization. Folding can entail many different points of (dis)connection in teaching and learning. There is also the possibility of unfolding, which means that literacy practices are insecure, the work to keep them naturalized needs to be sustained if those practices are to continue. Folding is also three-dimensional, where the boundaries are negotiable and not simply assumed to be at the edge of a context as container; boundaries and connections are made through the practices of folding.

The LfLFE project found that simple distinctions, such as informal/formal, vernacular/formal, contextualized/decontextualized, participation/acquisition and purification/translation proved inadequate for investigating literacies for learning. It suggests that the classroom context is an effect of network practices which exclude many forms of literacy. The project may not provide the detailed tracings that Nespor provides, but it raises questions about how we identify teaching and learning contexts and how we enact the concept of contexts itself. This is particularly significant in those situations where discourses of lifelong learning have taken hold as a way of mobilizing education. It is to these issues we now turn.

Teaching and learning contexts as network effects

Where does teaching and learning take place? What are the contexts of these practices? These questions may seem simple and straightforward, but if that is the case, it shows how successfully these practices have become black-boxed, to the point where it is simply taken for granted that (most) teaching and learning takes place in educational institutions.

When considering issues of teaching and learning, there is often a tendency to focus on the specific site of practices, for example schools and classrooms, so that all else becomes the context within which those practices take place. There is, then, a tendency to explore these external contextual factors as influences on what goes on inside the context. However, where and how we cut the network and what we take to be included within a specific context for elaboration, and whether we should cut the network at all, has both assumptions and effects. Thus, as Pickering (2001: 172) has argued, 'appeals to explanatory context in the human sciences run the risk of effacing fascinating manglings of "context" itself'. Similarly, although focussing on social practices more generally, and not the specifics of education, Lave (1996: 5, original emphasis) posed the problem:

> Research on everyday practices typically focuses on the activities of persons acting, although there is agreement that such phenomena cannot be analysed in isolation from the socially material world of that activity. But less attention has been given to the difficult task of conceptualizing relations between persons acting and the social world. Nor has there been sufficient attention to rethinking the 'social world of activity' in relational terms. Together, these constitute the problem of context.

Questions of context are not new, but are brought into particularly stark relief by developments promoted through a discourse of lifelong learning. If learning is lifelong and life wide, what specifically then, is a learning context? Are living and learning collapsed into each other? Does all of life become scaled as learning?

In this sense, learning contexts are distributed across the associational order and embedded in practices to such an extent that this order is itself already a learning context, and learning potentially becomes undifferentiated as a practice from other practices. Here, the associational order becomes, by definition, a learning order. In ANT terms, this takes work to achieve.

Insofar as we expand our concept of learning to mobilize apparently all aspects of life, we might be said to start to lose the conceptual basis for talking specifically of a teaching and learning context and the notions that these take place inside a bounded context. This raises important questions:

- What is specific to a teaching and learning context which is not to be found in other contexts?
- What characterizes a specifically teaching and learning context?
- What is the relationship between teaching, learning and context?
- Who names these contexts as teaching and learning contexts?

The final question is particularly important insofar as the discourses of educators, policy-makers and researchers are not necessarily shared by those who are engaging in practices within those areas identified as contexts of learning. All are struggling to assemble networks that give value to certain practices as teaching and learning. If, following ANT, we follow the actors, then we often find them translating their interests in ways other than they would be translated by others. Thus, for instance, studying family history may be considered a leisure activity by those who are engaging in it, when for many educators this could be considered a form of learning or research. The meaning and significance of practices can therefore be scaled and enrolled in various ways. For instance, insofar as people do not identify themselves as learning in different sites, they may not draw upon the things and relationships available to them for learning in other areas as was found in the LfLFE project where many students did not identify their everyday practices as involving reading and writing. Here, it is a question of what can be ascribed as teaching and learning by whom, rather than uncovering what is learnt. Teaching and learning are an effect of particular translations and mobilizations.

The question then emerges about how we understand a teaching and learning context, when these processes are not necessarily bound by a specific set of institutional relationships and structures, but emerge from specific mobilizations as network effects. For those drawing upon ANT, rather than context being a thing, it becomes an effect of practices and is itself a set of practices. Contextualizing rather than context becomes that upon which we would focus (Nespor 2003). This is where the practices of purification and translation are once again helpful, as learning is a specific effect of certain practices of contextualization rather than simply emerging within a taken for granted context. Contextualization here embraces practices of decontextualization – purification – and recontextualization – translating or hybridizing networks. As people and things move, different realizations of context emerge in what Nespor (2003) refers to as trajectories;

'schooling works by moving people and things along trajectories that ultimately situate them in spatial and temporal orders where only certain meanings, identities, and lines of action can be easily sustained' (Nespor 2003: 98). Thus, 'activities like schooling are in a large part constituted by struggles over which contextualizations or what kinds of contexts are to hold for participants in particular events, and what kinds are to count in institutional records of those events' (Nespor 2003: 104).

Once we look beyond the institutionalized contexts for education and training, such as schools, colleges and universities, and allow learning contexts to be extended into relationships between people, artefacts and variously defined others mediated through a range of social, organizational and technological actors, then the limitations of much institutionalized pedagogy comes into sharp focus. Pedagogy has, for some, been defined as contained within the 'spaces of enclosure' of the classroom, the book and the curriculum (Lankshear *et al.* 1996). Here, learners move from one classroom to another, one curriculum area to another, one institution to another in a linear step-by-step way. Learning is linear, bounded and cumulative. This is something that Davis and Sumara (2003) also point to in their study of the teaching of mathematics. They argue that Euclidean notions of linearity and the right angle inform much of the modern practices of teaching and learning.

> The modern school has been particularly underpinned by linear assumptions ... In matters of curriculum, their presence is perhaps most obvious in those projects that are aimed at direct, unambiguous, accumulative, and age-appropriate tours through neatly dissected collections of concepts ... The interpretative priority of the line is embedded in narratives of causality, certainty, optimality, progress, and efficiency.
>
> (Davis and Sumara 2003: 82)

Similarly, science educators Roth and McGinn (1997) argue that ANT is important for teaching–learning research as well as instructional practice precisely for its challenge to narratives of certainty. They show how ANT approaches can help educators and students together to deconstruct monolithic knowledge systems by examining their multivocality and precarious connections among things and people. ANT unpicks the apparent black boxes of much curricular knowledge and educational practice, and offers resources to trace the many webs and players and non-coherences embedded in them. It helps illuminate how particular knowledges, such as scientific 'evidence' and practices based on them, become powerful through obligatory passage points, gatekeepers, and supporting networks. It also reveals how what appears to be unassailable power is always some shifting and heterogeneous assemblage. Perhaps most important, suggest Roth and McGinn (1997), is teaching students how to critically analyse their worlds with an ANT sensibility: tracing the micro-strategies of power, the ways that entities including themselves can become translated into networks that normalize, and how all things are effects – unstable alliances – produced in continuous webs of action.

We have been examining some actual and possible uptakes of ANT in relation to researching teaching and learning. We now turn to how ANT is and can be deployed in studies of curriculum making.

Chapter 4

Entangling curriculum-making

In this chapter we explore how ANT can help to illuminate the complex dynamics, fractures and ambiguities in processes of curriculum implementation or making. 'Curriculum', what Pinar (2004: 5) declares to be 'the very organization and intellectual centring of schooling', is a slippery signifier at best. In early formulations that mobilized a dramatic turn in North American curriculum theory, Pinar and Grumet (1976) characterized curriculum as *currere* – running a course, in an active and holistic process bringing together teacher, learner and text in a particular situated moment to co-produce themselves, knowledge and culture. The 'running' is iterative and spirals across time, always circling back through the past and looping out to the future in its present moments of emergence. The enactments that are curriculum are described by Pinar (2004) as a 'complicated conversation', complicating sedimented knowledge, limited assumptions, over-determined subjectivities and certainty.

At policy levels of curriculum design and implementation in education, curriculum change is hotly debated particularly in terms of the purpose and nature of curriculum. Here, curriculum is often treated as subject content, desirable knowledge, skills and attitudes for students that are assumed to be identifiable outside of curriculum enactments and deployable through predetermined instructional technologies. Impatience with a perceived lack of change in the formal provision of learning opportunities, despite major policy innovation, is a continuing issue among certain publics. Curriculum reforms often disseminate outcomes-based prescriptions in what Pinar (2004) calls 'the nightmare of the present', where educators are losing control of curriculum to bureaucratic state elites. Yet, curriculum reforms are themselves complicated in enactments that do not always, or even often, produce what is desired or expected. So this chapter shares some common themes with later chapters on policy that examine the surprising complications of implementation. In relation to both policy and curriculum, the debate tends to be structured by a perceived *problem* of implementation, as though this is something that can be controlled and overcome in some way. In the chapters that follow, we explore how that problem is often addressed through the introduction of standards and accountability mechanisms.

ANT-informed studies of curriculum accept that such a degree of control is a temporary stabilization at best. While actor–network theory does not address curriculum theory, some studies have fruitfully drawn upon ANT concepts to explore how multiplicity is enacted through curriculum-making practices. In fact, ANT's conceptions of knowledge, bodies, identities and practices as continuously produced within webs of action are consonant with conceptions of curriculum as currere. ANT provides fine-grained analyses of the emergence, formation and growth of the networks that must be set in motion to mobilize change and stabilize the new curricula. In particular, such studies examine the tokens and intermediaries that are put into circulation, who sends them, where they suddenly appear, what they do there, how they are translated and put into further circulation.

This chapter will draw primarily on an ANT-informed empirical study of curriculum-making from schools and colleges in the UK (Miller *et al.* 2009, Edwards 2010). We will highlight the ways in which formal curriculum documents mobilize certain networks of individuals, things and organizations, both translating them and being translated by them. First, however, we will explore some of the broader background to research on curriculum implementation.

Curriculum change

Much of curriculum innovation around the globe over the past 30 years has tended towards the development of outcomes- and competency-based standards. In principle, such approaches provide for the possibility for ensuring consistency across settings, but also for multiplicity in terms of the curriculum routes to those outcomes. It is the inscriptions of outcomes statements that constitutes the prescribed curriculum, that which is intended. It is the possibilities for multiple routes to those outcomes that are often represented in the described curriculum (Bloomer 1997), those narratives of practice, often aspirational, provided by teachers, lecturers and students. It is in the observations of the enacted curriculum that we often witness tensions between what is intended, what is aspired to and what is achieved.

Over the years, there has been much written on the differences and similarities in the curriculum as prescribed, described and enacted (Bloomer 1997). There has also been much research into the factors that impact upon what happens as the curriculum is enacted. A simple heuristic identifies such factors as:

- contextual, e.g. national policy, funding arrangements
- organizational, e.g. nature and size of institution and subject department, styles of management, level and type of resources, locus of decision-making, internal or external assessments
- curriculum, e.g. the ways in which the curriculum is prescribed, nature of the curriculum, i.e. academic or vocational

- micro-political, e.g. collegial, hierarchical or individualistic, expectations of students and parents
- individual, e.g. professional formation and dispositions of lecturers and teachers, student backgrounds and prior experiences.

However, what such approaches to such issues can do is reify and black-box the curriculum as a taken for granted object, bounded by a context which (mis)shapes it in unexpected ways (Edwards *et al.* 2009c). These factors can therefore be positioned as in some ways external to curriculum-making practices and explanatory of them. A possible further inference of issues being posed in this manner is that, if these factors could be controlled, then curriculum-making would be much improved. The emphasis here is on explanation, on *why* differences in the enacted curriculum occur, as the basis for exerting control over it. In the process, curriculum-making may be reduced to a set of explanatory factors and education to a series of techniques.

Such approaches are part of the wider theoretical tendencies, to which we have referred, to work with a foundationalist ontology and a priori distinctions as a means of practising knowledge. An a priori asymmetry is built into such enactments, which produce explanations of the world which examine one thing in terms of the other and, through this, seek to order the world through human intentions and agency. It is these approaches that have been the subject of radical challenge from ANT. Where an approach of generalized symmetry is taken up, rather than reducing curriculum-making to a single ontology through explanation, its possible enactments are taken as multiple and heterogeneous, arising from the relating of the human and non-human in networks which have agentic effects. Instead of looking at the *factors* that can be positioned to explain differences between the prescribed, described and enacted curriculum to bring about their closer alignment, we need to examine more closely the actors in the multiplicity of curriculum-making practices. The emphasis, then, is on closely describing how things come to be the case without privileging human intention and agency.

This is where the ANT concept of translation becomes helpful again. Explanation and control are associated with a desire to *implement* the prescribed curriculum in its enactments in a linear sense. Early writings on ANT propose that practices are translated, changed in the process of changing, as 'to translate is to betray: ambiguity is part of translation' (Latour 1996: 48). Factors impacting upon the curriculum may be real, but they are not foundational explanations and to enact them as such is to miss the point of the translations to which they are subject. In other words, despite the attempt at standardization of learning outcomes in the prescribed curriculum, its uptake of individuals, things and organizations is multiply enacted and incapable of control due to the practices of translation (Mulcahy 1998, 1999). Standardization is therefore an (un)stable and precarious achievement. As we have seen, ANT analyses are descriptive of how things happen through the growth and shrinking of networks rather than attempting to explain them based upon foundational causes. It is itself enacted through empirical case studies and attempts to show rather than tell.

There have been relatively few studies of curriculum-making drawing upon ANT. What they share is a rejection of the discourse of implementation as too linear. They also tend to focus on detailed case studies of curriculum-making. For instance, Bisset and Potvin (2007) talk of educational programmes as 'negotiated spaces' in their study of the introduction of a nutrition programme into schools. For them, the nature of that space is also about the relationship between education and the community, which raises issues about professionalism and professional boundaries.

While such studies draw upon different aspects of and concepts from ANT, they all attempt to understand the ways in which the curriculum is ordered, assembled, distributed and performed through a range of material networks within which any object is interconnected, linked to institutional structures, everyday practices and policies in different domains. Curriculum-making can be traced in the processes of assembling and maintaining these networks, as well as in the negotiations and translations that occur at various nodes comprising a network. In this approach:

> the meanings of an event are constituted by hooking it up to moving networks of people acting, with, through, and by virtue of their entanglements with durable artefacts, structures and materials. Into these networks of action are woven so many commitments, identities and interests ...
>
> (Nespor 2003: 95)

It is through these translations that networks form, reform and dissolve.

> According to the latter (the model of translation), the spread in time and space of anything – claims, orders, artefacts, goods – is in the hands of people; each of these people may act in many different ways, letting the token drop, or modifying it, or deflecting it, or betraying it, or adding to it, or appropriating it ... When no one is there to take up the statement or token then it simply drops.
>
> (Latour 1986: 267)

However, translation is never a straightforward process; 'translation is always insecure, a process susceptible to failure. Disorder – or other orders – are only precariously kept at bay' (Law 2007).

The role of the token is important here. In early ANT, a token can be both discourses and things. The concept of token became reframed as a boundary object, which we outlined in the previous chapter. In later work by Latour (2005b) the token became differentiated as both mediator and intermediary. However, early Latour (1986) used the notion of tokens to challenge more conventional views that ideas and things diffuse through society in an unproblematic linear manner.

In this view, the idea or thing is unchanged by its movement within the associational realm. The token remains itself even as it diffuses. As Gaskell and Hepburn
(1998: 66) explain it, in a framing informed by diffusion:

> once 'discovered' or 'invented', the token moves through society unchanged
> encountering either people who use it and pass it on to others or people who
> resist it and don't use it. The path of the token is a product of the power
> of the originator of the idea and the frictions and resistances (lack of com-
> munication, ill will, opposition from interest groups, indifference) that it
> encounters.

Diffusion or epidemiological views treat implementation, change and innovation
as processes whereby some thing (idea, information, technology) is developed and
then transmitted in a linear fashion through an initial impetus by an authoritative
source. Such notions are challenged over their failure to attend to the multiple
micro-negotiations going on at each node in processes of translation. It is the
failure of such approaches on which ANT and ANT-influenced studies of innovation often focus (for example, Latour 1996, Law 2002, Suchman 2006). It is also
one of the reasons why participatory design has become very much more in vogue
in attempts to develop innovative technologies, as this brings more actors into
the development process as a whole. ANT challenges any notion of innovation
as being singular and immutable. As we have seen, recent ANT-related analyses
acknowledge the capacity for an object to exist as different things simultaneously
that all manage to remain bound as one recognizable thing.

The ANT concept of translation provides us with an alternative way of understanding these movements across space and time. Here, a token is not usually
passed unchanged, but can be ignored or taken up and translated as different
interests are invested in it. As a result, the token is itself changed.

> The path of the token is a product of the number and strength of the links
> that are established between it and a diverse group of other actors. It is not a
> product of an initial quality but of the subsequent actions of a multitude of
> others. In the model of translation, not only the token is continuously trans-
> formed as links with other actors are established but so are the other actors.
> As they take up and use the token, their actions and patterns of practice
> are changed as they see new possibilities with the token. Those associated
> with the token form a network through links with the token. The network
> is defined by the token but the token is also simultaneously defined by the
> network. The network and token co-evolve. As the token/network system
> stabilises the token is seen to be an unproblematic artefact or to define a part
> of nature, the network is seen to define a part of society and each is depend-
> ent on the other.
>
> (Gaskell and Hepburn 1998: 66)

These translations are possible because tokens are always unfinished and there are patterns of possibility that can be inscribed into them and that they inscribe in others, a dynamic that is explored also in conceptions of boundary objects.

In this ANT enactment, the co-emergence of token and network is an actor–network. Here, the changes that emerge across space and time are not a problem to be explained, as we see in much of the discussion about the differences between the prescribed, described and enacted curriculum. It is rather an expected part of curriculum-making as a network effect. As network effects, curriculum-making are enactments which are inevitably multiple both across different networks of action but also for those engaged in the practices.

In their study, Gaskell and Hepburn (1998) explored the way in which a particular curriculum innovation in Canada was translated in different ways in two settings to establish what they refer to as a 'coursenetwork'. They follow the official prescribed curriculum for the course innovation into the settings. Their understanding of this process is helpful:

> By focusing on the course as a token circulating and simultaneously defining and being defined by a network, and seeing the outcome as a coursenet-work, it is possible to understand the construction of different outcomes. An innovation tests the strength of the links in an existing coursenetwork. A successful innovation results in a modification to that coursenetwork. The stability of the innovation increases as the number of human and non-human actors linked to the innovation increases and as the strength of those links increases. However, the successful enrolment of additional actors entails translating their interests into the course through a process of negotiation in which the course and the actors are simultaneously transformed.
>
> (Gaskell and Hepburn 1998: 74)

In ANT studies, curriculum change is enacted as practices of network growth and the translations associated with it rather than as being simply about the imple-mentation of the prescribed to the enacted curriculum. Within this approach, the role of tokens or boundary objects in translating the interests, desires, aspirations, affordances of the many entities necessary to produce a coursenetwork is central.

Curriculum-making in college and school

The example of curriculum-making to which we now turn comes from Scotland (Miller *et al.* 2009). It is the outcomes-based Scottish Qualifications Authority (SQA) unit descriptors that schools and colleges mainly utilize when developing a curriculum in particular subjects. These provide the basis for the prescribed curriculum by specifying certain learning outcomes to be achieved at a specified level within a hierarchical system of assessment. At the level of the prescription, therefore, the curriculum is very standardized and rational, in principle enabling and supporting student mobility and the portability of credit within and across the education system. Such approaches are common around the world. In theory, there are many curriculum routes to achieve the outcomes and this provides the possibility for creative approaches to pedagogy on the part of institutions, departments and teachers/lecturers. This approach to the curriculum assumes that learning outcomes are the same despite different means of developing and demonstrating them.

However, research evidence from such systems suggests that there is less diversity in the described and enacted curriculum than envisioned or desired (Smyth *et al.* 1998). Indeed, many unit descriptors would seem to seek greater standardization, as they do not only specify learning outcomes, but also make broad statements about expectations in relation to teaching, learning and assessment practices to achieve those goals, thereby seeming to limit the possibilities for diversity. Further, a great deal of research points to a tendency for continuity rather than change in what goes on in schools and colleges in response to centrally mandated reform initiatives (e.g. Spillane 1999, Goodson 2004). For instance, Harris-Hart (2009: 116) suggests that 'teachers are often positioned to interpret policy texts in an unquestioning or non-critical manner and curriculum documents therefore give way to preferred readings'. Cuban (1984) identified a number of stability factors in schools that militate against changes in practice, for example, schools prize obedience over independent thinking, the existing culture of teaching, and the socialization of teachers through their own schooling. The availability of published textbooks and other resources, and teachers' existing frames of reference also act to enable and constrain curriculum-making in rigid ways.

Such factors and the persistence of established practices are positioned as contributing to the gaps between the prescribed, described and the enacted curriculum, despite the supposed standardization imposed through prescription. Research thus suggests that attempts to provide a standardized prescribed curriculum with equivalences across sites is not being achieved in the enacted curriculum. Different questions can be inferred from this conclusion. Research has tended to focus on providing explanatory factors for such divergence, with curriculum-making being taken as an object to be explained with the potential for future standardization and stabilization. Drawing upon ANT, we assume that heterogeneity and multiplicity are inherent in curriculum-making practices and therefore there is nothing to be explained (away) as such. It is simply the case.

In this section, we turn to a discussion of two brief case studies, adopting an ANT analysis to trace the curriculum-making processes that appeared. The cases were generated in two associated sites, a secondary school and a college of further education. The project explored three curriculum areas, hospitality, life sciences and technical studies, drawing data from various courses at equivalent levels at the two sites. Each unit within the individual curriculum areas had similar learning outcomes specified in the prescribed curriculum to enable as close a comparison across organizational sites as possible. The focus here is upon the hospitality cases.

In examining the enacted curriculum in this project, what became clear was the sheer abundance and importance of things to curriculum-making. Like those exploring the materialities of schooling (Lawn and Grosvenor 2005, Martinez 2005), the project began to focus on how objects become translated into particular forms of coursenetwork. Drawing on the principle of symmetry, the study was particularly interested in the unit descriptor, representing the prescribed curriculum, as token in the process of curriculum-making (Edwards 2010). The unit descriptors are themselves an effect of a lot of work to stabilize and bound a set of activities as standardized 'learning outcomes' that can then be taken up within different educational settings. Inscription is part of that process and also their authoritative location in an online library of units and qualifications. Their virtuality means that they are an outcome of the translation of a qwerty keyboard into code, which can then be retrieved online or in print as written text. Their availability is distributed across space and time, in order to regulate through the standardization of learning outcomes.

The college hospitality unit descriptor – *Cookery Processes* – had as its prescribed outcomes:

- Describe the cookery processes, their associated principles, and foods suitable for each process.
- Perform numerical tasks related to food preparation.
- Using commercial catering equipment, carry out the cookery processes to given specifications.
- Interpret oral instructions and standard recipes to carry out the cookery processes on a range of foods.

The school hospitality unit descriptor – *Practical Skills for the Hospitality Industry* – had as its prescribed outcomes:

- Prepare a range of food using appropriate techniques and equipment.
- Cook and present a range of food to an appropriate standard.
- Work in a safe and hygienic manner.

The similarity in the two units is emphasized by a certain commonality in the more detailed expectations of teaching, learning and assessment activities associated with each of the descriptors. Both of these descriptors or tokens therefore focused on enabling students to prepare food in a safe and hygienic way using appropriate equipment and techniques. In order to do so, the tokens needed to mobilize a variety of people and things in particular settings in order that they could have an existence.

Both units were part of courses with very similar overall aims. The college course – *Professional Cookery* – aimed to provide 'a thorough introduction to the techniques, skills and knowledge required to operate in the kitchen areas of a wide variety of commercial establishments'. The school course – *Practical*

Cookery – aimed to provide 'the development of techniques and skills required for food production appropriate to domestic and hospitality situations'. The difference between the two courses is in the way in which the home is mobilized as a setting for hospitality as well as commercial settings in the school. This is because of the history of cookery in the school curriculum as part of home economics. The institutions can ostensibly 'choose' which course at this level is most appropriate to their own organizational and curricular aims and best suited to their staff and student profiles. However, the tokens make themselves more available to one setting rather than the other through the ways in which they inscribe the outcomes to be achieved.

The short cases attempt to illuminate curriculum-making as network effects, in the process showing how similar unit descriptors (tokens) were translated into different coursenetworks as the prescribed curriculum was enacted in the different settings.

The college setting: hospitality coursenetwork

In the college, the unit descriptor mobilized and was translated by the lecturer, Malcolm, an ex-professional chef with many years of experience in different kitchens, who had gained his occupational qualifications part time. His enrolment into full-time lecturing at college was gradual and importantly influenced by personal reasons, in particular the desire for more family-friendly working hours. Prior to becoming a lecturer, Malcolm had worked in a variety of UK and overseas commercial settings. He moved into tutoring while working in a restaurant, initially one day per week, gradually gaining his teaching qualifications. In this arrangement he was both extending his initial networks but also being enrolled into that of teaching. Mulcahy (1998: 28) identified similar moves in her research on vocational education:

> Switching between, and combining, the tools and materials of competency-based training (for example, textual representations of competency; pre-set standards) and the tools and materials of their practice worlds (for instance, bodily representations of competency; negotiated standards; 'process' approaches to curricula).

The unit was taught over two lots of 18 weeks, with three kitchen-based sessions and one classroom-based session per week. Attendance by students was erratic – Malcolm identified one or two of the nine students as 'not good attendees', their enrolment into the coursenetwork being incomplete. The unit descriptor was translated within the college in three adjacent spaces – a large kitchen, a small kitchen and a more conventional classroom. The kitchens simulated the environments to be found in commercial hospitality workplaces. Each of these spaces was mobilized at different times for different purposes. A lot of the work in the kitchens involved preparing food for the college restaurant which was open to the public. The interests of the public's desire for food and the standards of the industry therefore had to be enrolled into the ways in which the token was enacted in the practices of Malcolm and the students.

Malcolm initially taught the students by focusing on building on their basic skills in cooking. When they reached a certain level, they then started preparing the food for the restaurant, the interests of the customers being used to shape the practices of the kitchen. The professional orientation of this enactment was embodied in the clothes of staff and students when working in the kitchens – white coats, hats and trousers. These clothes were provided to students at the start of their course, along with knives and a cookery book containing all the information they needed to pass the assessment for the unit.

The cookery book was an obligatory passage point, as it inscribed the outcomes of the unit descriptor, but translated them to embrace the full range of knowledge, understanding and recipes that were required. The token was translated into the activities associated with working in this occupation, but also became invisible, as references were to the cookery book and not the unit descriptor itself. The cookery book, therefore, became a key actor in curriculum-making, a focus for activity that brought together the lecturer, students, things and ingredients to rehearse the practices of commercial hospitality kitchens.

However, there were also more conventional educational outcomes to be achieved. Thus, the unit descriptor also mobilized certain things from the conventional classroom within the kitchens. A flipchart and textbooks, which would not be in a commercial setting, were enrolled in the coursenetwork. The flipchart displayed the menu the students were working on and the number of portions needed. The textbooks were open and the students followed instructions on food preparation from Malcolm. Students also had access to a folder with the recipes for the restaurant menus which they used for recipes for large numbers of customers, but for instructions around processes for smaller numbers they referred to the textbook. There was an immense textual mediation of the curriculum, which was perhaps unexpected given that Hospitality is an arena often associated with limited literacy (Ivanič *et al.* 2009).

The spatial ordering of the curriculum was also significant. In contrast to the kitchens, the classroom was laid out with tables for students forming a rectangle, with the lecturer at the front; a particular ordering space and possibilities for interaction. A range of things were available in the space to be mobilized. These included a digital screen, audiovisual equipment and an overhead projector on the lecturer's desk. As well as class-related items on their desks, the students often had mobile phones, drinks and iPods visible, giving a certain informality to the atmosphere, translating their interests as individuals and not merely as students into the curriculum space.

The classroom informality contrasted with the formality of their work in the kitchens which needed to be clutter free of personal items for health and safety reasons. This change in activity and use of space was also signalled through a more chatty style which punctuated the more focused instructional discourse of the classroom interactions. In the kitchen, the whole focus was on the food prep-aration and any talk between teacher and students tended to be about, or related to, the task in hand.

Outside speakers from the hospitality industry were brought into the college to talk with students, encouraging them to have part-time jobs in hospitality while studying in order to build networks in the industry. Here, similar to Nespor's (1994) management students, there was a clear attempt to mobilize dispositions and practices that would stand the students in good stead beyond the course. In this way the hospitality coursenetwork was expanded beyond the college and that prescribed in the token in order to make it more durable.

In the large kitchen, people and things were mobilized in a number of ways, for instance, to support learning by doing by the students, and through the demonstration of cooking techiniques by Malcolm, which the students watched. In one session, the students were preparing for Christmas dinners in the restaurant. Here, the annual celebration was mobilized as the rationale for a particular set of recipes. The students used their textbooks for guidance and there was less demonstrating than previously. The lecturer became less central to the working of the coursenetwork, as students referred to books and each other in order to coordinate their activities. The importance of teamwork in a kitchen was emphasized. The students were encouraged to make full use of the immaterial in their cooking. Smell, taste and look were therefore invoked as important aspects of cooking, as well as the proper use of pans, knives, mixers, etc. Here, the embodied experience of food was mobilized as a way through which students could learn.

We therefore see that the token, the unit descriptor, takes up and is taken up in a networked array of practices in enacting hospitality in curriculum-making in college. It becomes a hospitality coursenetwork.

The school setting: cookery coursenetwork

This unit descriptor in the school both translated, and was translated by, Pauline as a teacher of home economics. She had started a degree in food, health and welfare and, following a brief placement in a school, decided to become a teacher. She trained at university and then obtained a temporary post at the school in which she taught. Her practical experience of hospitality was domestic rather than commercial and this was reflected in how she was mobilized in the enact-ment of the curriculum. It was domestic scales which were translated into the learning outcomes of this token. The hospitality industry became largely erased in the translations from the prescribed into the enacted curriculum. Here then, despite similar learning outcomes to those of the college unit, a cookery rather than a hospitality coursenetwork was enacted.

The unit descriptor was translated in one room in the home economics depart-ment of the school. The department was on the second floor and the corridor was filled with displays of posters promoting healthy eating and a prevailing smell of food and cooking. The classroom was divided into many kitchenette areas, each with a sink, oven, cupboards to store equipment and a work surface. The doors of the cupboards had diagrams on them to show what should be stored there. There was a walk-in cupboard at the front of the class which held fridge freezers and large containers. The scale was domestic rather than commercial, as were the number of portions of food the students produced. The kitchen combined as a classroom with a teacher's desk at the front with a digital board and a rotating white board. The computer in the classroom was used by Pauline to display the learning outcomes of that class, to access emails and so on, but also to search the internet for information. The display of the learning outcomes made the token translated but also very visible in each class. This display was central to the mobilizing of activities in the coursenetwork.

However, the translation process also meant that certain aspects of the unit descriptor became invisible. Thus, the full title of the unit was only placed on the inside cover of the teacher's workbook, and on all other school produced materials (e.g. student workbook, support notes and the recipe booklet). The unit was simply called *Practical Cookery*. This, alongside the scale of cookery in the class, suggests that the occupational relevance of the unit was untranslated or pushed to one side by more powerful interests. As it was her first time teaching the unit, Pauline worked entirely from the school produced packs, which, like Malcolm's cookery book, were mobilized as a translation of the unit descriptor into the classroom setting. Such packs themselves become tokens, the translations that brought them into enactment and the erasure of the hospitality industry being glossed over. Indeed, the hospitality industry is black-boxed and excluded through its silencing as it is translated.

There were four students for this class, all female. Two were very interested in home economics, while the other two were doing the course as a respite from their more academic studies. This contrasting enrolment was reflected in attendance, degrees of interest and the interactions of the teacher with the respective students. The small class contrasted with an equivalent class in the school, which had 18 students. The different size of groups arose from timetable issues within the school, the timetable being a major actor in the coursenetwork in terms of ordering people into specific spaces at certain times. For Pauline, the small group allowed for a more informal and interactive style of teaching than normal. Ostensibly this might have supported strong enrolment within the coursenetwork but this did not occur, reflecting the different degrees of interessement and enrolment of the students. Those with an interest in pursuing home economics beyond school were enrolled more strongly than those for whom it was positioned as a break from their main academic focus.

The unit descriptor translated Pauline, who placed the learning outcomes for each class on the digital board and went over them with the class. The scale of the servings was small – four. Because of the constraints of the timetable, not all aspects of the processes being engaged with were contained within the one class. Working within the time frames of the hospitality coursenetwork can be contrasted with the constant running out of time to complete activities in the cookery coursenetwork. To run out of time in hospitality is to fail occupational norms.

Time seemed a fairly constant actor in trying to translate the unit descriptor in the curriculum. For instance, when the students were making cakes, Pauline instructed them to whisk the cream with an electric mixer once the cakes were in the oven. In principle, they should not use the electric whisk for this task but time was short. Pauline had the students set timers for the cakes (which ended up burning), and the students washed up and put away equipment. There was an even greater sense of hurriedness to this session than previous ones.

Once again, in this example we witness how a large network is translated by and translates the token of the unit descriptor as it enters a particular site. By contrast with the hospitality coursenetwork in the college, the school can be characterized as a cookery coursenetwork. We also witness how ostensibly similar learning outcomes are enacted multiply through the translations to which the unit descriptors are subject, mobilizing different spaces, people and artefacts as curriculum-making.

It is clear that any notion of implementation or diffusion in the enactment of the curriculum is misplaced, given the range and diversity of the interests, identities and things, as tokens are translated and translate, betrayed and betray. The case studies clearly indicate the ways in which the token of the prescribed curriculum is translated as it mobilizes and is itself translated by a range of other actors in the network. The prescribed curriculum is enacted as a hospitality and cookery coursenetwork respectively in the examples above. This cannot be reduced simply to human intention, or other factors as foundational explanations of what is occurring. Similar prescribed learning outcomes result in very different types of educative enactments. In the process, the prescribed curriculum in its translations has varying degrees of visibility as it is enacted. Curriculum-making is heterogeneous and multiple from this ANT enactment and not an object within a context.

Although ostensibly taking similar units within a standardized curriculum framework, it is clear that the enacted curriculum in hospitality varies significantly as it is translated into the different settings of school and college. We may infer from this one case that schools and colleges may provide similar opportunities at a formal level, but they are very different organizations serving different student groups, often with different types of staff with varying professional backgrounds and formations. Curriculum-making is multiple because the prescribed curriculum mobilizes different and often conflicting networks. Difference and multiplicity in the curriculum is therefore to be expected and described rather than be identified as problematic and explained (away). This raises important educational questions about the status and equivalence of learning outcomes within a standardized curriculum and the type and amount of work that is necessary to exclude multiplicity in the name of standardization.

Inferences

We may, therefore, begin to reframe some of our research focus from examining factors to explain differences to exploring actors enacting those differences through symmetry, translation and other concepts from ANT. To examine curriculum-making as a network effect in which no a priori status is given to certain objects is not an easy approach to grasp, or to represent adequately. What it does point to is that there is more to curriculum-making than we might imagine and that what is enrolled and translated into it makes a big difference in terms of both practices and what is taught and learnt. This also goes beyond cognitive and social understandings of the curriculum, both of which are based on the search for foundational explanations. This may not be a comfortable space, but it is a necessary one if we are to make sense of the curriculum-making practices in education.

It is the emergence of curriculum through its practices that lead some to position teachers not as curriculum-makers, therefore, but as curriculum performers. Such a positioning:

> acknowledges the agency of humans and non-human actors that influence the ways in which teachers perform curriculum; (2) allows for a more temporally inclusive examination of the curriculum (the enactment of the curriculum involves multiple rehearsals and performances over time; and (3) highlights the importance of audience – the ways in which teachers perform curriculum can be contextualized more clearly in view of varied audiences (colleagues, educational leaders and students for example).
>
> (Harris-Hart 2009: 120)

One thing that is crucial to ANT is the active role of things in having effects. In this chapter, we have drawn upon a study where the thing to be followed was the unit descriptor, something which itself became more or les visible as it was translated in the enactments of differing coursenetworks. We now turn to a set of things that have and are having a profound effect on education. These are the new technologies of information and communication. As these have started to have effects, and as network metaphors have become central to their translation into education, it is now time to explore what ANT analyses of technologized learning enact.

Chapter 5

Networking technologized learning

For the purposes of this chapter, we use the notion of technologized learning (TL) to denote the use of information and communications technologies (ICTs) in education. Education here continues to refer to activities ranging from school classroom teaching to workplace learning, and TL issues ranging from the implementation of system-wide technologies to learners' engagement with so called web 2.0 environments, and from the role of ICT in the managing and administration of organizations to the use of assistive technologies. Tracing the genealogy of the different terms deployed to frame our understanding of ICTs in education would itself be an interesting task, but one beyond the scope of this book. E-learning, networked learning, online learning, open learning, distributed learning, virtual education, digital media and technology for learning, technology enhanced learning, are all used to enact the entanglements of computing and education. Each in their own way is trying to characterize particular relationships among electronic technology, teaching and learning – as, for instance, different pedagogic spaces, different pedagogic relationships and identities, or simply a more efficient technology for teaching and learning.

Here, it is important to point to the way in which the technology in TL is often reduced to that associated with computing. However, it does not take much sense of the historical to realize that education has always had material technologies associated with it, ether directly or indirectly: technologies to which ANT studies in education have attended with particular interest. Directly, through such items as pens, cookers, Bunsen burners, slates, chalk, etc., and indirectly, through such things as mass produced textbooks that rely on the printing press, electricity networks that power the infrastructure of institutions, or the roads and buses that enable teachers and students to journey from home to institution and back – with no doubt occasional loiterings along the way. Each technology in education is therefore always already an assemblage. So, for example, in relation to the uptake of interactive television (ITV):

> The ITV technology and equipment in many 'smart' classrooms and distance-learning facilities enlist a host of participating actants. The hosting institution sets aside funds and employment; the academic and facilities departments

fill those employment slots; the telephone company provides technical consultants and account administrators; glossy advertising copy draws in audience support; clocks regulate labour hours; darker shades of paint ensure appropriate background contrast; and any number of other actants come together to ensure that ITV functions within certain parameters.

(Waltz 2004: 169–70)

Thus, while technology has always been part of modern education, it is almost as though it is only with the spread of computing that technology has become visible along with all the lash-ups that make it possible.

However, despite the importance of technologies, both psychologized framing of learning as largely individual and cognitive and the sociologized framing of education as an engine for social mobility and reproduction have seemingly passed over the 'hard stuff' of the material in their rush to explain. This is particularly interesting given the uptake of ethnographic approaches from anthropology in the new sociology of education in the 1970s. Anthropology, traditionally, has tried to understand cultures partly through the objects and artefacts that are integrated in meaningful social practices. The material matters in the understanding of culture. Phenomenology has, therefore, been integral to anthropology as a discipline. Objects have traditionally been taken to be those givens that particular groups invest meaning with, usually natural objects of one sort or another. Artefacts are usually taken to be crafted in some way, such as pots and jewellery. There has been much debate about the distinctions and significance of the differences between objects and artefacts. This has been complicated further by questions about the role of tools, for artefacts require tools to be crafted, however close those tools might themselves be to objects, such as a sharp piece of flint. We can extend this complex picture further by asking what or how we perceive technology to have a role in all this. When do tools become a technology? When do tools and artefacts require a technology to support their production? For some, the notion of technology is associated with industrialization and the loss of craft in the production of artefacts. However, it is also possible to frame artefacts, tools and even objects as technologies. These debates are played out in discussions of the nature of materiality in understanding practices (Miller 2005, Henare *et al.* 2007), debates which themselves have been influenced by ANT and, in particular, the work of Latour.

There are complex conceptual issues here, which themselves impact upon our enactments of education, but remain largely silenced in the major focus on human interaction and meaning in the enacting of teaching and learning. It may well be because computers have come to interrupt that humanist notion of interaction in such a significant way that it has become noticed as a technology and therefore given voice through TL and its multiple enactments. This has given rise to much exploration of post-humanist positions wherein the human and technological are entwined. Technologies can be internally embedded in the body, e.g. pacemakers; externally amplifying the body, e.g. glasses and watches; or periodically interacting with the body, e.g. kettles, iPhones. A favoured metaphor in such approaches is that of the cyborg, and cyborg learning is one enactment of TL. Indeed, as we indicated in an earlier chapter, some have suggested the cyborg as a way of intervening in education more generally.

> The idea of rhizomANTically becoming-cyborg signifies my desire to imagine teaching and learning as material-semiotic assemblages of sociotechnical relations embedded in and performed by shifting connections and interactions among a variety of organic, technical, 'natural' and textual materials.
>
> (Gough 2004: 255)

To become-cyborg is, therefore, to accept the general principle of symmetry in educational pursuits. However, as we will explore, this somewhat exotic notion of TL is challenged by research which shows its often mundane character in everyday lives (Peterson 2007). Of course, Gough, and others influenced by ANT, might well argue that becoming-cyborg is itself an expression of the mundane in the materiality of education. This is especially so given the proliferation of technologies of, for instance:

- social networking (e.g. Facebook, Twitter)
- information sharing (e.g. Delicious, Flickr)
- identity construction and marketing (e.g. blogs)
- collective knowledge construction (e.g. wikis)
- immersive ecologies (e.g. Second Life)
- multimedia product creation and gaming (e.g. fan video making, mashups, blogs).

Here, to be human is the exotic categorization, purifying humanity of the non-human elements that make its own existence possible. Indeed, it may be in the affordances of interconnections, content creation, remixing and interactivity that we could become more human, as 'humanity' is able to become more mobile as material set of practices rather than as a transcendental category. Educators seem to be constantly trying to catch up with the practices of these technologies, and, of course, their implications for education. ANT provides a basis for tracing the former, although implications for the latter may be less clear or even.

ANT is not the only framing of education that attends to the role of tools, artefacts and technologies. Both situated learning theories and activity theory have given voice to their roles in learning as a practice. However, they both also give primacy to the human, and to human participation, practices and cognition in their framings of the role of the material in learning and teaching. In relation to emerging forms of TL, they also fail to give sufficient attention to the creative as well as participative aspects of practices, where there are opportunities for authoring, multiple identity enactments and the transgression of the narrative substructures written into the software. Boyd (2007) argues that online identities produce new forms of public space characterized by searchability, replicability, persistence and invisible audiences. Traces of the self are available more widely and to wider audiences than would have been the case in earlier eras. Within such spaces and practices, of course, there remain questions of their educative value, of access to and equity within these ecologies and of the potential for abuse (e.g. grooming) and the reproduction of traditional divisions.

Over the years, we have also witnessed the specific development of human–computer interaction (HCI) studies with a focus on ICT as a particularly significant technology for humans. Some of these have been influential in ANT in drawing the distinction between the planned development and implementation of technologies and the situated actions through which they are shaped and enacted (Suchman 2007). This has given rise to the notion of participatory design in developing technology and also TL, whereby users of the technology are engaged in the processes of its design. However, this is not easy, nor always with the desired consequences, given the different ontologies within which computer scientists and users may dwell. In educational uptakes of ICT, for instance, we may have educationalists, computer scientists, cognitive scientists, subject specialists, managers, students, parents, professional bodies and employers negotiating the particular design requirements in specific sites and settings. The relationships between, and notions of, designer and user have therefore become more precarious as the technological possibilities proliferate, and some users (e.g. students) may have skills equivalent to or greater than some designers (e.g. teachers). It is common to frame these all as having different perspectives on the same design. Drawing upon after-ANT, we may consider the stakeholders as dwelling in different ontologies where the design will never be singular, but rather a temporary assemblage.

In considering TL we also need to look beyond the computer, which might itself be taken to be a black box. An important part of the relationality and communication in and between computers remains hidden in many studies of TL, as it sits within the software that enables them to operate and be networked together (Lanzara and Morner 2005). It is the communication associated with coding that, with the hardware and electricity, makes ICT perform. The work of software pervades the world. Thus, as Thrift (2005: 240) observes:

> software has grown from a small thicket of mechanical writing to a forest of code covering much of the globe ... Code runs all manner of everyday devices, from electric toothbrushes to microwave ovens, from traffic lights to cars, from mobile phones to the most sophisticated computers.

It might, therefore, be argued that it is not ICT that is transforming learning and teaching but the codes that support different possibilities dependent upon the alliances and networks of which they are a part. Similarly, with increasing amounts of information being gained through online search engines, such as Google, it is important to recognize that the results of such searches depend upon the 'tagging' of data in ways that make it accessible to search engines, rather than on the quality or accuracy of the information per se. Yet, if ever there is an area that is black-boxed, it is software. For most educators, computers simply do things, and how they come to do those things is not examined. Software is performative and not representational and thus its importance, which is perhaps also reflected in its absence from debate.

Only a selection of issues associated with TL can be explored in this chapter and it is fair to say that there is scope for much more ANT analysis in TL given the multiplication of the latter and the many educational issues it raises (Greenhow *et al.* 2009). First we will focus on how computers have been viewed in education. We will show how it is precisely, as a technology separated from society, that they are deployed in institutional settings. Second, we examine the diverse uptakes of ANT in various studies of technological implementation to show the sorts of questions and approaches that researchers have enacted through ANT perspectives. Then we will focus upon one curriculum development initiative to introduce videoconferencing into a higher education setting in Australia. We will also point to some of the emerging possibilities for ANT studies of ICTs in education.

Are computers different?

It is often a surprise to consider how recently computers have become a ubiquitous part of our practices of educating. Many of those working in educational settings began their careers in the era before the PC became a standard part of working life. The original PC is about as distant from the wi-fi multifunctional computer that we have now as a supersonic jet from a First World War biplane. The technologies of Web 2.0 and the possibilities of the semantic web provide the possibilities for forms of interaction, learning and knowledge production stretched across space and time that were barely imaginable ten years ago. Mobile technologies are providing possibilities for endlessly reconfiguring the space–time geometries of education (Edwards and Usher 2008). However, we should not get too carried away, as much education still takes place using multiple technologies which are not ICTs.

So how did computers find their way into education? This is an issue explored by Bigum (1998) in relation to schooling in Australia. And here he used ANT to identify the ways in which computers were enacted as a technology separate from society in order that the cases for and against their use could be put forward. Bigum was therefore pointing to the importance of separation or purification in the work to introduce computers into schools. His study was based upon a discourse analysis of 'the educational roles that have been assigned to computers and related technologies in schools' (Bigum 1998: 587). He identified within these discourses that computers are given certain intrinsic qualities – qualities which rest in them as separate things – and that these, then, were deployed to assign roles to the institutions and persons that use them. Computers were therefore enacted through essentialist accounts which:

distinguish human and nonhuman elements ... What remains is a machine with a set of intrinsic, fixed, essential properties and human elements that are temporary – the providers of a context in which the technology is used ... The separation of 'the social' and 'the technical' sustains a framing in which the inherent capacities are not at issue.

(Bigum 1998: 588-9)

In other words, the discourses purify the technologies from the social. This results in and from an essentializing of their capacities and turns them into black boxes – things with taken for granted characteristics – where the work to enact them in this way is already lost.

In his analysis, Bigum was attempting to open the box, to show the work done to enact technologies in this way precisely through attempted purification. He identified four such discourses through which computers are enacted. The dominant is what he termed booster discourses. These 'promote a strong sense of inevitability about using computers in schools and demonstrate unshakable faith in the capacity of computer technology to solve most, if not all, of the problems of schooling' (Bigum 1998: 589–90). The essentialized capacities of computers – for example, interactivity, responsiveness and engagement – are positioned as resulting naturally in the enhancement of learning and teaching. Where this enhancement does not take place, it is a 'problem' of implementation, for example inadequate resources or resisting teachers.

The second set of discourses Bigum identified was of the anti-schoolers. In these discourses, computers could revolutionize learning to the extent that schools and teachers become redundant. Computers represent 'speed, efficiency and convenience' while schools are 'inefficient, slow, industrial age social structures' and teachers 'dull and boring' (Bigum 1998: 591). For anti-schoolers, computers have an inherent capacity to revolutionize rather than enhance learning.

The politics of computers defines the third set of critical discourses. Here, it is the loss of jobs, deskilling and surveillance associated with the deployment of computers that is of importance. However, computers themselves, the technology, are often positioned as neutral. The ways in which they are used in different social orders shapes them and is the issue. A subset of the critical discourses was what Bigum referred to as doomster discourses. These discourses share with the anti-schoolers the notion that computers are a revolutionizing technology. However, they are strongly opposed to this revolution and its effects. Here, the introduction of computers into schools was decried for its impact upon education.

While Bigum's piece was published in 1998, the discourses he identified are still rife in contemporary debates about TL. While they rely upon a purification of technology as separate from the social, Bigum offers a different analysis of how computers came to be taken up in schools based upon the alliances and networks that were formed in and through them. These alliances included teachers, schools and children, but also parents, home and computer vendors. This has seen the extension of computer use not only into schools but also into homes to the extent that it has become a mundane technology in many households around the world. In the process, the attribute of computers to enhance learning, which was the vaunted claim of computer vendors and boosters in and around schools, has itself been translated into a more diverse set of possibilities associated with gaming, social networking and communication.

While Bigum used ANT to explore how computers are positioned within schools, Fox (2000, 2001, 2005) used other aspects of ANT in relation to conceptions of networked learning. In challenging the notion of communities of practice as adequate to framing practices in networked learning, Fox (2001) identified the different ways in which technologies have been taken up to enable the spread of standardized practices and order. He did this firstly in relation to the printing press which made the mobilization and immutability of inscriptions possible. As the practices associated with printing spread, so standardized texts become available in centres of learning and libraries across space and time. A canon of knowledge therefore becomes possible through the wide availability of printed texts. For Fox, this standardization results in a privileging of knowledge as abstract, as a uniform typeface replaces the particularities and idiosyncracies of handwriting. The advent of the internet further provides for an enhancement of both mobility and mutability. However, it might also be argued that this depends on the ways in which the technology is configured. In relation to the amount of authoring on the internet there is, then multiplicity is also at play alongside forms of standardization. It may, therefore, be that simply extending the argument from the printing press to the internet in our understanding of education may be over simplistic. The logics and screen and page differ, as writing, mashing up and interaction as well as reading are more available through web-based discussion spaces for a (Kress 2003) and social networking is now identified as an online activity that can contribute to learning.

This interplay of the exotic and the mundane is significant in the discourses of TL and ICT and the internet more generally. All the discourses identified by Bigum suggest computers to be exotic in their inherent capacity to revolutionize. Indeed, Waltz (2004) pointed to the way many decry the way ICT is absorbed into the existing places and relationships of education, reproducing many of the power relations that some see TL as challenging. Emerging technologies provide the basis for learning ecologies in which people dwell and create in multiple sites and settings, based on, for instance, interest and affinity as well as necessity, the boundaries of which are insecure and mobile. Where and how learning is mobilized within such practices is open to question and raises challenges for educators.

More recent work has tended to show how computer use has become a far more mundane part of daily practices, at least in the areas where broadband has become available. In his small-scale study of students' practices in Denmark, Peterson (2007) suggested that broadband enacts the internet as mundane alongside kettles, televisions and fridges in how it is used. This is not to say that there are no changes associated with internet use: there are. Peterson suggested that the space and time of the everyday are reconfigured, as some of the traditional categorizations of what was done where and at what time no longer hold. There is 'a weakening of the usual structure of everyday life differentiated into different zones of work, study and recreation' (Peterson 2007: 86). The students will therefore surf the internet while boiling an egg. The alliances of the technologies with the human begin to raise questions about the categorizations that have been used often to structure our understanding of the everyday and of ICTs.

This mundane usage contrasts with the exotic discourses of ICT identified by Bigum. Yet, it is in tracing the alliances and networks of ICTs that we are able to identify the everyday ways in which TL is enacted. These are the situated actions to which we referred, where design, however participatory, might be said to constantly escape the limits of its own enactments. It suggests that the use of the internet for learning far outweighs the scope of the designers of TEL (Lepa and Tatnall 2006), because the everyday has an excess when contrasted with the attempts to stabilize associated with developing education. And that excess is often positioned as exotic. How, for instance, do we position the practices around creating an avatar in online environments? To be other than oneself in being oneself is not a new phenomenon if we think of the ways in which humans perform both a disclosing and hiding of themselves on a daily basis – at work and at play. But to be other than oneself through projecting into the avatar rather than in (un)masking entails a different set of networking practices and different ways through which to sustain an identity. Learning how to be an avatar and learning through being an avatar might be contrasted as a simulation rather than a real experience. But in ANT terms they both are material enactments; the real cannot be purified from the simulated. The attempt to sustain such a distinction is itself an effect to be traced.

The technological device

Tracing the development of TL has become an important area of research in education, perhaps receiving more sustained interest than in many other areas. This use of ANT is not in itself surprising, for historically ANT has been preoccupied with the processes of technical innovation. As Nespor (2010) reminds us, Law and Callon (1992: 46) argued that the success of a 'technological project' depends on whether it can: (1) construct 'a global network that will for a time provide resources of various kinds in the expectation of an ultimate return'; (2) construct a 'local network using the resources provided by the global network to ultimately offer a material, economic, cultural, or symbolic return to actors lodged in the global network'; and (3) 'impose itself as an obligatory point of passage between the two networks'. In education, the increased use of ICTs have resulted in increased attention specifically being given to TL, even while we are questioning how that has emerged. In a sense, technology is black-boxed as ICT through the framing of such practices as TL. This black-boxing effect may be one reason why technology studies have yielded such a surprising variety of enactments of ANT, some perhaps unrecognizable as ANT logic.

Another thing that may have influenced the uptake of ANT in the study of TL is of course the concept of network. Some of the folk who are identified as contributing to the development of ANT bemoan the network concept with which they are lumbered (Law and Hassard 1999). This concern takes two forms. One is about how well the original French concept is actually translated as 'network'. Given Latour's notion that to translate is to betray, perhaps we should be suspicious of all works that we read in translation. The second concern is that, when originally used in the 1980s, the concept of network was viewed as rhetorically radical in trying to reframe conventional sociological debates over structure and agency. However, the concept has now been overwhelmed in good part by the spreading influence and practices associated with ICTs and other globalizing processes, where the concept of the network is now ubiquitous. And indeed there are many network theories and forms of networks to draw upon in education, and not just ANT, as Carmichael and his colleagues (2006) point out. Thus, in the discussion of TL we need to be cautious about the various ways in which network theory is deployed because not all are influenced by ANT, but draw upon, for instance, social network theory, theories of the network society, etc. (Knox *et al.* 2006, Thorpe 2009). What becomes important from an ANT perspective is the specific framing of the network – its making and unmaking as an ambiguous, contingent and often incoherent entity – within the socio-material enactments of TL. As we have indicated, in order to maintain the centrality of relationality in understanding practices, while not becoming entangled in the connotations of the notion of network, various writers have developed alternative such as the lash up (Molotch 2005) or meshwork (Ingold 2007).

In fields of organization and management studies (e.g. Walsham 1997), ANT itself has proven a powerful analytic device that can decentre ICT as both a central objective and a naturalized controlling environment in learning. Studies of e-learning working with ANT have unpeeled the intermeshing of certain forms and assumptions of learning with the development of certain technologies.

> As vehicles for social arrangements and political intention, artefacts stand in for humans – or, rather, social intent is embedded in their materiality by virtue of the work they perform to establish one or another kind of order in the world. In this sense, one can attribute actions to things and call them *social* actions.
>
> (Waltz 2004: 161, original emphasis)

Network processes of expansion, contraction and transformation can be traced to understand how the internet, social networking and ICTs are producing new cultural worlds through lifelong learning (Fox 2005). Here, the possibilities that the particular configurations of technologies, people and pedagogies enact can be subject to detailed analysis, not least through an examination of those that are implicitly designed into hardware and software. Drawing upon ANT, we can examine the ways in which different configurations work to produce differing possibilities for knowledge generation, both mobilizing and stabilizing in particular ways, proving possibilities for actions at a distance. We can also explore the status of learning objects drawing upon the work of Mol (1999) who suggested the possibility of 'ontological politics', and Law and Singleton (2005), who expanded the notion of objects to explore possibilities of fluid and 'fire' objects, objects as always indeterminate, emerging, blended, and even flickering between ontological states. These ideas can help open our conceptions of the ways in which learning is performed differently in different networks and with what effects. Positioning learning objects as tokens or boundary objects provides ways for researchers to trace their particular uptakes and fallings apart, even as they might be used to spread a unified curriculum across space and time, as we saw with the unit descriptor in the example in the previous chapter.

Wide uptake of ANT is evident in studies of technology implementation in educational settings, particularly those examining system-wide implementation of a particular device (e.g. Simpson 2000, Roberts 2004, Samarawickrema and Stacey 2007, Hussenot 2008, Luck 2008). What is interesting in such studies is the way in which ANT ideas are appropriated, and the phenomena they are employed to understand. Typically, the broad notion of implementation as diffusion seems to survive undeterred, alongside assumptions about the existence of analytic constructs such as user–producer binaries, 'adoption', 'motivation' and 'buy-in' focused on humans as distinct from technology. This is despite ANT insistences that humans are mingled with non-human objects and technologies in an array of hybrid relations, and that new practices emerge through an unpredictable series of contested translations resulting in associations and links that are precarious at best.

For example, Samarawickrema and Stacey (2007) employed ANT unapologetically alongside diffusion theory to study the implementation of Web CT-Vista at Monash University in Australia. Specifically, they cited the translation notion of ANT as useful for understanding human motivations to engage or not engage the new technology. However, most of the entities described are left analytically intact as the black boxes that ANT actually had intended to unravel. Similarly, Hussenot (2008) used ANT to analyse implementation of new pedagogical software for student evaluation, intended to promote many changes in teaching practice, among 45 teachers in France. Again, the researcher borrowed the analytic tool of translation and sets it against, surprisingly, structuration theory. Thus the major categories of the study – technology, organization and institutions – are left intact as self-evident entities, each with a distinct set of 'structural properties' that are said to mediate the social action: facilities of use, rules and norms, and interpretative schemes. ANT's translation concept, intended to offer a wholly different ontology to one of structures and naturalized categories, is used here to explain users' adoption of the new software, in this case, tracing dynamics of controversies, spokespersons, compromises and intermediary objects. ANT critics and purists may cringe at such uptakes. However, such cringing is in fact a gesture of reification and boundary patrol. The point is that one particular ANT approach was found to be useful, in these cases, the method of tracing highly particular, moment-to-moment 'translations' occurring among heterogeneous materials, as a way to understand technological innovation and large-scale implementation. Thus, ANT concepts themselves undergo the processes of translation that other writers take up to understand other ICT phenomena: mutation, disassembly, incoherent and ambivalent linkages, and surprising alliances as its network of influence expands.

In a very different uptake of ANT, Nespor (2010) finds that its insistence on the network character of thought and agency, coupled with its attention to the centrality of artefacts as they order space and time, leads to challenging questions about the processes involved in technological 'implementation' in education. How are things actually related? What are the different types of associations (e.g. in sequence, pace, substitution, elasticity and changing mix), and how do these serve different ends? To get at these questions, Nespor demonstrates the analytic power in tracing a technological 'device' itself through its assemblage and various mutations over time. In one case, Nespor follows the many translations enacted in setting up instructional television at one university during the 1970s, and its evolution in subsequent decades to interactive video. The translations link global networks such as the ITV device itself, broadcasts, visions for educational technology, etc. with local networks such as classrooms, curricula and the technology unit in the university. Nespor finds that some of these translations are reversible or short-lived, while others are irreversible and persistent. Similarly, some networks, such as technological product development, are 'speeded-up', while others, such as behaviourist pedagogy, are 'slow, congealed'. He shows that the challenge for those entrusted with managing this educational change is to articulate these different networks at play to bring them 'into sync' at appropriate times for different audiences such as professors, administrators, programmers and the State Commission. In this case, ICT development takes on the characteristics of the multiple ontological position from Mol (2002) that we outlined in Chapter 2. Work is necessary to lash up the different networks and ontologies that are at play in the spread of ITV in education.

Nespor (2010) contrasts this example with a moving narrative of developing assistive technology for a boy with severe cerebral palsy to enable him to take tests in school. The technological device emerged through translations such as physical 'tinkering' and experimenting, articulating with and attempting translations of other global networks, such as administrative record keeping and the exclusionary practices of segregating special education students. In both cases, Nespor shows how devices translate the ways that phenomena produce major changes in their organizations and orderings. Yet the relative 'success' of the devices is ambiguous, and the devices themselves, their contexts of production and the changes they generate, differ dramatically.

In both cases, the device or token mediates various changes as it moves about, making associations and bringing about changes. Nespor proposes that we consider the type of trajectory that a device enacts as it changes over time:

(1) progressive, where later devices substitute for earlier ones but maintain the same function; (2) transformative, where later devices extend, elaborate and transform the functions of earlier ones; or (3) biographical coupling, where a progression of artefacts becomes interwoven in a particular human biography to transform the function or even the category of both person and device. Overall, as Nespor (2010) points out, ANT's encouragement to trace the technological device in change initiatives such as TL innovation can unsettle the very ways we consider educational change.

We now turn to a very different extended case study of a specific innovation in TL from a university in Australia where such a tracing was undertaken. The device in this case is interactive videoconferencing.

Action at a distance

Luck (2003, 2004, 2008) examined the processes of implementing an interactive videoconferencing (IVC) system in an educational institution, Central Queensland University in Australia (CQU). She drew upon Callon's (1986) original moments of translation and the notions of agnosticism, generalized symmetry and free association in the attempt to show the enactment of the innovation without privileging human intention and meaning. Luck offers useful insights about the ways in which a new network of usage grows and the different spatial enactments entailed. She traced how the network moved in education among highly diverse groups of actors – faculties, support staff, technologies, facilities and students – distributed across multiple geographical sites and already enrolled in durable networks of teaching–learning practices. Here, she found similar responses to the introduction of videoconferencing as Bigum did in relation to the introduction of computers in schools more generally.

This analysis is particularly useful for, as Busch (1997) has argued, university knowledge disciplines and practices are heavily black-boxed and particularly resistant to new translations. Using an ANT analysis, Busch argued that universities consist of highly durable actor–networks held in place by linkages among vast networks of equipment, architectures, other institutions and historical relational patterns. In relation to the innovation that Luck (2003: 84) studied, this is highly pertinent as 'the videoconferencing rooms were designed and built to replicate a tiered classroom such as those used for face-to-face teaching with the addition of cameras, microphones and television monitors'. In other words, if we see the IVC technologies as tokens, they were translated into an existing network of university education, as well as attempting to translate the latter.

The CQU innovation process began with certain activities at the university level (videoconferencing trials, forming a steering group, writing a grant) that created loose local networks. These local networks aligned with national networks pressuring for reduced spending, increased student access and a unified national system in higher education. This not only granted these more distant networks material presence and strength in the university, but helped to strengthen the local networks. Luck shows the importance, perhaps particularly in hierarchical institutions such as higher education, of a heterogeneous engineer who exerts sufficient authority to define the problem in ways that other actors will accept. In CQU, she presents the university's senior management as this engineer. However, a simple decree from managers rarely accomplishes implementation. In this case, a 'future directions' document circulated by senior management problematized existing teaching–learning systems and convincingly linked these with the funding and viability problems of the institution. This document became a key intermediary – an actor that can translate thinking and behaviour – in the form of an immutable mobile. It was an inscription that itself represents a translation of a series of events and actors and that has achieved sufficient durability to circulate across far-reaching space–times.

This document combined with various objects to problematize existing practice and began a process of interessement and enrolment. These additional objects included, for example:

- a logo – 'Vision 97' for the initiative
- grants made available to install the new IVC systems in classrooms
- letters sent to students and parents guaranteeing that they could complete a degree at home and avoid relocation costs
- prospective promotions for support staff involved in implementation
- demonstrations of the higher quality and convenience of the proposed IVC systems comparative to existing temporary cabinets rolled from room to room.

As Luck (2008: 181) notes, 'once there are rooms, screens, wires, microphones, policies and training schemes in place, [the IVC implementation] is more credible and compelling as a useful system for performing teaching activities'. The active circulation of these objects throughout CQU's distributed sites occurred not only through mail, media and announcements, but also through the establishment of a 'walking group'. This group visited all constituents in all regional campuses to engage them directly in the initiative, talking about and touching components of the IVC. Luck's analysis shows how what goes on at these different nodes of circulating things and humans – the attempts to translate through problematizing, persuading and enrolling at the far-flung edges of the network's potential reach – actually builds the new network of practice bit by bit.

Actors' enrolment in the network is, however, precarious, and needs to be stabilized if the network is to endure. Luck showed the multiple negotiations that continued to occur throughout to inscribe the various actors into certain roles that became stabilized in a configuration that could perform the new IVC teaching–learning system. Much of this negotiation was at the linkages of objects and technologies with human intentions, expectations and attempted actions. Each of these linkages embedded endless numbers of artefacts, mediators and inscriptions negotiating connections that gradually became locked into the new network. For example, sound issues of the new system entailed speakers and speaker adjustments, recordings, variable control panels, refinements to microphone size and links to manage the unique classroom demands on the IVC, carpet installation to address noise concerns, technicians, designers, trials, written concerns about cost escalations, and so forth.

Luck's study in effect traced the various forms of ordering that can hold precarious relationship in place. Durability, which is ordering through time, can be achieved by delegation to the most durable materials that can maintain their relational patterns, and to other networks to hold in place these durable materials (technicians and repair agencies hold microphones in place). Mobility, which is ordering through space–time, can be achieved through immutable mobiles that travel, binding various locales into central modes of calculation. Centres of calculation and translation order direction, voice and representation, often by anticipating the responses and reactions of the materials to be translated. Finally, the scope of ordering is extended when strategies of translation are reproduced in a range of network locations.

Overall, Luck's network reading helps illustrate how, in TL innovations, insufficient attention is often granted to the active role of objects and technology. These tend to be treated as brute things to be installed rather than dynamic actors. To grow a network, relationships need to be built carefully and flexibly among the mix of objects–technologies–humans, attuning to non-human actors' capacity to act back in ways that network engineers may not have anticipated. Luck points out various strategies through which a fragile new network of these relationships is extended and strengthened in a successful educational reform. For example, key actors are employed as intermediaries, as many actors are added as possible, and alignments are made with other, distant networks such as national priorities and international discourses in education. Such strategies contribute to the extension, durability and even irreversibility of a new network, with perhaps undesired forms of entrenchment. But the network is also experiencing continual challenges and shifts at its multiple micro-connections as actors discover and exploit weaknesses in inscriptions, or enact anti-programmes. Constant attunement to these shifts and flexible adjustment is the essential everyday work of those actors interested in sustaining a network of innovation. The work is ongoing not only at these nodes but also in the overall shape of the educational institution as the new networks stretch and translate its appearance, its functions, and its extensions into spaces that appear to lie beyond it.

Luck's (2008) analysis of a TL initiative showed how an ANT reading can reveal important socio-material negotiations, particularly the importance of things and other non-human elements exerting force in these negotiations. The early-ANT model she employed also helpfully traces distinct moments through which change occurs. She also (2003) has drawn upon after-ANT notions, particularly those of Law and Mol (2001), to examine the multiple topologies of IVC use – region, network, fluid and fire.

The class is described as a single class but in many ways each physical class-room performs as a separate *region*. It was noted that this particular course was team-taught. The teaching team performs as a *network* across three campuses. The university wants to have the same model of teaching independent of the campus that the students are enrolled in. This means that teaching using IVC is performed as a *fluid*. When lecturing staff are preparing to conduct classes using the IVC they are performing within a *fire space* – there will always be students whom lecturers cannot see but must take into consideration in the conduct of their classes.

(Luck 2003: 89, original emphasis)

Larger changes emerged through minute changes as elements assemble, connect, translate one another and gradually become a durable network of practices and materials entwined with people. In this way, the implementation of a videoconferencing teaching–learning system is understood at the micro-level of ongoing, unpredictable, often difficult transactions and 'strategic uncertainties' (Luck 2004).

This is a very particular case study. But it is part of a much wider set of processes associated with globalizing practices that secure action at a distance through the multiple interlinked enactments.

To be a cyborg is to be human

The proliferating infusion of technologies into every aspect of education as well as workplace practice draws particular attention to the issues of what makes objects of knowledge distinct, what constrains enactments of knowledge, and how different enactments of the same object function together. They point to different emerging practices, multiple subjectivities, a multiplication of author(ity), and different cyborgian embodiments of what it might signify to be human or a teacher/learner. How the practices in these multiple sites are or might be mashed up as learning in an educationally worthwhile way is a major pedagogic question – as are questions of whether they should be. Many of the issues identified at the start of this chapter have yet to be adequately researcher in education (Greenhow *et al.* 2009). Network ontologies, such as ANT, help us to illustrate the capillaries that enact cyborgs, the hybrids of humans with information technologies, and new forms of knowledge, such as those that emerge through Twitter formats based on highly limited communiqués and the imperative to attract net-surfing followers. Tracing networks also reveals the knowledges that become distinct when organized pedagogies are distributed across multiple regions of learners and teachers. Becoming-cyborg, in Gough's (2004) terms, does not seem to be an option. We already are. To be human is to be cyborg.

Chapter 6

(Un)making standards in education

> Without standardization in things like railroad gauges, electrical amperage, and coins (and, of course, weights and measures) the related artefacts (locomotives, toasters, vending machines) would have been all but impossible.
>
> (Molotch 2005: 119)

Standards have become integral to educative practices and in the process, both making certain effects possible and also excluding other possibilities. Through the assessment of students we set standards for them to achieve. These are sometimes based upon norms and sometimes upon outcomes. Standards are also used to assess individual performance, and the performance of organizations and systems more widely. In this chapter, we will explore the work of standards in translating and mobilizing certain educational practices.

The purpose of standards is to achieve orderings of practice at a distance. Standards aspire to ensure consistency and comparability in the everyday conduct that occurs at diverse locations and across time, in which a whole constellation of relations meet and weave together in particular ways to constitute practice. For any idea, such as a standard for practice, to be 'mobile, durable and capable of inciting action at a distance' the idea must 'have the form of a trace, an inscription, a representation' (Bowers 1992: 117). Formal standards that attempt to define levels of competence across locations have taken a variety of trace forms in educational practices: curriculum documents stating standards of content and performances for classroom activities, assessment instruments and accountability systems determining standards of achievement for learners, and government-mandated professional standards of practice for teachers and principals.

Decades of educational research have examined and critiqued the processes of creating and applying universal standards to multiple and localized educational practice. We now have many studies and arguments showing the perspectives of ideologies and meanings at play, the power and politics invoked to perpetuate particular interests, influences on pedagogy and identities, inequities produced, and the tensions of multiple practices coping with more universal standards.

Furthermore, it is by now widely argued that an increasing move to large-scale educational change is being conducted through dispersing specific standards for teaching and curriculum. All of this is part of wider assemblages that Power (1999) dubbed as the 'audit society'.

As Fenwick (2010a) has argued, ANT brings two main contributions to these debates about standards. ANT-inspired studies trace the ways that educational standards achieve and maintain some durable form as a consequence of the relations in which they are located and performed. Further, ANT analyses reconfigure the terms and assumptions involved in considering educational standards. Such analyses signal rifts and disjunctures in statements of educational standards and so called implementations. These rifts open new possibilities as well as recognition of important ambivalences, jugglings and transgressive enactments that are all contained within standards in practice. In focusing on standards, we therefore, once again, witness attempts to understand the multiplicity of practices as they are spread across space and time.

ANT does not consider the terrain as configured by 'powers that be' which create and impose a set of standards. Instead, standards, as well as these powers, are understood to be effects that emerge through a series of complex actions. Of course, many non-ANT educational analyses also analyse processes of standard-setting and standards-usage as emergent, multifarious and discontinuous. However, to view a particular set of educational standards themselves as a series of networks is to recognize the many negotiations that lead to translations of entities at each knot of the political decision enactment: specific terms of language, materials, coalitions of people, existing documents, disciplinary bodies of knowledge and so on. ANT helps locate the many inclusions and exclusions that occur in assembling these networks of standards, which can be easily obscured in references to standards that appear to exist as inevitable and immutable.

Star's (1991) oft-quoted story of McDonald's hamburger with onions standards is but one example. The standard McDonald's burger excludes onion-allergy sufferers. Like Star herself, these excluded actors may nonetheless include themselves in the network of McDonald's customers, but scrape away the onions. Thus, Star translates herself into becoming part of the network, but changes the standards, and therefore the terms of enrolment, in one simple action. Star's analysis shows something else that network accounts bring to bear, which is the interruptions and unruliness of standards in action. Star describes her encounter and negotiations with the standards travelling through the McDonald's network for her as chaotic, confusing and unpredictable. This is far from the smooth enrolment into a network where particular standards seek to translate her behaviour in particular ways. As a space of learning that is inherently unpredictable, educational practice is filled with these sorts of interruptions and inventions, with difference that refuses or misunderstands or circumvents any attempt at standardization.

Further, the socio-material emphasis of ANT has inspired educational analysts to seek beyond the politics of language and the negotiations of ideologies in standards debates to focus on the ways that material things and actions are implicated in the play of standards formations. The examples in this chapter show how standards are performed in diverse socio-material forms, indeed in spaces between diverse and distributed forms, forms which are constantly in tension and moving. One author examining the work of standards in vocational education (Mulcahy 1999) argues that the human body itself can be seen as a distributed object of politics among these forms.

Within classic ANT analysis, a particular list of educational standards might be described as an 'immutable mobile'. The network(s) of invention, resistance and negotiations that produced these standards are rendered invisible. Lists of standards appear to be immutable, fixed, self-evident. They are treated as a black box, an immutable object that can travel across distances of geographic, cultural and political spaces to regulate activity. A list of standards for learner achievement can be transmitted from a centre, such as a government department to school districts, teacher associations, textbook publishers and even, through international organizations such as the OECD, to other governments. The logic is that an immutable list would be more powerful, as it travels around these spaces, in dictating terms and even shaping the actualities of knowledge and action that constitute acceptable educational competency and performance.

However, given the diverse forms proliferated through standards in practice, ANT helps illuminate the multiple heterogeneous possibilities that are embedded within any formal iteration of educational standards inscribed in texts. In practice, these possibilities emerge and jostle in unexpected ways. The possibilities emerge as different actants are introduced into practices of standards development and use, as different material limitations and cultural expectations contribute to and resist the ideas contained within written standards, and as one set of written standards collaborates with other forms of standards at play in any region of educational practice. Thus, what may be characterized in certain analyses as local resistance to standards is viewed by ANT as one visible instantiation of a whole series of possibilities and transgressions. ANT shows that these are not added to the list of standards by particular people, but that heterogeneity is contained within the standards themselves. The mobile is not as immutable as it appears, but is far more open and fluid than common analysis tends to acknowledge, capable of multiple unfoldings. This is a central observation of ANT, as everything at play embeds so many mappings of memory, association and performativity that immutability is impossible. In this way, ANT reveals the *uncertainty of standards* as both rhetorical positionings and as bases for judgement in the governance of educational activity.

This line of thinking emerged in after-ANT discussions (Hetherington and Law 2000). When studies of networks created through orderings of standardization began to focus on standards that failed, it became clear that the immutable mobile concept was not adequate to describe what was happening.

ANT became too managerialist in its early versions as it thought about objects. Its intuition about the importance of relations was right, but it got itself too concerned with standardization, with the rigidities of immutable mobiles that, if they exist at all, exist within rather specific and rigid networks that try to reach out over long distances and achieve centralized control. Perhaps, then, we need to be looking at networks that are more relaxed, networks where such control is less important. Perhaps we need to be looking at networks where objects precisely have to adapt and change shape if they are to survive.

(Law and Singleton 2005: 339)

This points to the fluidity of things, that they are constantly unfolding as and in practices. Educative practices are closely influenced by standards on all fronts – curriculum, governance, student achievement, teacher performance. However, as the stories in this chapter show, the networks through which these standards are enacted, when they actually succeed in translating behaviours of people and things, appear far more ambivalent and loose than the early-ANT notions of centrally-controlled networks would allow.

ANT analyses also step outside conceptions of local–global scalar distinctions in considering educational standards. A common view is to see standards as imposed from higher to lower hierarchical levels in an organization or community, or to understand globalized standards as needing to be implemented locally. This is to accept an ontological distinction between these scalar levels, but as we have shown, ANT recognizes no such a priori distinction. Instead, it traces how a network becomes extended, through a proliferation of networks and links, to function across far-flung regions of space and time. The question is not what occurs at local and global levels and how they influence one another; it is rather to focus on how networks become more or less long or more or less connected, performing comparable (if often distinctly different) practices. Network length is the effect of how various materials became assembled to allow it to function and achieve some stability. What appears as difference in size and scale is simply the end product of network extension actions. ANT analyses examine the extended networks of what may be viewed as one common educational standard and how these play out in the diverse practices and regions into which they worm.

The interesting question is how to conceptualize these playings out. If ANT analyses eschew the notion of global standards being produced somewhere and then implemented locally, with inevitable resistances and transformations, how would a network analysis account for these tensions? What actually circulates among the different settings in the name of standards? To what extent do translation strategies succeed in replicating the protocols intended to prescribe consistent practice in different contexts?

Three educational accounts inspired by ANT are featured in this chapter. Each addresses these sorts of questions about standards and how they work in everyday professional practice. First, Timmermans and Berg (1997) argue that universal standards, even in the most high stakes, tightly controlled instances, are always local universality, performed in a particular, contingent and situated crystallization of movements. Second, Murdoch (1998) suggests that different networks of both standard prescription and more open negotiation are entwined in each instance of practice. Third, Mulcahy (1999, 2007) works with the conceptualization of standards as actually existing in different ontological forms, as representations and as performances. All three conceptions highlight the spaces and disjunctures that open between a formal standard and the press of everyday demands and priorities in educational practice. All three show these spaces as generative opportunities where invention and adaptation emerge to enrich standards.

Local universality

One enactment on how standards work shows how even the most strictly defined protocols are always performed in unique ways in practice (Timmermans and Berg 1997). Thus, the supposed universality of the standard is always local universality. In practice, a protocol functions not as strict performance of a standard but as the outcome of negotiation processes among various actors. We will take a closer look at this argument.

In a typical standard of practice, a protocol is specified in a text, such as a procedure with written directions and possibly accompanying tools. A protocol is defined by Timmermans and Berg as a technoscientific script that crystallizes multiple trajectories. They examined medical resuscitation protocols such as cardio-pulmonary resuscitation (CPR), and found that:

> The protocol designers, funding agencies, the different groups of involved physicians, patients' hopes and desires, organizational facilities, laboratory capabilities, drug companies, the patients' organs' own resilience, and so forth, all come into play in the negotiation processes leading up to the 'final' protocol. What kind of drugs are used, how they are to be dosed, who should receive them: all these 'decisions' are not so much a product of consciously developed plans as a result of these continuous, dispersed and often *contingent* interactions. The actual shape of the tool, in other words, resembles no one 'blueprint' but is accomplished 'in-course'.
>
> (Timmermans and Berg 1997: 283, emphasis added)

Classroom activity also embeds a range of protocols that illustrate how pedagogical activity is far more a result of contingent interactions than consciously developed 'plans', despite the much loved lesson plan of teacher education. Protocols in the classroom also show the various trajectories that come together in its performance. For example, a common mathematics lesson involves the teacher presenting a standard protocol, such as how to multiply rational fractions, in a 'chalk-talk', after which students practice applying the formula by solving a series of paper–pencil problems at their desks using a prescribed textbook. Each entity involved in the protocol or performance of the standard has its own trajectory (Nespor 2003). The student who is struggling with fractions may have past failures, present requirements for acceptance by the watching peers and future worries about facing disappointed parents. The teacher's actions are situated in a series of mathematics curriculum plans and management processes for a class of children with an eye to standardized tests in the near future. The maths text itself contains a trajectory of curriculum research established about scope and sequence of mathematics education, problems and tested solutions compiled by the writers. The teacher invents activities using plastic blocks, and perhaps supplements the textbook problems in favour of a few she develops herself. Students, excited about the upcoming school dance, cannot settle into the lesson in any case, so, on the spot she invents a class problem using fractions related to the dance.

Protocol as a standard interferes in these different trajectories of actants, changing these trajectories in the moment when they are brought together. This moment not only gathers and transforms, but also creates visibility of all the trajectories and roles and purposes of those involved. This is why Timmermans and Berg call it a 'crystallization' of multiple trajectories. As a network moment, a moment of translation, this transaction is contingent and temporary. Whatever is performed in that moment is not guaranteed to have any stability or prescriptive power for ensuing action. In the 80 different cases of CPR they observed, Timmermans and Berg (1997: 288) found that in most cases, professionals adapt the standard: 'seen from their perspectives, it is the protocol's trajectory which is secondary and which is aligned to their own goals and trajectories ... it is dealt with in terms of their local specificities'. Nurses act beyond their scope by dropping hints to inexperienced physicians, which may prompt more aggressive treatment by the physician, new drugs not specified by the protocol are introduced, and strict directives of the protocol are altered in situations of 'the very hopeless patient'. Tight control is also unreasonable for non-human elements in medical situations where machines break down, X-rays can show unexpected images, and blood cells can behave oddly. The protocol's explicit demands always need tinkering, a notion that intuitively is also the case for educators.

In another example reported by Mirchandani (2004), call centre workers are trained not only to follow standardized telephone protocols, but also to adopt accents and first names that are consistent with the country to which they will be providing a service. This is a challenge when trainees are geographically separated, such as callers in Bangor, India learning to serve the southern USA. The educational challenges are further complicated when standardized disciplines must hold across disparate regions and cultures, as when trainers located in Melbourne, Australia are teaching the learners in Bangor to serve Atlanta, Georgia (Farrell 2006). Call centres are notorious for close, constant supervision and even punishment to ensure worker compliance with the protocols. However, as Mirchandani reports, workers seem infinitely motivated and capable of producing variations on this protocol. One example occurred over a market survey of breakfast cereal. The callers were supposed to use a script that began by asking who in the household ate breakfast cereal, then questioned the brands of cereal used. However, the customers tried to explain the details of who ate what cereals in ways that the survey could not manage. After some further experiments, the workers quietly created variations to the script that allowed for these unanticipated responses. The point is that a universal text circulating among different networks prompts unanticipated things to emerge that challenges the standard. If disciplinary action is imposed to prevent this translation of the standard, such as a supervisor punishing the call worker and insisting on use of the original protocol, which is what happened in the case reported by Mirchandani, the network has already shifted. The fragility of the ordering attempt has been exposed in the possibilities for reinvention.

Educators nod with recognition. They know that the lesson plan prescribed in the teacher's guide or the model presented at an in-service session is incomplete and ill-fitting and must always be adapted. What this conception of ANT adds is explicit recognition of what is actually going on in this translation of standards. In the moment of translation, the protocol is one actor with a historical trajectory, in a commotion of actors each with their own trajectories. These are drawn together in the press to perform that protocol with some reasonable outcome aligned with their own desires:

> Local universality, then, implies a context of practice, of multiple crystal-lizing and dispersed trajectories, of reappropriation, repairing, combining, and even circumventing the protocols and standards, of leaving margins of freedom, of reminding, of long processes of negotiation, of diverse interests, and so forth.
>
> (Timmermans and Berg 1997: 298)

This conception helps shift the focus from standards as an exercise of domination and submission or resistance, to an interplay and scaling that is performed anew in each setting.

Networks of prescription and negotiation

Formal standards can also be enacted as a regulatory network flowing and unfold-ing alongside, and even entwined with, the adaptive and resistant flows. For example, Star's (1995) studies of nurses show that, while they understand clearly the evidence-based standards meant to govern their practice, on the wards they are continually trying to carve out spaces of discretionary practice within the clas-sification of competencies scheme. Eventually, a standardized network becomes enacted out of this localized informal practice, and then superimposed on that practice. The ward, therefore, is not a site of resistance to the standards but a network of alternate orderings. Thus, Star views the stabilization of standards occurring through a series of tradeoffs between generality and local uniqueness, between network builders and enrolled entities, who must reach agreements or compromises if a network is to be stable through time and space. Along this line, Murdoch (1998) conceptualizes 'spaces of prescription' and 'spaces of negotiation' that coexist and loosely correspond, not in opposition but in duality. Spaces of prescription, tightly ordered and normalized, are created through networks where entities are pulled closely together into assemblages that clearly exclude certain actants. These are pushed out to form alternate assemblages. Spaces of negotiation are created through networks where links between actors and intermediaries are provisional and divergent, where norms are hard to establish and standards are frequently compromised. Various components of a network continually negotiate with one another, forming variable coalitions and assuming ever changing shapes. These two spaces of network configurations, prescription and negotiation, form two sides of same phenomenon and cannot exist without one another. Further, both spaces can flow from the same network.

We can see examples of this in workplace education, particularly in staff training in relation to paperwork protocols that must be performed as part of implementing prescribed International Standards of Operation (ISOs). The international standardization movement seeks 'global solutions to satisfy industry and customers worldwide' (ISO 2009) by specifying standards (over 16,500 to date) to regulate every aspect of workplace production and relations. This growth is fed partly by the status achieved by an organization that attains 'ISO certification', and partly by transnational corporate concerns to guarantee consistent quality and efficiency across distributed international sites and diverse settings. Training across these different sites becomes a particular challenge when the objective is to eliminate variation and unpredictability.

One story told by Belfiore *et al.* (2004) follows hotel workers through their education in total quality customer service. Front of house staff were trained to interact with hotel guests using standardized protocols. To the management's frustration, the workers routinely altered the protocols because they believed guests were more satisfied with more personal communication. As the computer systems organizing front of house staff's records were constantly changing with the new implementation, workers informally developed and shared shortcuts together to get on with their everyday tasks. Cleaning staff were also required to use standardized forms which supervisors cross-checked through more lengthy paper-based procedures. However, the workers kept adapting the forms so they could document as quickly as possible what they determined to be the key issues of room standards. These women workers had formed close local ethnic groups bound by a shared 'housekeepers' culture, holding pride and skill in high quality cleaning and effective systems for controlling their own work. One group adopted a system of dots that was dismissed as meaningless by the floor manager, but was difficult to eliminate.

While a network of prescription was clearly in force and attempting to enrol the staff and their paper assessments, another network of negotiation was also in play. Also in play were the close sociocultural networks of the staff, and the pre-existing network of practices that, for them, defined good work in which they took pride. These networks unsurprisingly entwined with one another. The prescriptive network of the new ISO protocols and paper assessments did not simply enrol the staff, the cleaning equipment and the clip charts, but nor was it simply rejected. In fact, the new standardized procedures and texts actually appeared to prompt invention, as the hotel workers spontaneously adapted them to produce the required assessments, maintain their own associations, and continue to collectively perform a practice they defined as quality work. Standards may, therefore, produce a result that is consistent with its intentions, but not in the ways intended. They may be necessary for ordering practices, but the translation is never complete.

The different ontologies of standards

Here is where the notion of an immutable mobile, while helpful to show how a list of standards, moves in and around different networks of practice, enrolling them into one extended network across sites separated widely by time and physical space, becomes limited. Standards become transmuted at these different sites as much as they transform and mobilize actors. The relations are not immutable, and the networks are sometimes more incoherent than coherent. And yet, the official standards, whatever they may have been originally, appear to hold a recognizable presence across these sites. The code is understood and is visible throughout the network. Actors themselves, such as the call centre workers developing a new script to replace the standardized protocol, believe that they are performing the standard, even when the objects and actions they produce deviate in fundamental ways from the standard's inscribed purposes. How can these multiplicities be explained in the name of standardization?

Writers who puzzled through these anomalies with ANT-related theories (Mol and Law 1994, Law and Singleton 2005) suggest that the problem may be with our perception of difference. We attempt to see a thing holding a stable shape in the networks it acts upon. These writers encourage us to reach beyond these notions, and to consider how objects themselves are sometimes far more variable, unfolding and fluid, than fixed. Law's oft-cited example of the Zimbabwe pump studied by de Laet and Mol (2000) points to the fluidity of this sort of thing as it changes gradually and gently over time. Parts that break down are replaced with different things at hand, the pump's uses are adapted and reinterpreted, functions are assessed differently, what counts as clean water changes in different situations, and practices linked to it shift over time as new practices emerge. The pump both changes and stays the same. It does not morph into an entirely different thing. In fact, the success of the pump depends on its fluidity and adaptability. Here, then, is a notion of a 'fluid object' that maintains some consistency but whose internal structures and boundaries shift over time and through its negotiations in different networks. As a fluid object, a standard for practice or for learners' competency can mobilize and link together extended networks that maintain key continuities even though practices at different nodes or knots may vary.

Mulcahy (1999, 2007) uses these after-ANT concepts to tackle the same issue we have explored here and in previous chapters, that of the discrepancies and apparent incoherence that opens in the moments of educational practice between formal prescriptions of standards and the inventive adaptations of practitioners and students. Through her analyses of competency standards prescribed for the vocational curriculum in an Australian context, cooking, in this case, and professional standards of practice prescribed for school teachers, Mulcahy formulates a conception of standards as actually inhabiting different forms at the same time in particular contexts. Practitioners learn to juggle these different ontological forms. For Mulcahy, these jugglings and the spaces across which they fly are in fact not spaces of control and subjugation, but generative spaces of possibility.

In Mulcahy's (1999) tracings of cookery teachers working with students in kitchens, she shows how different forms of competency standards are present and held in tension in a series of embodied relations. The set of national industry standards, normally represented on a piece of paper, also lives in teachers' interpretations of such standards in their demonstrations and directions to students. Also present, as we saw in Chapter 4, are teachers' embodied and very personal professional standards of practice. These are too materially complex for formal representation as competency, such as predicting the effect of a flavour on a particular dish. Further, local standards of adaptation come to bear as teacher–cooks have accommodated practices over time to particular contexts, shaped by such things as faulty equipment or unavailability of good quality ingredients. Further, teachers draw from accumulated experience of watching and assessing students' growing capacity, for example, knowing when students have come to embody acceptable performance in some aspects of a skill, while they may not quite master other aspects. Teachers' work with students folds through embodied negotiation of these different forms of standards, such that no one formal standard or term of competency becomes privileged over another.

> Standards are accomplished face to face, through interactional work. They are not so much read off the written specifications and then applied, as recreated on the job, using the written specifications as a resource or guide. Achieving competence is a matter of using embodied skills, face-to-face communication, and collective negotiation by which the outcomes of the work can be taken into account.
>
> (Mulcahy 1999: 94)

These various representations of standards incorporating bodies in motion, equipment, ingredients, dishes produced, politics, talk and texts are not static and separate, but flow constantly in movement and relations in the site of teaching and cooking. Indeed, Mulcahy (1999: 97) argues that teachers knowingly engage in a 'strategic juggling of representational ambiguity' among these varied standards. This juggling translates the formal competency standard into diverse representational forms of competency that settle the 'problem' of difference at the local level.

Another example of this strategic juggling can be seen in workplace education related to implementing ISOs. In a textile production plant described by Belfiore *et al.* (2004), workers were trained in a new ISO-regulated system that increased production quotas and imposed more efficient, consistent procedures. Non-compliance report (NCR) forms were one of the many new textual activities introduced to regulate this process. However, workers learned to be very careful about how and with whom they wrote up 'incidents' where ISO standards were not met. These reports required the assignation of blame or at least figuring out the cause of a complex problem. Workers were also caught between the time consuming form filling process and supervisors' urges to hurry production. They often simply circumvented the form and masked the issue. Self protection, solidarity and small revenges were all played out at the site of the NCR form. When managers became aware of what was viewed as worker non-compliance with the form, the problem was interpreted to be a gap in worker knowledge and further training prescribed. It is unlikely that this training would have ensured the desired outcome, given that the workers' adaptations were about sustaining the existing associations and negotiating the material conflicts embedded in the new production process.

In her analyses of standards for teachers implemented in Australia (2007), Mulcahy shows how they function in socio-material practices. Standards take different forms in different settings. In the policy setting, standards function as textual representations that move among practices of consultation, revision, political consensus-seeking and approvals. Stakeholders are the primary human actors in these material networks. However, in school settings, standards for teaching and learning exist as embodied, messy interactions. Students are significant contributors within these interactions. The point is that the embodied standard is not simply the enfleshment or the imperfect imposition on action of the textual representation, but that the two function as related but distinct forms. These forms jostle in a continuous tension in all settings. Just as the policy representation winds through embodied classroom activity, so do these messy practices act to recreate and translate the specified standards. Mulcahy concludes that seeking to reconcile these different ontological forms would create an undesirable closure, replacing the dynamism of various enactments of standards with a rigid consensus that offers little more than the original formal prescribed standard. Instead, Mulcahy argues for holding differences in tension. These include different practices of standards, scales and settings.

In another example of prescribed standards for teaching, in the Canadian province of British Columbia (BC), we can see how the different ontological forms of standards are created *within* the different networks of practice forming the educational system. These include the policy-making networks linked to the ministry of education, the BC teachers' federation protecting teacher interests, the BC College of Teachers (BCCT) which provides certification for teachers, the universities which determine graduation standards for teacher education, and the school districts which evaluate teachers for promotion. To focus on one of these, the BCCT originally prescribed a set of 13 standards for teaching after extensive consultation with stakeholders other than students, including universities and teacher agencies. Universities, exercising their autonomy to establish their own curricula and academic standards for graduation, negotiated an agreement with the government such that the provincially prescribed standards would not dictate university programmes. The alternative was that they would be 'recognized' in evaluation assignments and criteria used in their pre-service teacher education programmes (UBC 2008). Students in these programmes must create a portfolio of artefacts that demonstrate achievement of the teaching standards.

This agreement functions as yet another textual representation exercising its own authority to prescribe standards. Every university teacher is provided with a copy of the BCCT list of 13 standards as well as the university restatement of the role of teacher standards in the curriculum. However, the enactment of these formal standards varies widely. At the University of British Columbia in Vancouver, a separate but complementary set of standards was devised to show students ways that the university expectations exceed the BCCT prescribed standards. In one university course, the BCCT standards are used as pliable starting points for interpretation (Phelan 2007). Students are directed to complete assignments focusing on questions such as 'What assumptions about teaching and learning are implicit/explicit in the standard?'. They are asked to assemble artefacts from their teacher education that demonstrate 'tensions or difficulties or dilemmas that may surround the standard in practice'. A new, fluid form of performed standard emerges in such practice, distinct from but existing alongside the prescriptive authority embodied in formal representations of standard statements such as 'Educators value the involvement and support of parents, guardians, families and communities in schools'. However, in response to the various forms assumed by teaching standards in practice, the BCCT undertook a revision of the formal representation of teaching standards four years after their implementation, reducing 13 to eight standards. At the time of writing, amidst debate about what has been rendered absent in this reduction, the standards literally exist in different ontological forms of representation as well as embodied enactments. Each is present to the other, even if not explicitly recognized through compliance, avoidance, subversion or critique.

As different forms of standards jostle together in different settings of practice, their tensions produce healthy fissures, tunnels, folds and unmapped spaces. Inventive possibilities emerge continuously at these fissures. This is why, as Mulcahy (2007) argues, best practices for particular contexts can only occur when these tensions are held together. Attempts to reconcile different forms of standards, different networks of prescription and negotiation or different enactments of local universality close these possibilities. Murdoch (1998) claims that actors will naturally seek the cracks, rifts and folds for manoeuvering within networks, finding the contestable lines and sites where they can invent themselves differently. This is how individuals negotiate their incorporation into networks mobilized by standards formed by powerful centres of calculation.

Conclusion

In an ANT analysis, standards attempt to create comparability by controlling conduct across space and time. This is accomplished through traces and representations that can fix an idea and move it around through specifying texts, required tools, or mandated protocols. However, for standardization to actually work, as Bowker and Star (1999: 232–3) suggest, there must emerge a difficult balance of comparability across sites alongside 'margins of control', and spaces of 'intimacy' for actors in practice. High levels of control and maximum visibility threaten the very intimacy that can enable standardization to come to life in the networks of action at each site. The ANT accounts of standardization attempts in education make this abundantly clear. The concept of an 'immutable mobile' of standards travelling around different regions and insinuating itself into different messy negotiations among actors in ways that translate all into an extended network is inadequate to describe educational practice, or arguably any practice.

Different assemblages are possible in the network of standardization, assemblages that emerge among the nodes and folds of extended networks, but not as stable entities. These assemblages themselves are continually emerging and shifting and dissolving into new forms as the actants encounter interruptions and discover new approaches. Local network negotiations will always be pressed by actors' and objects' creativity and limitations, and other networks functioning in the same space that reinforce different meanings of quality and priorities. These all jostle alongside and modify a standard's demands for compliance. These assemblages often bear sufficient comparability to sustain the most necessary dimensions of consistency. However, they also demonstrate Law's (2003) admonition that there are no orders, only orderings, which are always precarious.

The negotiations are always marked by struggle. As the examples in this book illustrate, attempts at ordering can never be complete. First, comparability across an extended network threatens the manageability of each unique network or system sharing particular contextual exigencies. Members of these networks act in ways to achieve what is uppermost for them, what glues together their network, whether that is saving a patient, producing the best tasting dish for this clientele, maintaining tight cultural reciprocities, pleasing this hotel guest, or creating a critical intellectual dialogue. Learning may be implicit to all of these, but is not necessarily the practical focus around which they revolve. The standards network is one thread woven into these networks. Regardless of the attempts to control conduct at a distance, network members appear to be constantly adapting and inventing, translating and being translated for themselves and finding spaces and openings so to do.

In after-ANT analyses, standards exist in multiple ontological forms that are performed simultaneously and that, as networks themselves, are continually changing shape. Educators, like other practitioners, are quite used to juggling these shape-shifting forms and their tensions of simultaneity within the high voltage dynamic of everyday commotion. In these ways, an ANT analysis highlights the limitations of conventional accounts of standards as globally formed ideals troubled by imperfect local implementation, or as cases of domination and subjugation that require local resistance to top-down exercises of power. ANT analyses also avoid framing issues of standards as a problem in achieving consistency across domains by reconciling local and global enactments. Instead, the analyses here show just how precarious attempts are at ordering, how immutable mobiles are always mutable, and how the network spaces that proliferate around instantiations of standards always generate uncertainties, transgressions and wonderfully generative ambivalences.

In discussing the 'mess' that is characteristic of all practice, Law and Singleton (2005) caution against closing network spaces through managerialism, which can be exercised by educational researchers seeking to contain and explain standardization as much as by educational managers and policy-makers seeking to mobilize particular standards:

> Managerialism, we noted, finds mess intractable; indeed unknowable. Perhaps more radically, managerialism makes mess, not in the nasty and motivated way that is the most obvious way of interpreting such a suggestion (though no doubt this happens), but simply because it, in its nature, demands clarity and distinction. That which is not clear and distinct, well ordered, is othered. It is constituted as mess, like the plants that are turned into weeds by virtue of the invention of gardening. Perhaps, then, mess is like invisible work except that it is not invisible. Instead it simply does not fit: it flows around and exceeds the limits set by immutable mobiles.
>
> (Law and Singleton 2005: 341)

For educational researchers interested in standards and processes of standardization, ANT urges a focus on this mess, on the interplays that occur at the most local levels of practice, in ways that resist the urge to clarify, unify, order and distinguish. The examples in this chapter show the insights produced when we trace the interplays not only of a particular standard attempt to become universal, but of all the other standards and their networks that intersect with the universal. They focus on the different strategies and inventions that emerge. Some respond to one another, but others simply coexist together, being juggled by educators and students. These include strategies invoked to enrol actors into networks that extend universal standards, as well as actors' strategies to react to or reinvent these networks. Standardization networks will adopt the strategies that best ensure stability, and, as Murdoch (1998) argues, take the shape that will be most durable whether this is a more open network of negotiation, a messier network that enfolds ambivalence and incoherence, or a more closed network of prescription. And, of course, ANT maintains an important insistence on tracing how things in education influence and even project these strategies. Thus, for instance, from his analysis of standardized curriculum standards and testing in US schools Nespor (2002: 376–7) concludes that:

instead of seeing some participants as 'reformers' and others as 'contexts', the idea is to account for all in the same terms by viewing them as historically and geographically stretched out in materially heterogeneous networks that overlap and interact with one another ... Implicit or explicit, battles over how things in the here and now will be articulated with (or conceptualized in terms of) settings and events distant in time and space are at the core of the struggle for educational justice. The key questions for educators in this struggle are how different kinds of schooling will entail different kinds of trajectories and pathways for students, what kinds of socio-cultural geographies these pathways collectively define, how the pathways and geographies are made visible to teachers, parents and children, and how different groups use them to contextualize and make particular kinds of school events meaningful.

Murdoch (1998) also notes that ANT helps address a central question of why actors permit themselves to be enrolled into networks promoting standardized practices, particularly reflexive human actors. Educational analysts featured here also show how ANT concepts can be modified and opened to trace complex shifts and manglings in these negotiations around standards. These accounts reframe the debate around standards significantly, abandoning the attempt to track implementation (and correlated coercions) of universal educational standards that simply maintain focus on the most powerful actors and reinforce managerialism. These more open, flexible ANT analyses focus on the ineffable moments of performance, on the ephemeral bodies and representations that emerge in the intransitive educational events that occur at the confluence of networks. The analyses unpeel these network joints to explore the tensions among different representations of standards embedded in the movements at these joints. They trace the emergence of different ontological forms of a particular educational standard coexisting in a particular region of practice.

Chapter 7

Educational reform and planned change

In previous chapters, we drew upon ANT-informed studies to explore separate aspects embedded in networks of ongoing educational practice. In studying planned educational change, such as school improvement projects or curriculum reform initiatives, these aspects usually need to be considered together as they respond to major agendas and interventions that can produce all sorts of antici- pated and unanticipated outcomes. ANT has been widely employed in examining planned change in the broad field of organizational studies. However, aside from a few accounts of educational innovation and policy drawing upon ANT, litera- ture on educational change in the main offers little uptake of ANT concepts. This is unfortunate, given ANT's capacity to trace complex micro-politics and materi- alizing processes that are so central in educational change.

Working from ANT and after-ANT concepts and an extended example of educational change, this chapter first addresses the question: what does a network analysis contribute to understanding educational change efforts? It also considers: what can be understood about educational reform by stepping *outside* a network analysis, which, while important for illuminating certain dynamics, can become a singular and totalizing representation that obscures others? In other words, how might after-ANT readings of educational change help us to appreciate the spaces or blanks *beyond* networks, the partial and ambivalent belongings, and the otherness that cannot/should not be colonized by a single (networked) account? The argument ensuing from these questions suggests not only that ANT-inspired readings open important questions for researching education, but also that an educational consideration opens useful spaces for the ongoing development of material semiotics and other after-ANT explorations.

ANT and educational change

Before examining what ANT might offer, it is important to acknowledge the different kinds of questions attracting inquiry into educational change. One kind are critical questions about hegemonic reform purposes, the warring inter- ests, agendas and exclusions embodied in certain state-initiated reform efforts (Taylor *et al.* 2002), and the oppressive regulatory effects on life in schools and teaching–learning processes. While important, these tend to focus solely on the social rather than the socio-material, and are based on a priori assumptions about social structures and subject categories that ANT readings call into question. A second kind are questions around the processes themselves of educational reform: how does it work over time and place; how do different actors respond; what rhetorical and material struggles ensue, and what actually changes? Some educational inquiry moves into managerial formulations of these sorts of questions, examining what promotes success or failure and even 'lessons learned' in educational change initiatives. Overall, this second kind of question may be viewed as merely functionalist. However, they remain important because educational change projects are typically premised on a functional logic of implementation and measurement. These are usually directed towards changing pedagogy and other educational structures in ways that will increase student participation and achievement. Thus, it is also an expensive, politically visible and complex enterprise that can attract the close scrutiny of the media and public and a range of suspicious engagements from educators and educational administrators.

If we remain with this functional logic for the present, acknowledging its value given the high stakes for all involved, one common framing of the 'problem' of analysing educational reform is how to conceive (and thus provide recommendations for the management of) the organizational change process. As we also saw in Chapter 4, volumes of educational change literature have addressed this problem. Conceptions borrowed from organizational studies range from episodic event-oriented transformation to incremental process-based recursive change (Weick and Quinn 1999). Reform processes range from various iterations of strategic planning to epidemiological diffusion. In the former, the focus is on preliminary explicit goals, stages of planned implementation including management of resistance, and evaluated outcomes. In the latter, innovation is dropped into the container of the environment and gradually spreads through incentives and social processes, such as persuasion and knowledge-sharing. Selected notions of complexity theory, such as emergence, self-organization, recursion and fluidity adapted for educational managers (e.g. Fullan 1993) have attracted popular appeal. Related models of the 'professional learning community' (DuFour and Eaker 1998) centre educational change at the site of the teacher, framing teacher learning as the problem and conventional, if ambiguous, romantic ideals of knowledge sharing in community as the solution.

The difficulty with this problematization of change processes in an organization is its starting point of conceiving the classroom, school or school district as distinct homogeneous organizations, and furthermore, organizations that are essentially social. Thus, the category of the thing to be changed is established a priori as an entity, separate from the thing that is understood to carry within it the force for change. Furthermore, the emphasis on personal and social processes, as important as these appear to be in constituting the cultural, emotional, political and psychological relations at work in education, completely ignores the material presences that exert force and are entwined with what appears to be human intention, engagement, resistance and change. A second problem, as Nespor (2003) elaborates, is the conception of an educational innovation as a seed that is dropped into the pre-existing context of the school or school district. This presents context as a container and innovation as an origin that will grow (to use an arborescent metaphor), spread (to suggest an amorphous diffusion process), or be 'rolled out' (to use common parlance suggesting flattening of school landscapes with heavy machinery).

What, then, escapes analysis in the container–seed conception is the actual form and outcome of struggle negotiated at each of the myriad knots of the process – each interaction between human elements (desires, pedagogical knowledge, attachments, intentions, etc.) and things (such as textbooks, laboratory equipment, assessment forms, policy statements, parent newsletters, databases). Furthermore, the diverse ongoing work required to sustain, or even to stabilize, any new educational change is often overlooked. The conventional story is that after implementation, whether it is conceptualized as growth, spread or roll out, there is institutionalization (Crossan *et al.* 1999) or, alternatively, failure, and that appears to be the end of the change tale.

In contrast, Nespor (2002: 367–8) argues from an ANT-ish approach:

> The point is that we need to understand 'school change' as at least partly about the ways school practices are made mobile, and what and how they connect as they move. What are the structures of connections or linkages? What materials are they made of? How do things change as they move? How do connections change with this movement?

The naturalization of a notion called 'educational change' can be traced as an actor that was built over time and is now held in place by other actors and chains of ongoing effort. The more extended the network, the more entities that become enrolled into its links and translated or transformed in ways that support its work, the more likely it is to endure over time and to extend across regions.

An ANT reading of educational change offers useful concrete insights about what goes on in the dynamics of change. In the field of organization studies, ANT analyses of innovation and change processes have proliferated (Latour 1996, Czarniawska and Hernes 2005). These both trace failures, showing how networks have imploded or failed to enrol sufficient entities to survive, as well as successes, showing how the networks of 'macro-actors', large initiatives, associations, bodies of knowledge or practices, have expanded and thrived. After-ANT readings focus on the material practices that become enacted and distributed, but also on the otherings that occur: the fluid spaces and partial belongings that can comprise what appears to be a powerful network. In relation to educational change, ANT-ish inquiry might ask:

- How does a new state initiative seeking to generate 'school improvement' produce itself into an identifiable 'thing'?

- How does 'it' (or they, for 'it' may be multiple things) become enacted over time and across different regions?
- What diverse negotiations and responses are generated through material practices, and how do these affect its durability and force?
- What exactly becomes engaged and connected, what becomes excluded, and how do these involvements shift over time?
- Where and how does power accumulate through these negotiations?

Nespor (1994, 2002) carefully distinguishes this approach from that of social network analysis, which treats actors as well defined entities pre-existing their social relations, and network ties as static and neutral. He treats networks as assemblages of heterogeneous things, such as written curricula, videos, human actions and buildings that can move educational practices across space and time. Things themselves are neither solid objects and subjects, nor clearly separated from their context. They are each an effect produced through a set of relations that is constantly in motion. The network that appears through the linkages among these things is a trace, reasonably stable, of a series of translations that have changed and continue to change each entity participating within the network. In fact, network effects work on, and are exercised by, things that may not be enrolled into a particular network.

Nespor (2002) argues that a network reading shifts the tendency to view certain participants as 'reformers' and others as 'contexts' to understanding that all are part of materially heterogeneous networks that have unfolded geographically and historically and that overlap and relate with one another. Reforms and contexts mutually create one another. Reforms are 'contingent *effects* of struggles and negotiations in which groups try to define themselves and their interests by linking up with other relatively durable and extensive networks' (Nespor 2002: 366). Elements that appear to lie outside a school's networked activity, such as a parent for example, are in fact connected to and partly produced by it. For example, Nespor shows how a school's network of reform extended into a parent's actions and identity through a child's homework. The homework was treated by the parent not just as an object of performance circulating within the school, but as a comparator to the child's homework produced years earlier. This representation was then hybridized within the terms of the national curricula debates, which reterritorialized the homework and rescaled the local school into part of the national problem, while translating national level debates into specific critiques of the local school reform. The mother does not, therefore, just participate in school change but actively reframes it into terms that she can accept and oppose. The early-ANT model she employs also helpfully traces distinct moments through which change occurs. The larger change emerges through minute changes as elements assemble, connect, translate one another and gradually become a durable network of practices and materials entwined with people.

While useful, this model is not without its critics. One criticism is the tendency for any theoretical approach to itself become sedimented into an explanatory frame that is imposed, a priori, on the data. This is especially problematic for ANT, which has striven to maintain a fluid, decentred and exploratory approach that challenges a priori concepts and structures and honours complexities of immanent, emergent phenomena. However, in response, McLean and Hassard (2004) argue that the four-step moments of translation model can be viewed more as an analytic heuristic or sensitizing concept adapted to make sense of complex observations. Analysts of educational change should not slavishly impose four steps and expect a linear process, but appreciate that translation is ongoing, iterative and disorderly.

Two further critiques of early-ANT involve the problems of centrality, or a focus on 'big actors', and the problem of difference or otherness. The issue of centrality emerged when so many ANT studies focus on the development of large, powerful networks such as major policy initiatives. While ANT concepts are clearly helpful in illuminating the movements resulting in success, or failure, depending on the perspective and interests of those judging, of a major reform, the danger is lack of reflexivity about what the analyst is including and excluding. The ANT decision to establish boundaries around an object of inquiry is problematic, if it simply adopts the categories of its subjects and focuses on what appears to be most important and visible. This was Nespor's (1994) difficulty with ANT applied to education in ways that focused on big projects and ignored those with less visibility, fewer strategies or complex relations to networks.

This issue opens out to a whole series of questions about otherness in ANT, which Hetherington and Law (2000) summarized in a special journal issue devoted to the topic. They argue that the metaphor of the network can presume to colonize all dimensions, elements, layers and spaces of a phenomenon, as though everything that exists is drawn somewhere, somehow, into the relentless knots of networks extending infinitely. A network reading potentially 'leaves no room for alterity and allows for nothing to stand outside the relations that it orders through its descriptions of the word' (Hetherington and Law 2000: 128). This problem extends further than colonizing or 'speaking for' marginalized humans and things. The problem is also about dividing space and action according to issues of relation and difference: what becomes connected and mobilized into a network and what remains different according to that network's terms and relations. What of alterity that is blank, unexpected, novel and ambivalent? What of otherness that lies within or flows across network alignments, that is incoherent or non-representable? These questions warn the ANT analyst from presuming to offer any single account of events, and alert attention to spaces and discontinuities that may be enacted through certain, conventional network readings.

However, as Clarke (2002) has argued in her analysis of a major literacy policy initiative in the UK, education continues to struggle with 'big actor' reforms that do threaten to enrol wider constituents, including critically challenging actors and counter-networks of resistance, sedimenting all of these heterogeneous elements into powerful networks that can function oppressively. ANT analysis is particularly useful in tracing these power relations, showing how connections and translations among materials as well as language and social processes can appear to lock hegemonies into place. Clearly, ANT readings need to move as carefully and reflexively as possible, mindful of their own tendency to create obligatory points of passage, cautious in neither totalizing nor ignoring phenomena unfolding, and mindful of both their own highly provisional accounts and the entanglement of these accounts in enacting the phenomena being read.

Mobilizing and making change durable

Let us consider an example of an educational change examined by Fenwick (2010b). The initiative was launched in 2000 in Alberta, Canada and is still thriving, rather astonishingly given some of its precepts, at the time of writing ten years later. Why? How? In the following ANT-ish reading, certain concepts appear useful to go some way to address these questions. ANT helps illuminate moments in the enrolment and translation of actors, the importance of particular mobile inscriptions that travel about ordering particular activities, the problematization and relations that establish centres of calculation and translation, and the overall gradual assemblage and strengthening of a network through various strategies. However, the case also resists an overly tight emphasis on network building, for non-networkable spaces and otherness can be glimpsed when we probe what is going on in the unfoldings of this network. Indeed, certain otherings appear in some ways to be enabling the most visible network to proceed with its work.

The following account is not intended to collapse this complexity into a slick performance of (otherness enriched) network reading, but to suggest the potential for ANT-ish approaches to not only analyse how powerful networks become set in motion through educational reform, but also to gesture towards gaps and more fluid spaces within and among these networks. The case is an educational reform called the Alberta Initiative for School Improvement (AISI) which states its official goal as 'to improve student learning and performance by fostering initiatives that reflect the unique needs and circumstances of each school authority' (Alberta Learning 1999: 4). The initiative has made Alberta government funds available to any school or school district whose proposal for a three-year school improvement project is judged by the provincial ministry, Alberta Education, to be acceptable according to clearly communicated criteria. The criterion of particular significance is to improve student achievement, mostly through measurement on provincial standardized tests. The first three-year AISI cycle supposedly showed such general success in improving student test scores and meeting individual projects' student achievement targets, according to government reports (Alberta Learning 2001), that it was renewed for two more three-year cycles since startup.

The initiative is characterized by several features that are surprising in a context where bitter disputes between the government, school districts and teachers marked the six years of educational restructuring for accountability prior to 2000 (Taylor *et al.* 2002). During this period, school districts were amalgamated, standardized student testing expanded, and business planning introduced in a 'wave of top-down, seemingly ideologically driven package of educational reforms' (Burger *et al.* 2001: para 12). Perhaps the most surprising feature is the vast number of schools and districts that became involved and continued their involvement in the AISI reform, despite the history of stormy relations. A second point of interest is that AISI established a partnership of the government with all educational professional associations representing the teachers, superintendents and school boards. The sustainability of this alliance over ten years is worth noting given the rather wide range of ideology and interests represented by these organizations. Third, the government has committed more funds to AISI than to any other educational reform and further, in a historically unusual arrangement, granted these funds directly to school districts. Approximately C$500 million had been committed by 2008 to fund over 1,600 projects (of Alberta's 2,246 total number of schools) (McEwan 2008). The current AISI website, an exhaustive collection of individual project reports, province-wide meta-analyses and databases of 'lessons learned' in every curricular area, brings to the fore concepts such as 'evidence-based' education, universalized 'best practices' of pedagogy, and classroom-based research limited to improving teacher techniques towards outcomes-based student achievement. This raises a fourth surprising issue, as AISI has managed to actively involve university faculties of education in its projects, despite its emphases on measured outcomes and evidence-based practice, which might be expected to engender philosophical contestation and resistance from many academics.

The question of how AISI managed to extend as far as it had, enrolling and sustaining participation among such diverse constituents, is of particular interest. A network reading could show the importance of intermediaries, like money, in attracting participants. Superintendents, for example, after a decade of funding cutbacks and restructuring, were highly motivated by the offer of cash for improvement proposals, even when they were aware of their own translation in accepting the grants. One superintendent explained:

> The name of the game is conditional granting. They call it enveloping or whatever terminology you want, but it works ... because it creates the behaviour you want. In my instance for example, AISI [Alberta Initiative for School Improvement] money, politically I can't afford to let over a million dollars go. I would get crucified ... by my board, by our parents, because we let a million dollars slide. They don't care what has to happen to make it happen, just get it for us ... They say we want you to jump one foot and it works because the carrot is one foot off the ground.
>
> (Taylor *et al.* 2002: 476)

The attraction for teachers lay at least partly in the apparently open nature of AISI projects. The project problem, content and methods are left entirely to the discretion of the school or district applicant, as long as they can demonstrate an improvement to student achievement. Most early projects were oriented to improving student literacy and mathematics achievement. Other popular areas emerging over the years were developing pedagogies for English as a Second Language instruction, for integrating technology into classrooms, and for 'differentiated instruction' (instructional approaches to meet different student special needs and learning styles). In all of these projects, a stream of new materials came rolling into classrooms: class sets of mathematics puzzles and blocks, new computers and teaching software, textbooks and teacher guides. Teachers were intimately enmeshed in putting to work not only these student materials, but also the new instruments of data collection that each project needed to design.

Once districts and teachers were mobilized to design and apply for projects for which they had local affection and commitment, intermediaries began to circulate around the province that helped translate these energies into certain consistent practices. The project proposals, for example, demanded structures of pre- and post-project measurement of student performance. Each project was required to produce an annual report according to a template created by the government AISI office. This report focused attention on technical information, such as improvement objectives, key strategies, evaluation methods, student outcomes, effective practices, sustainability, what worked and what did not work, etc. (Alberta Education 2008). There was little space for exploring or recognizing complexity. These reports are all posted publicly on a searchable web-based database, an inscription which collapses, orders and translates complex multiplicity into one centre of calculation.

Other centres draw together the nodes of the projects to further reinforce the network. A province-wide AISI conference, sponsored annually by the provincial government, features presentations from teachers leading the projects. AISI coordinators, known as 'lead' teachers with credibility in their district, are trained for the role and gathered together throughout the year for support. These individuals represent more intense nodes of translation spreading throughout the extending network. Teachers became translated into collectors of data. Textbooks, plastic blocks and computer games became objects of study. Lesson plans became experiments. Everyday interactions with students became 'benchmarking'. Student assignments became AISI findings. In other words, the translation of teacher to (AISI) researcher fundamentally changes the pedagogic gaze, identity, and relationships.

To re-enact classroom work as an AISI project, the province's six universities were mobilized to assist schools with meeting the research requirements. Each was allotted sufficient funds to appoint its own AISI coordinator and office, which began generating websites about classroom research methods and distributing materials, such as measurement tools, in workshops and school visits. These were to show teachers how to collect and analyse their own data, and benchmark student achievement, and so on. In each of these moves, an ANT reading of available documents illuminates how the reform spread not through top-down imposition, but through the circulation of inscriptions, intermediaries, collaborations with objects and technologies, and a host of actors. These translated one another, assembling highly heterogeneous institutions, political interests, philosophies of knowledge and suspicions about change.

Clearly, AISI appears to have established and extended itself as a far reaching and durable network. It has mobilized hundreds of teachers and administrators, linked with classroom materials, databases, school timetables and equipment, as well as universities and professional associations, to accept their own translation into designated roles that extended and stabilized the network. AISI seems to work partly as a mediation between the local networks of schools and districts, and the more extended but distinct networks of the teachers' association, the university's education teaching and research programmes, and the government network. Each network maintained its own life and circulations while being bound up, for different reasons and to support different agendas, in the circulating inscriptions and translations of the AISI network. The government coordinator of AISI activities claims that 'multiple sources of evidence' show that AISI has had 'profound effect on education in Alberta', particularly in 'improved student learning, renewed focus on teaching and learning, better decision-making based on evidence, job-embedded professional development, and shared and distributed leadership' (McEwan 2008: 6).

Fluid spaces and ambivalent belongings

There is much that is obscured by this reading focused on centricity, on how the reform extended and stabilized itself. What beckons some acknowledgment, at least, are the spaces and the otherness shadowed away by bringing to the fore a seemingly immutable 'AISI network' as though it were cut into the province like a madly branching river. Different spaces, even different forms of space, can be discerned moving in and around this most visible network of power. Further, there seem to be different forms of belonging to this network and its tributaries. The simple question of how translation occurs does not reach far enough. What about partial translations? When and why do these occur? How do the resulting ambivalent belongings affect the overall network? These are some of the questions addressed in after-ANT work.

Returning to the teachers who appeared to become so widely engaged in the projects, it might be understandable that these in fact represented a rather open space. While the start and end points were shaped by the prescribed proposal and report templates, and while the objective was predetermined to be student achievement, the freedom to choose the content, activities and materials for the project opened an important space of local innovation and control. In other words, projects were widely diverse in their questions as well as their pedagogical content. Some schools worked with the prescribed provincial curricula and others focused on implementing what might be considered more popular (perhaps even theoretically questionable) initiatives, such as 'multiple intelligences'. Teachers tried new pedagogical practices, collected data in the classroom evidencing the success of these practices, and reported results.

The projects are referred to as 'action research' (Parsons *et al.* 2006), and appear to offer opportunities for teachers to engage creatively in generating and legitimating the classroom oriented, practice-based knowledge that advocates of teacher research have been promoting in recent decades (e.g. Cochran-Smith and Lytle 1999). Teachers were invited by AISI to become translated into knowledge producers and authorities. The university representatives were translated by AISI into roles that served, rather than disseminated, knowledge production. These local spaces of innovation and discretionary action are critical to maintain network extension by retaining 'intimacy in its detailed knowledge of the nuances of practice' (Bowker and Star 1999: 232). Too much standardized control and network imperative threatens its manageability and survival.

These spaces might be seen as the gaps between the network knots; if the knots are simply the visible parts of the project, the required reports that are calculated and gathered into dense sites. But like a fishing net, big spaces can open where these calculations do not specify type of pedagogies, direction of project, pace of implementation, enrolment of actors, standard instruments or texts, etc. Since the scrutiny of the text focuses most on the measurable student achievement, these spaces exist as an unrepresented other to the network. The actual materials used, the pedagogical approaches tried, the various experiments and failures and upsets, the everyday commotion of classroom action, the wide uses of objects; all of this swirls in a space outside the attention of the network. This other is assumed to be present by the network's reports, but is in fact absent. It escapes representation. Thus, what constitutes an AISI project, the thing that is linked into such an apparently durable network, exists in different dimensions. It exists as the neatly ordered project reports and all the meta-analyses generated from these. It exists as the funded set of materials and activities that teachers and administrators manage and plan. However, the AISI project, unbounded, is also the immanent, ineffable events of the classroom reality which as Thrift (2000) argues, always and necessarily live outside network space.

Perhaps the only central thing holding together the AISI network is the circulating insistence on increasing measurable student achievement. However, even this notion appears to slide in the messy spaces of the network. Stelmach (2004), for example, shows that at the level of parent and teacher discussions, impact on achievement was often overlooked and AISI project success was explained in rather symbolic terms. A perception existed that as long as the strategies that were implemented during the project had life beyond it, AISI had succeeded.

For the universities, the AISI projects exist as a research enterprise. Fluid spaces open here. Approvals for ethical research procedures, for instance, which the university regards as essential in any project that collects and represents data, fell into a space between direct grants from government to schools and university assistance to conduct research (Parsons *et al.* 2006). Teacher–researcher training, normally conducted by the faculties of education through accredited courses and programmes under their control, was permitted and indeed encouraged in spaces with no tuition, progression or clear disciplinary authority. In network logic, university personnel were simply enrolled into extensions of knowledge exchange reaching beyond the districts.

These extensions created fissures that generated complicated spaces where various dimensions had to be negotiated. These are regions, or perhaps other forms of spaces, that a strict network reading of the massive AISI reform cannot embrace. One of the most obvious of these is the othering of inquiry that reaches outside the a-critical and a-political AISI circumscription of particular forms and questions of research. Everything in AISI is geared to improving instructional methods for a narrow set of academic student engagements. Only rare projects address students' experiences beyond these engagements, or analyse issues of equity and justice. Few projects explored poverty or health, racism, homophobia, religious discrimination or social exclusion in schools. None critically examined educational policy, or analysed systemic politics and power relations in school practices, texts, relations, and so forth. Absent was educational research of post-realist, post-humanist, complexity orientations of the sort that scholars such as Patti Lather (2007) and Brent Davis et al. (2008) have been mapping. In fact, in one presentation to the Alberta school superintendents association, AISI was claimed to be the 'gold standard' of improvement models that sends a 'clear message' to universities that the only valid research is that which reflects student achievement results (Burger et al. 2001).

However, with the universities enrolled in extending and strengthening the AISI network, the appearance is created of scholarly approval and support for the AISI endorsed form of educational research. Further, 'action research' becomes converted to solving predetermined problems, an AISI formulation that completely ignored Alberta scholars' explorations of classroom action research as participatory, hermeneutic, emancipatory and emergent (e.g. Sumara and Carson 1997). Were the universities fully enrolled? When we examine their involvement, it appears that each of the province's universities had simply used AISI funds to cover partial salary of one faculty member designated as an AISI coordinator and provide some clerical support. Some, but certainly not all, of these university-based AISI offices became active in training teachers and school district AISI coordinators in research methods, maintaining websites to support research, etc. (Parsons et al. 2006). However, AISI activity and offices do not appear on the university websites. The university faculties of educational research can be described as belonging to the AISI network only as ambivalent members. They have accepted the funds and the attached responsibilities to promote AISI, they have maintained their names as full partners on the AISI website, but the translation of their roles has remained minimal.

Parents, too, were enrolled in ambivalent ways in the AISI network. While AISI projects required active involvement of 'parents and the community to work collaboratively to introduce innovative and creative initiatives based upon local needs and circumstances' (Alberta Learning 1999), there was general agreement that parent engagement in them was peripheral. They were often relegated to receiving special newsletters about project activities and attending show and tell events. Perhaps, not surprisingly, the general amount and nature of integrative parent involvement in schools remained largely unaffected by AISI (Parsons *et al.* 2006). One study of this phenomenon (Stelmach 2004) described a school district that installed a special 'Action Team' to mobilize parents in AISI participation, by creating home–school linkages and active parental engagement in project strategies to improve learning. However, the Action Team's discussions were kept separate from the teachers' curriculum meetings, and parents felt they were interfering inappropriately both with teachers' time and their legitimate authority over classroom decisions.

> As one parent suggested, 'I felt that we as parents didn't have as much to offer because, first of all we had to learn what the issues were'. When teachers came up with ideas, this parent admitted that the others on the Action Team agreed to go along with the teachers because parents and community members felt ill equipped to offer alternatives. In doing this, parents affirmed the cultural expectation that teachers are responsible for student learning.
>
> (Stelmach 2004: para 34)

The translation of parents was limited to highly circumscribed roles in the network, receiving personal invitations to student award ceremonies and special newsletters, attending designated parent lunches and the like. Issues of persistent parental marginalization through social class, racialization and culture were not even recognized. Still, some parents participated, even in the awkward dialogues inviting parent suggestions which they sensed were unwelcome. Meanwhile, as Stelmach (2004) notes, the school entrance sign continued to regulate all visitors to report to the office, announcing clear insider–outsider boundaries and control of territory. Despite parents' apparent inscription as network participants in various AISI texts and attendances, they remained actors at the edges. Their partial translation recalls Nespor's (1994) warning about ANT's possible presumption of ever-expanding fluid networks. The associational world of schools flows in very deep, durable channels.

What of the translation of teachers into actors in the AISI network? According to a government report, teachers have not only been converted into successful AISI researchers, but also into continuous learners with a focused 'what works' orientation. In other words, the complex spaces and pedagogic flows comprising what it is to be a 'teacher' have been converted into measures of teaching capacity based on application of evidence-based practice.

> Teachers now view themselves as learners and engage in inquiry related to the impact of their practices on student learning. They talk about gathering evidence of effective practices and use it to determine what works and what doesn't work for students.
>
> (Alberta Learning 2004: 48)

However, in one of the only studies available that actually followed the actors in AISI, a more complex picture emerges. Judah and Richardson (2006) show how teachers they interviewed were both excited by the opportunity afforded by AISI to creatively develop new knowledge with their students and colleagues, and dismayed by the regulatory strictures and mandated involvement of the projects. In other words, teachers were 'caught between competing discourses of personal empowerment and individual autonomy on the one hand and of the need to respond to externally driven measures of accountability and excellence on the other' (Judah and Richardson 2006: 69). The study also showed that teachers who were AISI coordinators struggled with imposing projects on their colleagues that seemed to be highly regulated, yet that offered potentially rich opportunity and time for professional learning.

Time itself became another space of complex enrolment. As AISI offered sufficient funds for substitutes to release teachers from classroom time, schools and districts could enable teacher gatherings for building curriculum and learning new strategy. For teachers, this was an especially welcome space for new emergences (Parsons *et al.* 2006). However, time away from the class is not release from the class activity, as all teachers know who have laboured late nights over substitute lesson plans for the next day of their absence. In AISI, as with many educational implementations, teachers must maintain simultaneous presence in different forms and in different spaces that are not all delineated by the terms of the powerful network. Teachers inhabit life in their AISI enrolment as both researchers and as learners of teaching practice, in their ongoing classroom responsibilities as immanent engagement in that practice, in their regulated accounting to the government, and in their defense of boundaries defining their knowledge authority and practice.

Not surprisingly, translation in educational change, such as AISI, is partial and diverse, representing ambivalent belongings rather than transformation and fluid spaces that escape network representation. Still, they are belongings, and the powerful AISI network in Alberta has become durable as an extended set of connections among highly heterogeneous entities. Within and among these connections, however, are multiple openings and ungoverned regions where local, creative and unpredictable activity and identities can play.

Conclusion

In examining educational change, the early kind of ANT analysis is useful to reveal the material interactions through which a major initiative is successfully mobilized. This is even where, as we have seen in the example we have examined, one might have expected it to inspire widespread critique and collective resistance. The approach of tracing the moments of translation and strategies of ordering practices and identities helps illuminate how the change, conceptualized as a growing network, gradually extends and becomes durable. In effect, the network inscribes a new geography of social and material relations throughout an educational system. This analysis is particularly useful in tracing how ideas, practices and new technologies that appear to be completely foreign and irreconcilable with existing networks can eventually insinuate themselves as the new norms. This analysis can also examine the myriad wider connections implicated in educational change. As Nespor (2002) asks, when the meanings of schools are connected to all sorts of things outside the border of the school, should not school change efforts address these relations?

However, within this reading, we can see how translations vary. Some entities are more partially enrolled, and some translations hold but are very leaky. The linkages often create ambivalent belongings, where people, things and collectives struggle to protect practices from inscription through these new connections at the same time as they work the connections for their own purposes. We also see the other spaces that are non-calculable, and in fact not even representable by network logic. In the AISI network, local spaces allowed district and classroom project invention in directions that the network did not attempt to order beyond allocating the space of design. These can be characterized as spaces within the network, held loosely between the ordering nodes. But other spaces also float alongside the network, unrecognized, uncaptured and unrelated to both its ordering processes and to the ANT researcher's network logic. These are the spaces of both ambivalence and of contradiction, where the direction and nature of action is undecidable and unpredictable. In these spaces, creative possibilities can emerge. However, they also can be contained and obscured through network strategies to block counter networks of invention.

The ANT-ish readings suggested here would trace not only the most visible movements of ordering in educational change, but also gesture to the elusive, more messy, more promising otherness of new possibilities. Attention to the socio-material connections and their patterns can discern not only closures but also openings in mass reform efforts, spaces for flux and instability embedded within and floating apart from the network. Most importantly, such readings can open inquiry into processes through which such possibilities can be protected and amplified, recognized, and perhaps connected together, where appropriate, to realize alternative educational changes.

Chapter 8

(Ac)counting for education

Like education, curriculum and pedagogy, evaluation practices are themselves organizations of activity that produce space and time by mobilizing and accumulating distant settings into present contexts and accounts. Accountability and accounting have been key themes for educational reform in many contexts in the last decades. Indeed, we can link the concern for standardization that we discussed in Chapter 6 with that for accountability. In efforts to ensure that standards are achieved, practices are accounted for, made both calculable and representable. Massive resources have, therefore, been poured into developing agencies to hold education to account and develop practices through which to account for what goes on in educational settings. This is the focus of this chapter.

Before going further into ANT inflections on these issues, any discussion of accountability in education or elsewhere must start by recognizing its various forms. For instance, there is:

- fiscal accountability
- legal accountability (compliance with explicit regulations)
- bureaucratic outcomes-oriented accountability (duty to the organization's mission)
- community accountability (duty to care)
- professional accountability (duty to a profession's discipline and ethics).

All of these forms are arguably active at the same time in educational systems, where processes from teaching and learning to professional integrity and financial governance are subjected to external measurements. These measurements require a conversion of living events, and their often unpredictable ambiguity into representations of certain scales. These representations are rendered so that they can be scrutinized and assessed, according to (usually) conflicting accountability demands by (usually) conflicting stakeholder interests ranging among educational managers, government departments, funding bodies, parents and the general public. As Robson (1992) explains, accounts essentially make living events visible; they provide a basis for calculation. This calculation and its targets afford a means for acting upon individuals to produce new processes. While

accountability enactments are by now profuse in educational research, ANT studies bring a new focus to the complex negotiations of power among human and
non-human elements in these processes. ANT analyses not only enrich but also
identify limitations in conventional readings of accountability, and point to some
new possibilities in researching evaluation and accountability in education.

Critics claim that accountability demands have escalated in education to an
unprecedented level, a fetish in Power's (1999) view, and a condition for justice.
Among accountability critics in education are Mathison and Ross (2002: 1) who,
in their analysis of the hegemonic forms, define accountability as:

> a means of interaction in hierarchical, often bureaucratic systems, between
> those who have power and those who do not ... Specifically, accountability
> is an economic means of interaction. When power is delegated and dispersed
> to those within a hierarchical system there is an expected return from the
> investment of that power in others. Those to whom power has been del-
> egated are obligated to answer or render an account of the degree of success
> in accomplishing the outcomes desired by those in power. Because of the
> diffuse nature of many hierarchical systems, accountability depends on both
> surveillance and self-regulation.

The project then, for many critical educational writers, becomes one of developing counter-hegemonic strategies on the part of the less powerful. These
strategies may include collective grassroots – energized resistances or the
creation of democratic participatory evaluation approaches to resist external
measurements wielded by those with more power. This view understands
clear distinctions between groups, those who have and those who do not have
power, positioned in necessarily antagonistic relations, until some effort is made
to achieve productive, if difficult, dialogues towards more democratic working
arrangements.

A different critical view is provided through the governmentality thesis
advanced by Rose (1999) among others. This relies on a more post-structuralist
understanding of power. Power is both productive and constraining of possibilities and is held to circulate through complex, shifting webs of relations rather
than being delegated to one group or another who must then negotiate across
their gap of power difference. In this view, accountability is achieved through
making constituents of a system visible and therefore calculable. In education,
for example, teaching and learning practices can be rendered visible through representational technologies, including publication of student test results, national
and international league tables, surveillance cameras in schools, individual student learning plans, and mandated teacher growth plans reviewed by supervisors.
These technologies, working through 'numbers and other "inscription devices",
actually constitute the domains they appear to represent; they render them representable in a docile form – a form amenable to the application of calculation and
deliberation' (Rose 1999: 198). People internalize these forms of self-regulation

through representations of their performance, according to this thesis. In effect, human actors make themselves into calculable subjects.

One branch of accountability research in education has centred on its different forms, attempting to identify the overriding *purposes* of educational accountability, or who is being held accountable for what and to whom. Other research has examined the effects of accountability on practice and policy. A third branch focuses on accountability systems already functioning in education, seeking to understand their micro-interactions that maintain a particular culture of accountability. For a summary of these literatures, see Webb (2005).

ANT analyses address all of these accountability processes and share a strong concern with how power circulates and what is enacted in these processes. However, ANT-related studies have shown that accountability is performed in far more distributed ways and with uncertain effects than some educational research would maintain. They also show how calculation and visibility circulates in far messier and more contested ways than some portrayals of governmentality would suggest. What ANT analyses contribute, first, is to highlight the often-forgotten things in evaluation and the different active roles played by different object forms in collaboration with humans producing dynamics of accountability. ANT explores the relations emerging at every point of a network as these things and players work upon one another, persuading, seducing, resisting, compelling. ANT seeks to explore the scaling of certain practices as *evaluating* by bringing together a range of human and non-human objects in one network.

Second, the ANT concept of translation is particularly useful for analysing what actually occurs in the processes of evaluation. After all, accounting creates a continuous form of control precisely because it can proceed without any interpersonal contact. Numbers can be gathered and transformed into measures of educational inputs and outputs that circulate through texts, codes, databases and pedagogical devices to govern activity. Some of these things and the accountability measures that become folded within them function as immutable mobiles that can travel back and forth between educational centres of accountability and local regions. These things can work to bind various locales into central modes of calculation that then can prescribe what goes in various locales. The process enables the 'conduct of conduct', translating standardized modes of regulation that attempt to render various locales visible, portable and accountable within an accounting network. However, as we have also shown in earlier chapters, just as different objects and texts as well as humans attempt to act upon and to translate one another, they also ignore, misuse, challenge and reinvent one another.

Third, ANT analysis is especially suited for conceptualizing the spaces of evaluation and accountability that are performed in varied educational environments, such as, classrooms, schools, school–community networks, student testing systems, educational policy committees, and so forth. The classroom, for example, is a calculative space of things – attendance rosters, homework checkers, anecdotal student records, binders containing students' individual assignment portfolios lined on the wall, displays of recent student writing and recent poster assignments on the bulletin boards. These interact together to shape the action and the space, as well as each other, in ways that perform continuous networks of evaluation. Finally, ANT ideas are also useful in rethinking evaluation of learning and education, encouraging questions about what connections assemble things and people into networks, what subjectivities and behaviours are translated by the network, what objects (of knowledge, practice, technology) appear to be held together by network processes, and how these objects dissolve.

This chapter will focus in particular on accountability processes at play in evaluating learners and teachers and in creating calculative spaces. ANT concepts help to trace important nuances in these processes, showing how they actually function as messy networks folded into spaces alongside other networks, and how injunctions of accountability are negotiated at different nodes of these networks.

Accounting for learning

Evaluations of learning and knowledge typically involve calculative processes conducted through texts and other objects that circulate among members of a community, whether their primary focus of participation is learning, instructing, assessing, leading or enacting routine practices. In our discussion here we will draw upon the concepts of actants and actors, and mediators and intermediaries, as introduced in Chapter 1. Actants are distinguished from actors as the latter are usually employed to refer to entities that are thought of in human terms, even when they are hybrids of the human and non-human:

> Whatever acts or shifts actions, action itself being defined by a list of performances through trials; through these performances are deduced a set of competences with which the actant is endowed; the Fusion point of a metal is a trial through which the strength of an alloy is defined; the bankruptcy of a company is a trial through which the faithfulness of an ally may be defined; an actor is an actant endowed with a character (usually anthropomorphic).
>
> (Akrich and Latour 1991: 259)

Mediators are human and non-human actants, such as measuring instruments, teacher guides, ideas about standards, knowledge about evaluation approaches, grades, charts, databases: they actively work upon events and entities. Mediators can form links, induce or prevent certain behaviours, interpret and transform action, and so forth. They can be tinkered with, adapted, interpreted and redirected. Intermediaries, both human and non-human, function more like a stabilized black box. They will transport a force or meaning without transforming it. However, an intermediary will break down and become a complex mediator that suddenly leads into multiple directions and mobilizes more mediators. Further, a mediator can turn into an intermediary that must be accounted for by more work.

In any practice of evaluating learning, mediators work and intermediaries circulate to produce networks of texts, classroom things, school routines, state rhetoric, social expectation and discrete student actions. These networks of evaluating learning outcomes then shape the practices of teaching and learning as well as the subjectivities of teachers and learners and their relations. Hamilton and Hillier (2007) point out that because these evaluation networks are themselves specialized literacy and numeracy practices, they reveal in particular the role of texts in these 'projects of social ordering'. As such a project, these evaluation networks gather people and things together, enrol their complicity, influence their behaviours, and forge connections among them. These connections can become so stabilized or durable over time that the network becomes institutionalized to appear to be a performance measurement 'system'. A system often becomes treated as inevitable and immutable by the participants enrolled within it. As we have outlined in previous chapters, resistance, partial compliance, distress and debate can all be contained within its networks.

An example of such a system can be pointed to in standardized tests of student achievement, something we explored in Chapter 6. Increasingly mandated across states and provinces in North America, and elsewhere, such tests help to link together massive networks through the movement of the test as an immutable mobile. It is an intermediary that embeds a history of network enactments, struggles and mediations which have settled into one fixed representation. Nespor (2002) describes how these tests' fixed items translate complex learning practices into limited categories, the calculation of which translates year-long and vastly different educational processes around the state into numeric scores. Teachers are bypassed as mediators of pedagogy and knowledge, and students are directly enrolled into subject matter that has been translated into the test's limited forms of knowledge. As the stakes are high in the calculative process (schools scoring less than a certain percentage lose their accreditation), Nespor shows that the test mobilizes a whole series of events and people to align with its forms. For instance, administrators force curricula to conform to the test's demands, teachers drill classes in test preparation, remedial classes are arranged to improve students' test achievement, and fear is mobilized among all. The result is a:

> funnelling, hierarchical network in which the state becomes a centre of accumulation collecting standardized representations of all the students in its political borders. The state can then summarize and compare students as a class, and more importantly speak for and act upon them.
>
> (Nespor 2002: 375)

Another example of such enactments are the evaluation networks that incorporate individual's reports of their learning goals and achievements, such as Individual Learning Plans (Hamilton and Hillier 2007) and Teacher Professional Growth Plans (Fenwick 2003). Human actors become mobilized by the non-human text of the 'plan' to shape their practice in ways that can be incongruent with the emergent nature of teaching and learning, and cause considerable confusion and frustration. The plan approach to evaluating learning also makes individuals visible and subject to the self-regulation that analysts such as Fejes (2008) and Fenwick (2003) have documented using a Foucauldian framework of disciplinary surveillance. The self becomes a subject of self-surveillance and calculation.

Hamilton and Hillier (2007) employ ANT in examining the network connections and mobilizations linked to individual learning assessments. Her focus is upon the Individual Learning Plan (ILP) used in England as a tool to record student literacy progress in adult skills for life programmes. The ILP functions as a paper form produced at each local education institution and filled out for each literacy student. On this form the teacher must record curriculum elements, short-, medium- and long-term goals (translated into 'SMART' targets), student 'learning style', and small steps of student progress. While originally intended as a formative assessment activity, the ILP became a performance measure tool for administrative purposes, and a measure of quality assurance. What interests Hamilton most is how these individual learning assessment practices work to align local practices and identities to global or systemic practices of literacy. For Hamilton, the ILP is a key thing in the process of ordering enacted through the English performance measurement system for literacy for three reasons. First, the ILP is a central nexus of practice where various discourses and policy strands meet. Second, it is highly contentious among teachers. Third, it is embedded in everyday face-to-face interactions of literacy education, literally at the 'heart' of teaching–learning practices.

Hamilton traces the student–teacher interactions. As might be expected, the ILP becomes incorporated in practice, not through straightforward mobilization of particular behaviours, but through negotiations of various responses and accommodations from teachers. This ranges from cynicism to strategic compliance to creative adaptation of the format. ILPs are mediators and not intermediaries. The ILP form itself can generate new things, bits of paperwork whose regulation and flow are complex to coordinate. These include initial assessments, tracking information, learning agreements, paperwork to synchronize practice across teachers, and templates to help teachers achieve consistency in reporting. Learning processes become shaped by the ILP's linear trajectory and predetermined emphases and levels. Students' experiences become shaped by the discourse of aspirations and achievements dictated by the ILP. Student and teacher subjectivities become shaped by the struggles to negotiate the ILP, to meet the inspectors' requirements, yet protect the emergent and diverse nature of literacy learning.

Hamilton concludes that while student involvement in the ILPs is more passive and compliant, the tutors become mobilized in creative bridging activities which are also, for them, ethically conflicting and deeply uncomfortable activities. The tutors must create bridges between students' activities and the ILP, the college administration, and inspectors that audit the ILP. In effect, the ILP generates a series of practices among tutors that:

involves actively co-opting tutors into the very processes they are skeptical about while they struggle to make the ILP experience better for themselves and their students – more appropriate and less unwieldy. Tutors are thereby incorporated, or enrolled, into the systems' goals as active mediators (Latour 2005b: 39) as their own core motivations and definitions of good practice are invoked: practical ease of use, collaboration with their colleagues and responding to students in a learner-centred way.

(Hamilton 2009: 239)

Another example of teachers finding all sorts of means to open the connections being wrought in surveillant-style evaluation approaches can be seen in Fenwick's (2003) study of Teacher Professional Growth Plans (TPGP). Mandated for all schools in a Canadian province, TPGPs required every teacher to create goals for professional growth at the beginning of each year, and record activities and achievements of the goals at the years' end for review by a supervisor. The visibility and display afforded of teachers' complex learning processes could be analysed as a clear form of pastoral governance where individuals are regulated by internalizing the self-improvement gaze of the TPGP activity. However, when the actual negotiations are traced among the various objects, texts and humans that become enrolled in these evaluative networks, a series of fabrications as well as mistakes and deliberate misrepresentations become obvious. Some teachers wrote 'goal' statements that described what they were already doing rather than what they aspired to learn. Some, such as one who claimed to write down 'learn PowerPoint' as his goal every year, created a deliberate pro forma performance calculated to appear compliant with the district's own goals, and thus to avoid attention. Some teachers treated their goal statements as personal affirmations rather than as evaluation. Some supervisors admitted to approving 'lots of latitude' in how and what teachers wrote, given their sense of the inherent uncertainty over what constituted legitimate goals of professional growth. In some schools, the whole TPGP process was turned into a collaborative dialogue among teachers and supervisors about what counts as teacher knowledge in different situations, what purpose is served by a goal, and how to know when one has learned. The TPGP text, while intended to function as an intermediary and transport particular protocols of teacher self-evaluation into different settings, actually behaves as a mediator, creating possibilities and occurrences, but being modified itself in all sorts of complex directions. In other words, the TPGP form, in the negotiations of practice, becomes a folding and fluid object. It is not a distinct and stable instrument of evaluation but an uncertain space that produces diverse and conflicting accounts.

In addition, and linked to the plan, is the portfolio. While portfolio practices and purposes vary, most involve the collection of artefacts (assignments, photos, creative products, others' documentation, etc.) that evidence learners' competency and intend to advance students' reflection and self-evaluation. The notion of life as linear and narrated is displaced into an assemblage, literally a gathering together of things that represent the multiplicity of the self.

In classrooms, portfolio practices in effect become networks that translate various dynamics of teaching, learning and evaluation. As new portfolio activities are incorporated, they translate the organization and rhythms of the everyday educational activity. The material demands of the portfolio, whether a cardboard folder to be filled with diverse things or an electronic collection of URL links to a student's digital creations, translates students' activities and knowledge into a particular production of visible things that then become gathered into some meaningful whole. The self is curated in the enactment of the portfolio. The pedagogical expectations of the portfolio translate teachers' practices as they learn to create activities that will result in portfolio appropriate artefacts, and to manage this new collection of things. Depending on the age and capacity of students, physical management of portfolios can be a formidable task that translates much student and teacher activity in the classroom to focus on organizing, collecting, updating, reviewing and recording. Pedagogical management of portfolios is also potentially formidable, as teachers and teaching practices become translated by the diverse expectations inscribed into the portfolio. Portfolios can act as mobilizers of diverse creative student expression, as everyday receptacles for activity, as demonstrations that state mandated standards have been met, as visible evidence of acceptable pedagogy, and as a cumulative student record that follows them year to year. They can be both actant and actor in the networks of evaluation.

In their study, Habib and Wittek (2007: 279) explore how the portfolio becomes a constitutive element of a classroom community, as well as the 'affordances and constraints that are related to its use'. They studied portfolio practices to evaluate learning used in undergraduate nursing and journalism programmes in a Norwegian college, and how the portfolio becomes an actor in the interplay between designers and users of new educational processes. They suggest that the artefacts or non-human tools that collaborate with humans to form what becomes visible as portfolio assessment practices could be differentiated according to the extent to which they participate in the translation process. That is, primary artefacts are those tools in the portfolio production process that have been more or less rigidly inscribed by some programme of action: a piece of paper can be written or drawn upon but also become part of origami. These artefacts undergo translation primarily through the meanings inscribed into them by users. Secondary artefacts are representations of primary artefacts, such as the written guidelines for portfolio use, or the routines built into the learning management system. These secondary artefacts participate in their own reinscription and definition as well as translating others. The student who reads the written portfolio guidelines and jots down her own list of things to include in her portfolio is being translated by the guidelines, but at the same time as she is translating them into something new. This is another secondary artefact. Tertiary artefacts do not usually bear heavy inscription, but emerge as novel and unexpected ways to think about or use primary artefacts. Habib and Wittek conclude that in portfolio assessment, these tertiary artefacts take form in the students' modes of thinking, and thus, their approaches to practices that have been influenced by portfolios.

For example, nursing students' engagement with portfolios may change their production of texts (planning, performing, using sources), their ways of envisioning a finished product according to portfolio assessment criteria, or their ways of documenting and thus performing their practice.

In conducting this analysis, Habib and Wittek combine ANT concepts of translation with what they call socio-historical theory. This entails understanding activities as deeply connected to the cultural artefacts that propel them as well as to the community that embeds the activity. Learning is mediated by these artefacts. However, what Habib and Wittek further point to is the degree of inscription and translation of the portfolio. In some instances, the portfolio might be heavily inscribed with external goals of school managers or ministerial agendas. In other instances, portfolios may undergo more significant translation by users. Different translations, they decide, are linked to different students' desire for and success in 'appropriation' (making an artefact one's own) and 'mastery' (knowing how to use an artefact), such as integrating portfolios into everyday working culture and practice.

Both Hamilton, and Habib and Wittek differentiate the involvement of students, teachers and types of non-human things. Both studies accentuate the extent and complexity of negotiation that occurs within the network, showing the mutual interaction of different actants on one another and the ways they shape human interactions, meanings and identities. However, both studies also show that very different negotiations at the network's different nodes affect just how, and how much, any non-human actant can inscribe or mobilize particular human actors and actions. Critics wielding particular ANT readings might not accept the way that Habib and Wittek treat artefacts as completely distinct from humans, viewing humans as 'users' of non-human entities and being affected by them to a greater or lesser extent. However, these ANT informed accounts clearly demonstrate how educational evaluation practices that are supposedly democratic and learner-controlled such as individual plans and portfolios are fissured with struggle and ethical conflict.

The various material interactions linked together in these practices shape the nature of students' and teachers' engagements with one another, with knowledge, with learning process and with the larger system or network in which they have become enrolled. Further, as Hamilton (2007) urges us to observe, these networks of performance evaluation work to *contain* the ruptures and fissures. They attempt to hold together the disjunctures of discomfort, ethical conflict and other negotiations and prevent them from becoming visible. Thus, while the circulation of texts in an evaluative network achieves consistency and comparability in the ordering of practices in particular ways, this achievement depends upon stabilizing only certain practices as the norm. For Hamilton, this amounts to an attempt to purify education of difference and multiplicity, which is akin to creating monsters in the attempts at ordering and calculation.

In these extended networks of evaluation and calculation, as Nespor (2002) points out, certain kinds of materials and people are assembled and translated to become aligned with the standardized form, while others, such as the testers, supervisors and the state, are not. The state becomes the monster. This may seem to present an almost hegemonic portrayal of the powerful state wreaking oppression upon schools, teachers, pedagogies and children. However, it is important once again to recognize that ANT offers a more open analysis. As Latour (2005b) points out, a war room can command and control anything only as long as it maintains connection with distributed sites of action through continuous transport of information. Evaluation and accountability 'is made only of movements, which are woven by the constant circulation of documents, stories, accounts, goods and passions' (Latour 2005b: 179). What the ANT enactment contributes is much greater focus on the objects and texts that mediate these evaluative processes, and the diverse and unpredictable negotiations that occur as these things intermingle with teachers and learners, even becoming part of them, in everyday micro-interactions. Most importantly, all of these links are precarious. Links can be dissolved, translations refused, and mediation attempts transformed into unanticipated directions. Whatever may appear to be an immutable system of performance measurement is held together very provisionally by myriad connections, as well as spaces between them, that can be identified and reopened.

Messy calculation and calculative spaces

All practices of learning evaluation are bound up within more extended networks of accountability. At the heart of accountability is calculation, what Callon and Law (2005) describe as the manipulation of objects within a single spatio–temporal frame. Calculation is an act of counting and judgment that typically follows a three-stage process. First, relevant things are sorted, detached and displayed in single frame. Second, these entities are manipulated and transformed to show or create relations between them. Third, a result is extracted such as a new thing, a ranking or a decision. Calculation does not reside in human subjects and become projected through their efforts as acts of agency. In this approach, calculation is enacted in 'material arrangements, systems of measurement and methods of displacement – or their absence' (Callon and Law 2005: 718). Calculation works through material practices that depend upon things like written benchmarks, inspection forms, pens, databases, newspapers, and so forth.

Callon and Law go on to suggest two helpful after-ANT framings for understanding educational accountability. First, they offer the term 'qualculation' to capture the ways that arithmetic and qualitative accounts are melded in acts of calculation. Things have to be valued in particular ways, they must *qualify* for calculation, which involves qualitative processes. And acts of qualculation involve all sorts of ways to manipulate things within a single spatio–temporal frame, only some of which are arithmetic. Second, they suggest that calculation and non-calculation are mutually constitutive. They rub together, rather than existing in separate spaces. They cannot be purified, but are always already hybrid or in between. All calculation comes about with and against non-calculation, and vice versa. The most important boundary is not between the acts of counting and the acts of judgment. The most important boundary, and the opening for educators feeling thoroughly subjugated by what they may perceive to be onerous, externally-imposed accountability systems, is between arrangements that allow qualculation, and other arrangements that make it impossible. This dynamic will be explored further on.

An example of these calculative complexities is richly unfolded in an audit tale, described by Neyland and Woolgar (2002), of purchasing a database for a university on the basis of value for money. While the process appeared to be arithmetic and logical, accountability in practice was highly contingent and uncertain. Audiences were difficult to identify and kept shifting, their expectations unclear and contradictory. Organizing principles for the process were improvised differently at different stages. Indeed, the very process of accounting involved the construction of accounts by the team to account for their actions as well as to account for the different stakeholder views in forms that would hold the database company to account. The research team's questions throughout this tale show the close relation of calculative and non-calculative spaces. 'Who wants this and what is the "this" that they want?' (Neyland and Woolgar 2002: 263). Are some kinds of practical action understood to be directed to particular audiences in particular accountability relationships? Can some practical actions be more accountable than others? Who says what and when and how can this be reproduced? Have we reached a decision and how do we know?

In another study that may aptly be compared to education, Cronin (2008) examines how calculation functions through advertising in outdoor urban spaces. As a persuasive discourse intending to enrol actants to act in particular ways and become part of particular networks of consumption, advertising is a powerful form of pedagogy, albeit for commercial purposes. Acts of advertising, like acts of teaching, bear at best only a loose coupling of cause and effect to others' changes in behaviour. Further, education is like advertising, as it calculates spaces with an eye to the future. Students exist in terms of imagined futures – the subjects they are going to become – that pedagogy seeks to produce, as well as in networks of existing activity. As Cronin points out, the resulting spaces of networks contain more than what Massey (2005) calls the simultaneity of stories-so-far. These networks fold together the stories-so-far with 'a temporal and spatial simultaneity of stories-to-come' (Cronin 2008: 2745). In terms of accountability, then, whether focusing on teaching or advertising outcomes, there will always be multiple networks of calculation attempting to represent or measure what is happening for purposes of directing it towards the future. To rephrase Cronin, accountability mechanisms do not produce a homogenous school space subjected to and governed by particular knowledge-producing activities, but multiple, coexisting time–spaces of pedagogy which are animated by a calculative energy.

Both of these examples illustrate the complexities of calculation and the elision of quantitative and qualitative practices of manipulating heterogeneous entities in calculative environments. Further, both examples show how calculation and non-calculation are closely connected.

Surveillance is a common feature of calculative spaces. In schools, teaching practices are usually surveilled either through surprise inspection visits to a classroom or object traces of practice, such as classroom displays, lesson plans, student portfolios, and student results on external tests. Self-surveillance is at the heart of the Foucauldian notion of pastoral regulation, where actors supposedly internalize self-regulatory representational strategies. Webb (2005) conducted an ethnography of one school, which had been identified as problematic through standardized student test results. The aim was to explore the effects on teaching practice of the school's new requirement to demonstrate significant achievement gains. In this 'anatomy of accountability', he shows how surveillance circulates as an assemblage of visible presences, a collaboration of things and actions, that invoke the absences of the teacher's actual work. Further, what he found was that teachers did not necessarily internalize the new injunctions to become self-regulatory, but rather began to 'surveil each other'. Teachers found themselves watching others who were 'pulling the VCR out more then they should be, spending a lot of time in front of the copying machine just copying everything off – get the feeling a teacher's slacking or is a bad teacher' (Webb 2006: 210). As for themselves, they became conscious of their own visibility in such things as the quality of their classroom bulletin board displays, or the comportment of their students. However, they were bewildered about what sorts of criteria were being brought to bear. When others are watching your class walk down the hall, are you supposed to make the students walk more quietly? Is quietness the criterion? When others study your bulletin boards, are your displays being judged for being too vivid or too simple, too entertaining or too didactic?

Not only were many teachers not internalizing self-regulation in their interactions within calculative spaces, Webb (2006) found that many also attempted to respond to calculative attempts with strategies such as fabricating performance. Fabrications were both coordinated and uncoordinated among teachers. They included:

- manufactured performances designed to exemplify particular standards
- ingratiation (using flattery to defuse another's judgment)
- deflecting the other's evaluative gaze (pointing out and amplifying other problems requiring attention)
- self-promotion (playing up particular abilities for effect)
- supplication (advertising one's shortcomings to be viewed as needy).

Alongside these strategies, Webb (2006: 208) also found examples of powerful strategies and forces of translation exerted on teachers' performances and subjectivities by the various calculative practices circulating in schools.

Beneath participants' use of fabrication lay professional knowledge that recognized how to present oneself within particular registers of meaning. However, because of the uncertainty of being evaluated differently by different agents, fabrications held approximate political capital for those who used them.

Webb concluded his study by wondering whether teachers' micro-political strategies of pretence and resistance were in fact examples of translation that folded them into the accountability network after all. And, of course, they would be. The fabrication even, or perhaps especially as resistance, is performed as part of the calculable arrangement. How the fabrication happens to be valued and calculated by particular observers in particular arrangements of a moment determines its force in the processes of translation. However, the ambiguities that Webb found in the effects of surveillance are notable interruptions in the networks of accountability. Surveillance in practice, in the different possible constellations produced in a particular region, does not necessarily create calculable, self-regulatory selves. This ANT analysis shows that in fact human and non-humans perform together in multiple complex and unpredictable relations, particularly given the increasing uncertainty in audiences, stakeholders, criteria and directions of educational surveillance. This multiplicity and uncertainty prevails against a single account, and in this interruption, any powerful centre or single powerful network or hegemony of accountability becomes fractured. A similar question about whether accountability mechanisms become internalized by subjects surfaced in Neyland and Woolgar's (2002) study. The university team they studied, like Webb's teachers, were usually confused by the ambiguous and even shifting criteria by which they were to build accounts that accounted for the effectiveness and fiscal soundness of their decisions. The researchers, therefore, refused an analysis of governmentality, stating that there was little evidence of any internalization of the values of audit.

Returning to the question of calculable spaces, Callon and Law (2005) maintain that the central distinction is between those arrangements that allow qualculation and those spaces that do not. This does not negate the supposition that calculation and non-calculation coexist and depend on one another. However, Callon and Law (2005: 720) claim that 'the power of a qualculation depends on the number of entities that can be added to a list, to the number of relations between those entities, and the quality of the tools for classifying, manipulating, and ranking them'. Successful resistance to this power is achieved in two distinct ways. One is through rarefaction, where the possibility of qualculation is undermined by withdrawing the necessary resources. The second is through *proliferation*, where the possibility of qualculation is undermined by the multiplying of accounts. We witness this clearly in Neyland and Woolgar's (2002) study, where the shifting audiences and expectations in the accountability process led to a proliferation of accounts that eventually undermined the calculative space. In fact, the project team decided that accountability processes in practice are:

a whole series of flows, circuits, connections, disconnections, selections, favourings, accounts, holding to account and attempts at analysis. The messiness of accountability in action persuades us that the simple idea of internalizing the values, processes and practices of accountability is insufficient ...

we suggest that more attention be paid to the ways in which the performance of community establishes the moral order that can be seen to provide the reference point for the mess of flows and connections.

(Neyland and Woolgar 2002: 272)

In other examples here, we have seen how this proliferation of multiple accounts, with their attendant ambiguities and confusions, spoil the power of qualculation. We have also seen rarefaction through teachers who, despite accountability measures, continue to practice according to energies that defy the logic of accountability. Teachers can be driven by standards of caring, passion for their work, and professional commitments. While these energies do not immunize teachers to the effects of calculation, they do create different pedagogical networks among the human and non-human elements at play, networks that are non-calculable. As Stronach and his colleagues (2002) found, teachers are clearly captured within various manifestations of an audit culture, and indeed actively support principles of calculation, of measurement, effectiveness and improvement, in learning and education. However, teachers are also animated according to professional dispositions, collective values and solidarities that escape calculation. Stronach *et al.* characterized this doubled space as an 'economy of performance' existing alongside an 'ecology of practice'. The non-calculable ecologies of practice circulate in the same physical spaces, even among some of the same things, as do the calculable economies of performance. In fact, calculable and non-calculable spaces presuppose one another. This mutual existence once again illustrates the multiple ontologies enacted through ANT analyses.

Conclusion

In this chapter we have outlined how ANT is helpful in drawing attention to the action and uncertainties of heterogeneous materials assembled into diverse cross-cutting networks of (ac)countability. In evaluation approaches, such as the learning portfolio or the professional growth plan, the tendency is to focus on one learning figure and relegate all its complex interactions to background. ANT returns the focus to the relations between things, not the things themselves. ANT not only directs attention to the things and movements colliding in these networks. It also traces how the connections between these become formed and the efforts that go into sustaining them. No agent or knowledge has an essential existence outside a given network: nothing is given in the order of things, but enacts itself and is enacted into existence.

ANT questions the powerful actors that appear to emerge in accountability frameworks, and follows the links that brought them into being and that extend them in ways that order educational geographies. These links are far more fragile and malleable than certain hegemonic accounts of accountability would suggest. Latour (2005b) explains that whenever there is mention of a system or structure, ANT asks: how has it been compiled? Where is it? Where can I find it? The ANT gaze discerns agencies occurring at a number of sites and conduits, as well as break-ages and twistings, and active spaces in the net. In Latour's (2005b: 44) words:

> action is not done under the full control of consciousness; action should rather be felt as a node, a knot, and a conglomerate of many surprising sets of agencies that have to be slowly disentangled. It is this venerable source of uncertainty that we wish to render vivid again in the odd expression of actor–network.

An ANT sensibility suggests alternative approaches to conducting educational evaluation. As ANT eschews approaches to learning as individual acquisition of knowledge and skills to understand learning as struggle within the emergence of connections, it suggests that evaluation of learning, like research, ought to 'follow the actors' in Latour's terms. That is, evaluation approaches would begin by tracking the emerging patterns among networks at play in activities intending to generate knowledge, drawing particular attention to what occurs in the background: the myriad fluctuations, subtle interactions, the series of consequences emerging from a single action. Assessment would also focus on providing feedback at various nodes and connections among humans and non-humans. A key element of evaluation would be to attune participants within any network to the emerging patterns and linkages that are forming, the mediations working upon them, as well as to its breaches and non-calculable spaces. Finally, ANT understandings would require any observer, such as evaluators, to also assess their own entangled involvements in the emerging networks of thought, things and action. The evaluation of learning becomes a question of how knowledge circulates to enrol, mobilize and stabilize as well as to open spaces of multiplicity and uncertainty within particular practices and ideas.

Among these uncertainties are the folds of calculative and non-calculative energies at work in the complex spaces of accountability. In ANT-infused studies of educational evaluation, we are invited to explore the many interplays and openings, not just moment of transgression or resistance or fabrication, but also the ambivalences between calculation and non-calculation.

Chapter 9

(De)centring educational policy

Powerful actors – whether dictators, myths, quarks or educational policies – become powerful through making numerous connections with others, those that are successful in enlisting as allies. They are all assemblages of disparate things: bodies, texts, tools and desires held together through fragile ties that demand a great deal of work to maintain them. This understanding offers an important breakthrough, argues Harman, from the human-centric limitations of much political philosophy:

> Latour's metaphysics is utterly democratic. Atoms and quarks are real actors in the cosmos, but so are Fidel Castro, Houdini, and unicorns. We cannot declare a priori that some actors are more real than others; all we can say is that some are stronger than others. But this strength is never measured solely in the currency of human struggles for dominance, since animals, stars and brute subatomic matter are engaged in the struggle for reality no less than are Machiavellian cabals. What Latour opposes is simple reduction ...
> (Harman 2007: 35)

When there is discussion of powerful actors in education, where centres of qualculation are ordered, then much of the focus is on the state, government and policy. Policy is a central concern for educational researchers, as policies at international, national, local and organizational levels are held to frame and contextualize the practices of education and training. Policy is often positioned as the originating source of practices and changes in practice in education, and therefore much is written about it. However, as Ball (2000) argues, the problem persists in discussions of educational policy that everyone assumes to know what it actually is, when in fact this is far from clear or consensual.

Simplifying greatly, there are two key foci for discussion of educational policy. The first is to do with policy making itself, the processes and practices through which something we can name as educational policy comes to be and, with that, its nature and significance. The state and governing are central to such discussions, as are the multiple ideologies informing politics and policy. Indeed, much of the discussion within this strand of research is based upon ideology critique of one sort or another. This attempts to identify and stabilize certain policies as having certain ideological assumptions and intents, in order to become hegemonic – the common sense of the moment. For instance, neoliberalism for the globalized knowledge economy has been a popular critique of much educational policy since the turn of the century. Here also, the role of international organizations such as the Organization for Economic Co-operation and Development (OECD) and transnational alliances such as the European Union (EU) have become a focus of debate, as the nation state is increasingly entangled in the webs of globalizing processes. This questioning of the sense of the sovereign state as autonomous actor in recent times has led to an increasing focus on governing rather than government, on the practices of governing wherever they take place, and less focus on government and the state per se (Rose 1999). For some, this is taken itself to represent a depoliticization of the political rather than extending politics into multiple domains.

While those engaged in ideology critique are attempting to tear away the veil of policy and uncover the 'real' interests being pursued, some ANT writers have sought to approach politics from an alternative framing. In particular, Latour (2005a: 19) has attempted to articulate a politics around matters of concern, which he contrasts with matters of fact.

> Where matters-of-fact have failed, let's try what I have called matters-of-concern. What we are trying to register here ... is a huge sea change in our conceptions of science, our grasps of facts, our understanding of objectivity. For too long, objects have been wrongly portrayed as matters-of-fact. This is unfair to science, unfair to objectivity, unfair to experience. They are much more interesting, variegated, uncertain, complicated, far reaching, heterogeneous, risky, historical, local, material and networky than the pathetic version offered for too long by philosophers. Rocks are not simply there to be kicked at, desks to be thumped at. 'Facts are facts are facts'? Yes, but they are also a lot of other things in addition.

Matters of fact produce, and are a product of, very literal politics, that which we might associate with such notions as evidence informed policy and practice, as though facts are unassailable. Latour questions the ways in which much critical thinking and writing has enacted facts because it involves the distancing of people from objects. This is a misrepresentation, an enactment of a particular form of critique, as the world is messier than suggested. Here, matters of concern signify the messy assemblages and attachments through which politics and policy can be enacted. While ideology critique tends to question matters of fact, it is itself usually positing an alternative matter of fact. For Latour, it is about completely reframing politics around assembling matters of concern. In this, he is following Foucault in trying to formulate critique as a trangressive ontological rather than transcendental metaphysical politics. This entails experimenting at the limits rather than seeking to break free of them; the latter being an impossibility. In everyday practice, Latour shows the hybrid that forms among matters of fact and matters of concern, the *facticbe* that smoothes away their distinctions.

The second foci of discussion in educational policy research is to do with implementation, in particular the perceived gap between policy intentions and their effects as they are translated into the contexts they are set to influence. As Ball (2000: 1834) writes, 'policies do not normally tell you what to do; they create circumstances in which the range of options available in deciding what to do are narrowed or changed'. We have seen how ANT analyses explore such gaps in a number of the earlier chapters. Policy evaluation is, therefore, a major strand of existing research. The implementation gap is not something that is of concern for educationalists alone. It is one of the key questions for all forms of policy studies. The fact that policy does not tend to produce the effects intended and/ or produces unintended consequences might make one wonder why states and governments bother at all. But bother they do, often seeking ever subtler ways of trying to secure implementation through such mechanisms, as we explored in Chapter 8, as accountability and audit regimes. However, their degrees of success are many and variable, given that policy enrols multiple actors and contexts.

ANT analyses offer much to help us understand policy implementation and how effects emerge from the networks of interests and actions that are brought into play in the making of policy and by policies themselves. For instance, as we outlined in Chapter 4, Hepburn (1997) explored the introduction of a new applied physics course in a British Columbia high school during the 1994–5 school year. The course was part of a provincial effort aimed at making science and technology education more responsive to the workplace. In examining the implementation of this policy, two actor–networks were identified at provincial and school levels. The teacher and other network builders attempted to enrol various human and non-human actors into the networks they were enacting in support of the course. The types of actors that were enrolled, the communities they belonged to, and what it took to convince them to support the course shaped the way that the coursenet-work was enacted in the classroom. However, the network that was enacted at the provincial level had only a minor connection to the one the teacher was con-structing at the school level. The space between the two networks meant that the interests of those who were involved in organizing the applied physics pilots at the provincial level were seldom taken into account in the course at the school. Focusing on policy in terms of networks and network enactments therefore points to new ways at examining the implementation gap.

Educational practices, therefore, can be seen as actor–networks in which participants and participation are ordered in time and space, for, as Popkewitz (1996) says of school-based reforms, changes in governing entails the reposi-tioning of actors and problem solving in the educational arena. Thus, parents, students and employers become actors in education and training by being posi-tioned as 'consumers' or 'with rights' in policy discourse. In different ways, different groups are positioned as having 'choice' in the spaces of education, thereby reconfiguring the relationships and exercises of power entailed. In the changing roles they are given in the governing of educational institutions in pursuit of policy goals, different networks are enacted.

In this chapter we will focus more on the policy-making process. Policy-making is about decision making and here we follow Dugdale (1999) in being concerned with its 'specificities and materialities'. For Dugdale (1999: 131), this implies 'a progressive shift from instability to stability, or from movement to immobility'. However, this is never complete for there are always oscillations in decision making processes (Hunter and Swan 2007). Dugdale pursues this issue in relation to the mobilizing of informed choice and the centred subject consumer in the context of IUD use. However, the material practices through which this is achieved, in particular through the production of an information leaflet, can also be identified in relation to some of the practices of consultation in policy decision making. 'The leaflet is a machine that produces the reader's decision as a flow to a single temporal point and as an origin that can be referred back to and judged when things go wrong' (Dugdale 1999: 128). Similar trajectories have been traced in relation to policy consultation documents (Nicoll 2006). We will examine later other similar strategies and effects of certain policy texts and practices.

In this chapter we also focus on a number of key themes in educational policy. First, we explore some of the uptakes of the education-for-economy policy discourse. Here, we can see how ANT approaches lead educational analysts to highlight the fragile and contingent assemblies that become manifest as 'authoritative' policy discourses. Our second focus is on the increasing ways in which international league tables are mobilized in national policy contexts to help frame the issues to be addressed through policy action. Here, we explore work that analyses the impact of league tables on literacy. The third focus is on the role of texts in translating the interests of the multiple into the singular, and some of the strategies through which those translations are made possible. Finally, we turn to questions of objects and enactments as educational policy analysts have tackled these, working with methods drawn from ANT. All of these negotiations carry power with them and have powerful effects.

Education-for-economy

We are witnessing a significant increase generally in questions of policy construction, implementation and impact, and the role of research and evidence in these processes. Governing and educational policy have become almost a form of hyperactivity, particularly in response to the global economic crisis from 2007. Here, the notion of the knowledge economy as a global policy discourse to which educational policy is subordinate has become crucial. Indeed, the knowledge economy is often positioned as both the effect of the contemporary phase of globalizing processes and also, supported by a neoliberal ideology, resulting in certain forms of globalization. There has been much critique of the idea of a knowledge economy from educationalists precisely for this latter reason (e.g. Olssen and Peters 2005, Robertson, 2005, Kenway et al. 2006).

A key area of contemporary debate among education policy analysts is the apparent educational consent to notions of the knowledge economy evident in a convergence of globalized education standards and values, and the authority exercised by supra-national agencies such as the OECD and UNESCO in these processes. Several of these analysts have drawn from the theoretical resources of ANT to trace the dynamics of this convergence and its authority, or to develop strategies to destabilize international educational policyscapes and mobilize alternative arrangements and networks. ANT is particularly helpful in showing the precarious and contingent nature of apparently powerful entities in educational policy, and for illuminating openings for resistance. Resnik (2006) for example, focuses on the rise of what she calls the 'education-economic growth network' during the 1950s and 1960s. She argues that through translation processes supra-national agencies became central allies that mobilized heterogeneous materials, including forums, human capital theory, artefacts of educational planning, and various experts (econometric economists, demographers, state representatives, international organization experts) to align with their interests. She follows some early translations through which understandings of education as producing economic growth became linked to practical education policy, which further translated into justifications for educational expansion and investment. Thus, Resnik claims, in contrast to neoinstitutionalist views characterizing supra-national agencies as mere vehicles of diffusion – receivers or transmitters of a preconceived educational model – ANT reveals these agencies becoming actors that co-produce the 'world education culture'. Resnik does not focus in any depth on the nature of these translations and their internal tensions, with the result that the different entities mobilized in the networks appear almost deterministically to be aligned in a coherent and predictable network. However, her analysis goes some way to challenge views that do not acknowledge the non-human actors in globalized convergence of education-for-economy policies. Further, she shows how power is exercised not through any one agency or actor, but through their ever-shifting alignments and ongoing translations.

Throughout the 1990s and 2000s, educational researchers identified a range of trends in policy that were having an increasing global reach and becoming part of the education-for-economy world education culture. Levin (1998), for example, in discussing schooling, identified a certain commonality of themes in the frameworks through which the substance of education policy was shaped. These were:

- the need for change largely cast in economic terms
- the increase in criticism of schools and their failure to deliver what was required
- changes in schooling being required without a significant increase in resourcing from governments
- educational reform being promoted through changes in forms of governance
- schools being required to work in more commercial and market-like ways
- an emphasis on standards, accountability and testing.

Carter and O'Neill (in Ball 1998: 122) identified five similar central elements in the reform of education around the globe:

* improving national economics by tightening the connection between schooling, employment, productivity and trade
* enhancing student outcomes in employment related skills and competencies
* attaining more direct control over curriculum content and assessment
* reducing the costs of education to government
* increasing community input to education by more direct involvement in school decision making and pressure of market choice.

Ball (1998) himself also identified the influences which were generating global similarities in policy. These were:

* neoliberal approaches
* new institutional economics
* performativity
* public choice theory
* new managerialism.

ANT provides us with a way of tracing how such themes come to be influential and authoritative in policy making.

In their analysis of globalization and education policy, Rizvi and Lingard (2010) suggest that the important nexus for focus is the linkage of authority (where does authority underpinning policy come from and how is it exercised) with values (how they are allocated and how this allocation guides practice). While Rizvi and Lingard concede that there is now occurring global convergence of values, this is not achieved through any top-down exercise of authority, but through the hard work of assembling and aligning connections among diverse conflicting values. In any policy process, they argue, values of efficiency must be balanced with those of social mobility, democratic equality, community and security. The question is, through what politics do these become assembled and sustained? Rizvi (2009) draws explicitly from ANT to analyse this messy process, using Latour's (2005b) notion of 'assemblage'. The assemblage is never stable but constantly moving as values are renegotiated. Such assemblages are matters of concern through which to challenge the matters of fact through which the education-for-economy is represented. For example, market values of education for economic growth are often rearticulated by conflicting values for social justice. Notions of equity and liberty are continually assembled, disassembled and displaced in the negotiations. Authority and values are not contained in any one actor in the assemblage that drives educational policies, nor can agency be traced from any particular source. Rizvi argues that the ANT concept of assemblage is particularly valuable in global policy analysis to show that there are no discrete values accorded privilege, but rather a messy shifting

entity comprised of ongoing material and political practices that establish a
precarious values consensus of the moment.

Translating league tables

We have been discussing the global assembling of policy discourses and the
attempts to scale educational policy to both global free trade and the knowledge
economy. Yet, within this similitude, there is also difference, as the global is
always already mediated and translated. As Ball (1998: 126) suggests:

> ... national policy making is inevitably a process of bricolage: a matter of bor-
> rowing and copying bits and pieces of ideas from elsewhere, drawing upon
> and amending locally tried and tested approaches, cannibalising theories,
> research, trends and fashions and not infrequently flailing around for any-
> thing at all that looks as though it might work.

Generic policies are therefore polyvalent, 'they are translated into particular
interactive and sustainable practices in complex ways' (Ball 1998: 127). In ANT
terms, these translations are dependent on the things and relationships through
which a policy-network is formed. As we have pointed out, increasingly influential in those processes of translation are the international organizations and
league tables which rank and scale national performance in various aspects of
standardized educational attainment. We have seen in Chapters 6 and 8 how
standardization and qualculation can be traced through ANT analysis. One tracing is of how they come to be taken up in the policy making process.

   In a study of the effects of the OECD Programme for International Student
Assessment (PISA) on EU and national governments, for instance, Grek (2009)
refers to the use of international league tables as 'governing by numbers', which
assume and promote 'the politics of comparison'. The PISA poses as its point of
attachment:

> Are students well prepared for future challenges? Can they analyse, reason
> and communicate effectively? Do they have the capacity to continue learn-
> ing throughout life? The OECD Programme for International Student
> Assessment (PISA) answers these questions and more, through its surveys
> of 15-year-olds in the principal industrialized countries. Every three years, it
> assesses how far students near the end of compulsory education have acquired
> some of the knowledge and skills essential for full participation in society.
>
> (OECD 2009)

The authority with which it asserts its own authority to answer the question posed
is part of the semiotic work of mobilizing a network. With the PISA, the knowledge and skills for the future focus on reading literacy, mathematical literacy and
scientific literacy. Thus, even in the identification of knowledge and skills, there is a

scaling in relation to literacy. Multiple forms of knowledge and skill become scaled as literacy as the basis for measurement of attainment. Cross-country comparisons are then drawn and countries can measure their performance across time.

For instance, in its 2006 report on science attainment, the OECD was able to announce that:

> Finland, with an average of 563 score points, was the highest-performing country on the PISA 2006 science scale ... Six other high-scoring countries had mean scores of 530 to 542 points: Canada, Japan and New Zealand and the partner countries/economies Hong Kong–China, Chinese Taipei and Estonia. Australia, the Netherlands, Korea, Germany, the United Kingdom, the Czech Republic, Switzerland, Austria, Belgium and Ireland, and the partner countries/economies Liechtenstein, Slovenia and Macao–China also scored above the OECD average of 500 score points ... On average across OECD countries, 1.3 per cent of 15-year-olds reached Level 6 of the PISA 2006 science scale, the highest proficiency level. These students could consistently identify, explain and apply scientific knowledge, and knowledge about science, in a variety of complex life situations. In New Zealand and Finland this figure was at least 3.9 per cent, three times the OECD average. In the United Kingdom, Australia, Japan and Canada, as well as the partner countries/economies Liechtenstein, Slovenia and Hong Kong–China, between 2 and 3 per cent reached Level 6.
>
> (OECD 2007)

Qualculation – value and measurement – and comparison are rife here and national governments can become enrolled in a game to maximize their countries position in the league tables. The effects of these enrolments are clear to see. As Grek (2009) points out, Finland had traditionally positioned itself as needing to borrow models of educational reform from overseas. The PISA results have consistently shown Finland scoring highly, so its education system has instead become the focus of other nations seeking to borrow from it. However, this has not been celebrated in the media, unlike in those countries which have done less well, such as Germany, where PISA results are mobilized as part of a national moral panic.

> The PISA results, apart from curricular reforms, brought a whole new conceptualization of the German school as a self-managing organization, in need of new quality control measures, applied in different combinations by the federal states: school inspections, self-evaluations, assessment tests and teacher professionalism have turned the German education system into a particular mixture of centralization and decentralization.
>
> (Grek 2009: 30)

The PISA results are enrolled and enrol others in a network of policy making which have very real effects. However, there is no linear way in which the results operate in relation to policy making. The reports are taken to be authoritative and can, when results are positioned as negative, provide the basis for forms of moral panic that harness governments into action. However, while we can often identify this influence in broad terms, there is little exploration or detailed tracing of the ways in which governments and states are enrolled by these international tables. Indeed, a comprehensive view of such processes would almost certainly be impossible given the range and multiplicity of actors involved, not least the media. However, ANT provides us with a way of exploring the practices of policy in the making, at least partially, by following certain translations through which such league tables enrol and are enrolled in policy networks.

Gorur (2010) has also adopted an ANT perspective to examine how the PISA emerges as one form of educational knowledge and expands to exercise apparent global authority in educational policy. She interviewed PISA's architects and decision makers to explore how PISA is being used to govern education transnationally and to translate complex educational processes into static data. Gorur is most interested in how PISA as a form of knowledge with apparent universal acceptance and impact came into being. She follows a method developed by Latour (1987) to trace how certain forms of scientific knowledge emerge and become powerful. Such knowledge achieves stabilization through everyday material practices that combine and align wide-ranging objects, ideas and behaviours. Working with these translation dynamics, Gorur follows how PISA knowledge is produced through processes of assembling and connecting a vast array of information from diverse locations and contexts into a single spatio–temporal frame:

> It has mapped the world, ordered knowledge and disciplined people into taking up their assigned positions at regular intervals. It has coded, classified and marked people and concepts, and produced new and interesting associations. When PISA becomes a matter of chains of translation, intervening at points along that chain, requesting verification or reference or challenging a translation become practical matters.
>
> (Gorur 2010, in press)

PISA as an entity of knowledge is shown through ANT analysis not only to be relational and continuously performative, but also precarious, held together through ongoing work that sustains its connections and enactments. Thus, what appears to be PISA's authority and universality actually depends upon fragile and provisional linkages. These linkages and the work they perform can be interrupted, weakened and even refused.

Hamilton (2001) has sketched these translations in relation to another set of qualculations, the International Adult Literacy Survey (IALS). Despite massive criticism of its underpinning assumptions, and methodological approaches, not least by Hamilton herself, IALS has nonetheless become a powerful actor in literacy policy-making. It is 'part of a solidifying international "regime of truth" which is developing through techniques of standardized assessment and testing and which in turn is organizing national and local knowledge about what literacy is' (Hamilton 2001: 178). The practices of the survey, therefore, seek to stabilize a certain understanding of literacy as literacy per se and use that for compara-tive purposes across multiple cultural contexts. It is only in this flattening out through standardization that such comparison becomes possible. These literacy practices are not those of everyday life, but those proxies, the test activities them-selves. Everyday practices are therefore translated into standardized tests within the survey, which change the contextual validity for the persons taking the tests. An irony here, of course, is that even as literacy is purified and naturalized as a specific set of standardized practices, literacy itself is mobilized to multiply scale a range of other practices, as we have seen above in relation to mathematical and scientific literacy.

In examining the impact of the IALS, Hamilton explores the ways in which power accrues as a network effect dependent on the size, number and status of the agents enrolled. This draws upon early forms of ANT analysis. She attempts to sketch the translations, framings and deletions in the trajectory of the IALS from the translation of everyday tasks into standardized tested tasks through to the development of curriculum documents for use in specific contexts. The test tasks focus on that which is positioned as universal and desirable in literacy by those involved in developing it and establishing its credibility. The vernacular and marginal are deleted in the process, even when it may be through such prac-tices that people enact and are enacted in the world (Verran 1999). These tasks are then translated into texts – books and stimulus materials – which are then presented to adults to respond to in tightly defined ways. The documents and practices of the test are black-boxed in the sense they are cut from the networks that made them possible and thus become representations of literacy per se.

The initial analysis of these tests is raw statistics. However, at the next stages there emerges both the influence of policy and the policy influences, as the raw statistics become subject to interrogation and interpretation by international organizations, national governments and other interested parties. These are trying to both position themselves within the policy debate but also steer it in certain directions. The raw statistics therefore begin to be translated into multiple explanations. As Hamilton (2001: 188) suggests 'a persuasive, carefully crafted interpretative framework is woven around the statistics, translating them from raw numbers to explanations' through rhetorical moves from correlation to cau-sation and the glossing over of contradictions. These reports, then, help to set the frame of policy discourse about adult literacy.

While Hamilton attempts to trace in broad terms the translations of policy, Clarke (2002) uses Callon's four moments of translation to examine the large policy network mobilized in the name of a particular meaning of literacy. Clarke also draws upon the principle of generalized symmetry as a basis for asking how the attributes of some entities in a network are assumed to be stable or natural while others are open to negotiation. This offers a systematic approach to the problem of both asserting linguistic equality, for example, and acknowledging the inequalities of power and status attached to particular dialects and genres. Generalized symmetry provides the basis for troubling the standardized view of literacy in the IALS.

Interestingly, Hamilton (2001) notes that behind the publicly available reports are technical reports, which point to all the limits of the data and their explanations, but nonetheless impact little on the public policy discourse. It is the latter which is then mobilized by and in the media. The discourse of the news media is mostly around simple messages rather than interrogating the assumptions and limitations of research. It is highly varied according to the media outlet with which one is engaging. Hamilton gives illustrations of how various newspapers translated the findings of one survey into a variety of crisis focused headlines. Given the powerful role of the media itself in framing policy issues to be addressed, such headlines perhaps inevitably position the government as needing to act.

She, like Burgess (2008), also points to the ways in which the assumptions mobilized by the IALS are translated into the curricular and their textual practices. Indeed, Hamilton goes on to point out that the findings of the survey can themselves take flight and be framed as common sense facts, the source of which it is no longer necessary to identify. This is familiar, as anyone listening to the radio or television will know, as there is often reportage that 'research says', where the practices that have mobilized that saying remain invisible and unquestioned.

Hamilton also points to the way in which a complicit network grows between government and literacy advocates and practitioners to maintain the crisis narrative as a way to support a policy action space and also the allocation of resources. Once black-boxed it becomes only the few who ask the question – what do these figures and explanations actually represent? To counter is to mobilize alternative representations. If 'representations are central to institutional ordering and reification, then to effectively counter those orderings and to enter the policy arena we must develop and embed alternative representations' (Hamilton 2001: 194). This entails trying to enact different matters of concern in gathering together people and things to intervene and interrupt.

Policy consultations

In liberal democracies, a major element in policy making is the consultation process. This can take many forms. In the UK, for instance, policy proposals are laid down in White Papers, but these are usually developed following the publication of Green Papers, and consultation on the proposals therein. These texts can be seen fairly immediately to be important in enrolling the interests of others into the policy process, however incomplete. Consultative processes have become ever more endemic as the limits of technocratic and expert forms of governance have been highlighted. Consultation may involve texts, conferences, focus groups, etc. Indeed it is in fact perhaps one of the ironies of contemporary governing in liberal democracies that the more consultation governments attempt, the more their own authority is itself undermined. Strategies to enhance the authority of governing therefore, such as consultations, can indeed undermine that authority, due to the different networks within which these practices develop. Thus, focus groups, for instance, may be mobilized more forcefully in relation to market research than political consultation, thereby undermining its capacity to enrol different interests through the policy consultation process.

Much of the discussion of the changing practices of governing have been developed from a Foucauldian governmentality perspective (e.g. Rose 1999). However, aspects of some of these discussions can be reread from an actor–network perspective. In her study of flexibility and lifelong learning, Nicoll (2006) provides a detailed rhetorical analysis of the 1998 Australian Federal Government report on *Learning for Life*. In particular, she points to the limits of the consultation undertaken, framed as they were by particular terms of reference. She also points to who engaged in the consultation, how they engaged, and the (lack of) response. In the process, Nicoll identifies the way in which the consultation enrolled different interests through the policy making process of consultation. In the discourse of ANT, we witness the enrolments and translations enacted through the inscriptions of the policy text and the consultations undertaken to spread the network of policy making in the attempted building of authority for the policy. We also see some of the holes in this process in the many who were not enrolled through the consultation.

Consultations can be dangerous for governing of course, as they may elicit responses that undermine the very policies to be promulgated. As Law (1994: 102) suggests, 'concrete walls are solid while they are maintained and patrolled. Texts order only if they are not destroyed en route, and there is someone at the other end who will read them and order her life accordingly'. Policy texts act as tokens or mediators. But in the process of consultation, they may become intermediaries, that is, subject to change.

Policy objects and enactments

Ball (1994) points out that policy initiatives in education typically privilege the policy-makers' reality and assume that teachers and schools and practices will adjust accordingly. As we have already indicated, policy continues to be discussed informally as a task of 'rolling it out', as though all the messy material complexities and political negotiations of policy texts in diverse enactments can be smoothed away like laying a carpet. However, in their study of one policy implementation in Scottish primary schools, I'Anson and Allan (2006) demonstrate how ANT slows down the analysis to attend to the particulars, especially the material ones, at play in policy enactment. Their object of inquiry was a new initiative to promote children's rights and active citizenship in Scottish schools, which was intended to enhance opportunities for pupil participation in decision making. I'Anson and Allan followed the complex negotiations enacted in different material spaces of the school – the playground, the classroom, the teacher–parent conference – compelled by the new focus and expectations on children's rights. They contrast these with the bureaucratic/pastoral spaces of regulation and subjectification created by the policy directives. Teachers juggled these simultaneous spaces through multiple experiments, distortions and changes in their practice. Furthermore, the Headteacher's focus was on the wider network involved in the enactment of children's rights, such as the janitor, community policemen, and school–home link worker. Each community enacted different versions of the children's rights and created different translations of the policy text. What eventually emerged was some coherence that the researchers could trace as it was 'patched' together among the different participants and groups – what the researchers termed professional *interstandings* (I'Anson and Allan 2006: 276) – which was enacted in between all, but not grounded in any one ontology.

The question of the thing that is educational policy, and the 'objects' that bring forth such policy, are approached differently by different researchers working with ANT. Some, like I'Anson and Allan, treat a single policy as something enacted in all sorts of different ways through objects interlinked in everyday practice, whether in bureaucratic boardrooms with flipcharts and sticky notes, public forums of critical debate, written guides for teachers, or moments of classroom practice. Mulcahy (2010) also shows, for example, that a new Australian policy specifying professional standards for teachers is *performed* simultaneously as a textual representation (a one-page list of statements), as complex classroom activity (where many other networks and standards interplay with the official teaching standard), and as political consultation processes. I'Anson and Allan treated the Scottish policy on children's rights in similar ways, as multiple enactments assembling heterogeneous objects in different ways. These were often at the same time and even in the same region. Mulcahy and I'Anson and Allan therefore show that the issue for educators is to not only negotiate among these enactments, but also to avoid the tendency to reconcile them into a singularity. As Mulcahy (2010) writes, following an ANT-and-after trajectory, the radical difference underscoring standards is far from problematic: holding differences in tension (rather than seeking to reconcile them) provides the best possibility for achieving accomplished teaching and learning'.

Others argue for separating the policy-as-text from the policy-as-enactment. There persists a discomfort with dissolving all separations of scale in what some characterize as the flattening-out effects of a network ontology. Rizvi (2009), for example, while, as we saw above, using Latour's analytic method of tracing policy assemblages, still casts these as contained within a larger 'context' created through collective social imaginaries and structures distinguishing the global and local. Thus, despite its assemblage, the policy is treated as a distinct object foregrounded against transcendent levels of powerful webs. For Rizvi, distinct scalar levels are important to enable analysis of how power flows in policy. This thinking is not unlike Ball's (2000: 1837) much-cited distinction of policy as text (distinct textual representations which, although encoded and decoded in complex and continually contested ways, are nonetheless identifiable and singular) and policy as discourse (a terrain created by interweaving policies: 'a moving discursive frame which articulates and constrains the possibilities and probabilities of interpretation and enactment'). Although Ball characterizes the one as embedded in the other, and obviously both realized through messy multiple processes, he still maintains the distinction of a thing in its context.

Ball does not work with ANT, but his influence on educational policy analysts including those using ANT is important to acknowledge. One who does use ANT and also recognizes Ball's distinctions in her policy analysis is Burgess (2008). With interests similar to Hamilton's (2001), Burgess centres upon the Individual Learning Plan (ILP), a textual instrument for assessing adult student literacy, as one object of classroom practice connected to England's Skills for Life policy. Burgess painstakingly traces how the ILP mobilizes different activities and encounters at various levels of an organization. In so doing, she shows that this one object, the ILP, mediates between classroom practice and the larger system and processes of the policy. It mediates across regions and scalar spaces, but also across time – it is heterochronous. Her analysis clearly separates the zones of local enactment from the more global region of policy in a rather un-ANT-like move, but she works with ANT to show how the object travels and produces networks across different networks and becomes changed in itself in the process.

In another educational policy study using ANT, Emad and Roth (2009) also focus on one object that crosses boundaries. However, for them, this object is the policy itself – the policy as text, in Ball's terms. Emad and Roth call this policy-as-object a 'boundary object' after Bowker and Star (1999): an interface between worlds that travels across the boundaries between communities and might even be used very differently in each. Thus, boundary objects 'inhabit intersecting social worlds while at the same time satisfying the specific information requirements and practices of each group' (Emad and Roth 2009: 20). These researchers focused on the national maritime educational policy in Canada, which must be developed to prescribe the certificate of competency for maritime workers, which in turn is supposed to direct training activities. In fact, all countries must develop their own maritime policy and articulate it externally with standards set by the International Maritime Organization, and internally with its diverse maritime training institutions. Therein emerged the problems. The policy in Canada was viewed, in brief, as vague, ambiguous, impossible to make into curriculum, locally incomprehensible, and incongruent with assessment practices. The boundary object of policy travelled but failed to mobilize and translate as it moved. Incidentally, the authors proposed that other boundary objects might have been chosen to mobilize the policy more effectively, such as a model course. In other words, the ANT perspective here focuses on the policy process as enacted in one object, an immutable mobile perhaps, that moves through and across different networks in an attempt to link them.

This approach is in marked contrast to that employed by Mulcahy and others who portray educational policy as multiple enactments – of which the performance of the policy-as-text is only one – in effect creating different worlds. These worlds are simultaneous, and often overlap, in a dance that Mol (2002) has called 'onto-logical politics'. The turn here is away from discourse and discursive fields where diverse meanings and conflicting ways of knowing are at play – an epistemological view – to a question of multiple ontologies. In educational policy, this turn opens the possibility for considering important new 'policy levers' as well as counter narratives and transgressions to the policy assemblages that appear to be emerging.

Chapter 10

Messy research

When we talk about ANT and its possibilities for educational questions and inquiry, we are inevitably asked: 'Yes, but how does one *do* ANT in educational research?' Students complain that published ANT studies tend to either obscure their actual approaches in the telling, or to insist that method is an inappropriate discussion for ANT. One writer who devoted her doctoral study to develop methods for studying the materiality of learning working with ANT, notes that 'The logical meaning and coherence of the concepts we use is less important: what is crucial is how they help us do empirical studies and analyses and the kinds of studies and analyses in which they result' (Sørensen 2009: 12).

Law's book (2004b) exploring the whole question of research methods, while not explicitly linking itself to ANT, is infused with its constructs, sensibilities, and examples from research that are inspired by or situated within ANT approaches. Law tellingly names his book *After Method*, and positions it to address the question: how might method deal with mess? This is not a question that is limited to those drawing upon ANT, and is consistent with debates and positions drawing upon, for instance, branches of post-structuralist and feminist research.

For Law (2004b), most phenomena of interest to social science research, such as education, are slippery, uncertain, constantly changing, emotional, vague and diffuse. In a more recent discussion, Law (2007: 596–7) writes that:

> In practice research needs to be messy and heterogeneous. It needs to be messy and heterogeneous because that is the way it – research – actually is. And also, and more importantly it needs to be messy because that is the way the largest part of the world is: messy, unknowable in a regular and routinized way. Unknowable, therefore, in ways that are definite or coherent.

Our approaches to research often fail to recognize important textures of these phenomena. Or worse, our research distorts or completely represses the very things we want to understand. Research methods are often designed to smooth away and simplify the messy lumpishness and most interesting complications of the world, in well-intentioned efforts to *know* them and make things clear. In other words, research itself purifies through its enactments. Furthermore, our research methods tend to enact as well as to *describe* the thing being researched, without always recognizing the implications of their own interference. Methodological rules tend to become naturalized in scientific debate. In the process, they tend to conceal all sorts of their own assumptions about what is important to examine and what kinds of information should be gathered. They also ignore the networks and practices through which they are held in place, such as journal and conference refereeing (Latour 1987). In contrast to research approaches that perpetuate problems like these, Law describes his purpose as raising questions about the kind of realities that *can* be known, or even should be known. He suggests that we explore research approaches that are 'broader, looser, more generous, and in certain respects quite different to that of many of the conventional understandings' (Law 2004b: 4). So what are these approaches?

Existing ANT studies represent an enormous array of empirical and analytic methods. It is important to bear in mind that one strand informing ANT has been the sociology of scientific knowledge and science and technology studies (Latour and Woolgar 1986, Latour 1987, 1999b). Empirical work here has traced the ways in which the messiness of scientific practices in laboratories and the like are translated into inscriptions that erase the messy work that has gone into those enactments.

In educational studies drawing from ANT approaches, researchers have often integrated other methods suggested by feminist, narrative, and curriculum theory, governmentality and other Foucauldian constructs, as well as auto-ethnography, arts based and videographic approaches. Most recent ANT writings are gravely concerned about becoming stuck in some immutable, static methodological framework, and would refuse anything calling itself an 'overall' statement. However, in the interests of providing some preliminary signposts for this chapter about ANT approaches, we offer some tentative observations.

ANT research often begins with Latour's (2005b) injunction to 'follow the actors'. That is, the focus is upon empirical research that meticulously tracks specific, material everyday details of a situation, site, sets of activities, practice, and so forth. This tracking is intended to understand how the things that appear to be actors, things exerting some force and influence in the world, are effects of multiple actants linked together in coherent (or incoherent) networks. Latour has indicated in his work that Garfinkel's ethnomethodological approach is a crucial stance for engaging in empirical studies. Indeed, the notion of following the actor was part of classic ethnomethodology, although ANT-ish notions of the actor are of a somewhat different order. We should also be wary of such labelling given the way in which ethnomethodology is now sometimes solely identified with conversation analysis in research. Some researchers, such as Fox (2008), have explored explicitly revised forms of ethnomethodology in framing ANT research. Many ANT studies are ethnographies of one sort of another. In particular, as noted by literacy researcher Hamilton (2010), there is preference for multi-sited ethnography where data can be linked across different geographic spaces and times instead of focusing on one site and assuming it to be a bounded entity. Hamilton applies this multi-sited ethnographic approach in her ANT study of encounters among teachers and learners in literacy education.

ANT-inspired ethnographies are distinct in one important assumption that they share: the local is all there is. The particular and local is not assumed or understood to be an instance of, nor situated within, a larger social system. Their forms of connectedness are what has to be empirically examined. As Clarke (2002: 112) explains in her study of educational policy:

> rather than aspiring to reproduce the 'real' world in a sociological representation, ANT acknowledges the role of narrative construction in research. All references are treated as 'simultaneously real, like nature, narrated, like discourse, and collective, like society' (Latour 1993: 6). So what can be observed locally are the ways in which 'out there' is produced in the patterning of relations between actors or entities in a network.

What ANT brings to its ethnographic methodological approaches is a sensibility for mess and it attempts to suspend a priori assumptions. ANT focuses upon the tiniest mundane details. This is not to find social patterns and structures, but to trace the micro-movements through which little humdrum bits, human and non-human, negotiate their joinings (or their un-joinings) to assemble the messy things we often try to ignore or explain away in our everyday worlds of education. ANT research attends to the following dimensions that will be discussed throughout this chapter:

- *Symmetry* – treating human and non-human elements as equally interesting, important and capable of exerting force upon each other as they come together.
- *Translation* – examining how individual things connect, partially connect or fail to connect to form nets or webs of activity, and examining how these things change through their connection.
- *Network assemblages* – attempting to trace the multiple networks at work, how they came to be enacted and what work holds them together despite blockages and counter-networks.
- *Multiplicity* – allowing for multiple ontologies and the relations among them, rather than explanations relying on multiple perspectives.
- *Ambivalence* – tracing the contradictions and uncertainties at play within and among these networks and the work they do.

ANT focuses, above all, on the relations between all these things, and between the things within these things. In particular, ANT analysis follows the orderings of human and non-human elements that produce things as configurations that vary in stability and durability. The problem, as some ANT critics have pointed out (e.g. Mietinnin 1999), is that ANT wants to follow everything at play in even a tiny slice of activity. Any object in an ANT study, as Latour and Woolgar

(1979) showed when examining one single scientific research article, embeds myriad networks of production through which experimental moves and mistakes, instruments, laboratory technicians, funding bodies, journal editors and other actants have been gathered, linked and translated.

Recognizing all of these connections, let alone following them, is simply unfeasible given the constraints of research projects on one hand, the infinite proliferation of networks on the other, and the limited capacity of human researchers to even apprehend all these networks. The issue, we suggest, is how to viably adopt and sustain an ANT sensibility throughout the modes of research process: delineating a question or focus and the boundaries of inquiry, observing and recording information as well as processes of gathering this information, understanding and representing some analysis of this information, and recognizing and tracking the researchers' implication in all that is enacted – from realizing the question to producing a representation. In this, we have to bear in mind that these are themselves network effects in the enacting of the educational-research-net. What this points to is that all research is a form of reduction or purification, but the specific translations at play in these practices need careful articulation and consideration in marking the boundaries of what constitutes 'good' research and 'good' research practices.

What, then, might be useful or productive approaches to empirical research suggested by ANT? In this chapter, we will work through some examples of studies already mentioned in this book, examples that we have selected either because they offer helpful considerations for questions particularly pertinent to educational research, or because they illustrate methodologies in ways that can extend useful framings and language for educational researchers. Sometimes we have selected ANT-associated pieces whose methods, or questions or critiques about methods, seem to us to offer interesting complications for ongoing conversations about educational research. Our purpose here is to offer experiments, interruptions and transgressions – not to prescribe techniques.

Finding a focus

All researchers must, at some point in their study, select a focus. Some call this the object of inquiry. For all researchers, this involves issues of where to set the boundaries of limitations, which means deciding what to include and what to exclude in one's purview of observation as well as the analysis of those observations, which can spin off into indefinite directions. In ANT studies, the problem with following actors is to identify and choose *which* actors to follow in their trajectories. What networks should one start with? Which trajectories of which people, objects, practices or discourses should be followed? Or another way to begin is to ask, what assemblages should be studied to determine how they became assembled and how they are continuing to be enacted? The problem quickly turns into which networks and which links can possibly be excluded, in the vast array of linkages that begin unfolding and fraying. Where should one 'cut the network', as Strathern (1996) characterized the question? For such a cutting is necessary. It is the where, how and with what effects that are the important questions.

The inclusion and exclusion of things is particularly difficult when the primary assumption is that there are no predetermined categories. An ANT perspective might argue that a researcher cannot simply start out by choosing, say, a particular college to study, or a particular practice such as learner evaluation or racism in schools, or a particular thing such as science curriculum or the implementation of a technology. Such choices presume that the thing under study already exists as a particular object with inherent attributes, causalities, consequences, and so forth. The ensuing research, then, will simply confirm the boundaries defining this thing rather than engaging in precisely what ANT is more interested in: exploring the micro-links and rivulets flowing within and across what we take for granted to be this thing or that. Thus, for example, in the LfLFE project discussed in Chapter 3, the researchers began the project focussing on 'literacy practices' as their object of study. However, because of the ANT sensibility adopted in certain parts of the project, they ended up identifying a range of 'micro-literacy practices' through which their original object of study was assembled in multiple ways (Ivanič et al. 2009).

ANT is not saying that categorization should be eschewed, but that categories should not be taken for granted. Bowker and Star (1999) provide a series of case studies of the practices through which categories and categorization are enacted. One criticism of early-ANT studies was the tendency to choose macro or 'heroic' actors to study: major policies and implementations, ICT structures, the emergence of a major phenomenon, and other 'large' things presumed to have significant impact. Not only does such choice tend to reify what are already powerful actors in the world, but it obscures its own assumptions about what things and actors already exist. In fact, such an approach can also reify an ANT world: creating a network ontology and overlaying it on the world's lumpy messes and shadows to impose a different kind of control and singularity. This is what happens when ANT is treated as a theory to be applied or a heuristic framework for analysis, as is actually the case in a large number of its uptakes in educational research, including some of our own.

Law (2007) reminds us that othering is a ubiquitous and unavoidable activity in research. To bring something into presence, for example by representing it, is to make other things absent at the same time. He distinguishes two forms of absence: manifest and otherness. Manifest absence is the sort that is acknowledged explicitly, even though it is absent. A teacher's actions might be described, with a mention of the way it embeds her particular professional education, previous pedagogical experiences or her educational philosophy. This background is absent, but its absence is noted explicitly. Otherness is unacknowledged absence. It might be unacknowledged by actors in a particular site but enacted by the researcher; or it might be unnoticed and unacknowledged by the researcher; or it might be noticed by the researcher but bracketed out of the research focus and its report. Law suggests different 'styles' of this othering: invisible work that goes into a research report; things that seem uninteresting or irrelevant; things that seem so obvious they are not worth a research focus or representation; and things that are repressed. He argues that researchers tend to repress in their writing everything that does not fit assumptions of commonsense realism.

Different ANT studies featured in this book have chosen different entry points to focus their study. This choice, deliberate or not, will always be based upon presuppositions about reality, as well as cultural–historical influences shaping a researcher's selection of what question, actors or network is most worth following. This choice will always affect the viewpoint that goes on to shape the study and the research narrative that is finally produced. When the starting point is a specific initiative (Fenwick 2010b, Nespor 2002) or policy (Hamilton 2010), the researcher bounds the terms, territories and trajectories of the inquiry in a particular way. These boundaries and the choices made en route are very different than when starting with a set of practices occurring in a particular region, such as Verran's (2001) study of Yoruba children learning science in Nigeria, or Edwards *et al.* (2009b) observations of cooking classes. Some ANT studies begin with a very tight focus, as in Hunter and Swan's (2007) study starting from the point of view of one actor who is marginalized or Other, to explore how inequity works in practice. And of course, it is common for researchers to begin with one problem and research purpose only to find themselves, through an ANT approach, dealing with messes that destabilize and even derail the original problem. Law and Singleton (2005) describe this very occurrence in their project to map the health care responses to alcoholic liver disease, described in Chapter 2. As the study proceeded, they gradually realized that such a mapping was impossible. There was no 'typical trajectory' of a patient, nor were there coherent paths available through the different clinics, surgeries, and community agencies serving the patients. Regardless of the starting point, an ANT approach focuses as soon as possible on the most local, particular details of a thing or actor as they go about the micro-activities of their day.

What detail does one pick to start following? One ANT approach is to choose a site and just sit in it for a while or wander about in it, watching, listening, thinking, perhaps talking with people in the site, until something of interest emerges. In one study that ended up focusing on boxes, the researchers explain:

> Part of our tactic when looking in detail at the activities that happen with really rather dull anonymous cardboard boxes was to wait to see what it would give us of interest, rather than ... exploiting a kind of thing that might be taken to be interesting already, like 'big decisions' at headquarters.
>
> (Laurier and Philo 2003: 102)

Laurier and Philo (2003) wanted to examine everyday practices of mobile workers, which offer insights useful to educators. Like the mobile consultants in that study, educators often must travel about to different work spaces for teaching. They transport a complex assembly of equipment, dealing with travel and vehicles and books and boxes in ways that routinely produce those regions that become pedagogic spaces. The researchers began with a specific interest in pursuing 'the relevance of particular varieties of objects as they are implicated in practices' (Laurier and Philo 2003: 88), often humble and mundane objects whose handling goes unnoticed. They chose to follow six mobile workers, and they focused in one article on the detailed everyday movements of just one woman, Marge. As the researchers followed her through the minute and often tedious actions of her daily calls, they took careful notes about the way she interacted with the different products she was showing to customers, the ways she moved through the warehouse selecting items, and how she packed and unpacked the boot of her car. Eventually, they found themselves focusing on this routine of unpacking as it produces a region, joining things in practical embodied activity through hands, boxes, car boots and so forth.

Another approach to picking a thread to follow is described by Roth (1996), who studied children in a science class learning to create bridges using toothpicks. Roth was interested in how knowledge circulated and developed as the children talked, worked together and were assisted by the teacher in constructing their bridges. Drawing upon ANT, he conceived the classroom as a complex multiplicity of networks. Some were entrenched, some being assembled in front of him in the bridge activities, and many reaching into the classroom from outside. To find some focus, Roth chose what he called 'tracers' – specific practices and productions – and followed them over time through the various networks in which they participated. How the researcher selects a particular tracer is important, but perhaps more important is the painstaking detail through which the researcher follows and documents that tracer. Roth began by observing students' use of things (toothpicks, tape, glue gun, geometric concepts), through analysis of videotapes, classroom interactions and field notes.

As we outlined earlier, one of these things, the glue gun, attracted his interest. Of all the tools available, it was the glue gun that reconfigured student groupings, dramatically affected bridge construction, and reorganized the collective student knowledge about building bridges with toothpicks. In following the glue gun as a selected tracer, Roth was led to observe a number of innovative configurations and new knowledge emerging through translations of children, concepts and things that he might otherwise have ignored if he had concentrated solely on children's use of the geometric concepts that the teacher was trying to prompt them to incorporate. Other tracers Roth selected for comparison allowed him to compare the pace of translation and the relative impact on the overall composition of the classroom. For example, artefacts, such as the novelty of placing a flag on one's bridge, were adopted easily and quickly but with little impact on the community's functions. Similarly, students' verbal expression of the triangle concepts were quickly incorporated but had little impact on the bridge construction. The practice of glue gun usage, on the other hand, was comparably slow to translate the classroom's actors, but had the greatest impact on reorganizing the community's action, spatial orderings and knowledge.

In these ways, ANT approaches can actually assist the researcher to highlight what is being included and what is excluded in any focus of inquiry. Because an ANT sensibility helps to expose myriad trails and ties among all the minute objects, actions, texts and talk in an activity, the researcher is forced to explicitly choose and declare which will be followed and which will be excluded. Such choices are bound to be far more mucky and uncertain, and subject to backtracking and red herrings, than researchers might wish. Furthermore, in ANT's preoccupation with how some elements are included through translation into any given network, and others are excluded, its very approach is useful for illuminating at least *some* of the inclusions and exclusions and their effects created by the research process itself. Indeed it is possible to draw upon ANT to explore the ways in which it has itself been multiply taken up and translated in differing networks of research.

Such illuminations will be incomplete and fallible, of course. Things that are excluded from network processes, as well as things that are excluded or Othered by the researcher's own necessary choices and selective attention, cannot often be known. Even when these Othered presences can be sensed by the researcher, they cannot easily or satisfactorily be represented – and perhaps it is presumptuous to even try. The best that any researchers can do is to attend closely, be reflexive about what we attend as relevant and what we ignore as irrelevant. As we cut the networks to examine one thing, we need to document our own culturally-shaped practices of ordering and excluding, and try not to mistake our own magnified focus of inquiry for a category independent of myriad external networks seeping through it. Many distributions outside our focus resist becoming realised, known and inscribed, and will always remain invisible to us.

Gathering information

Educational researchers working with ANT gather information in various ways. Most utilize some form of field observation following well-known ethnographic approaches: immersion in the site, focused observation of particular events or time periods, systematic note taking in real-time and/or videorecording of action, collection of documents and artefacts, and site conversations with participants, perhaps audio-recorded and transcribed. Some researchers combine field observation with analysis of relevant policy documents. More rarely, others such as Mulcahy (2006) have worked entirely from interviews, analysing the diverse networks that can be inferred in the discourses and narratives expressed by people. Latour (1999a: 20) has emphasized that in talking with human participants, the focus is upon understanding what things and people do, not what they mean: 'actors know what they do and we have to learn from them not only what they do, but how and why they do it'.

The point is to trace complexity and heterogeneity, and to escape the tendency to homogenize and unify. One way to proceed, suggested by Law (2004a), is to 'look down'. Looking down involves focusing on specific material details. It is 'a concern with the sensuous materiality of practice and the scale-destabilizing implications of this materiality' (Law 2004a: 21). For the researcher, '*there is no distinction between the individual and the environment.* There are no natural, pre-given boundaries. Instead there is blurring. Everything is connected and contained within everything else. There are, indeed, no limits' (Law 2004a: 23, original emphasis). Links between things are examined as 'uncertain, contingent, to be explored, and are not given in a general logic of emergence' (Law 2004a: 25). He contrasts this 'baroque' approach with a 'romantic' sensibility, using a distinction proposed by Kwa (2001). A romantic approach 'looks up', trying to achieve an overview and pattern for the whole. It tends to abstraction, treating natural and social entities with the same analytic vocabulary in ways that homogenize and control as it seeks coherence. Law notes that some early-ANT studies fell into this tendency to abstraction and looking up. However, a 'looking down' approach is content with non-coherence and lack of closure, accepting the fact that complexity cannot possibly be modeled and explicitly represented as a whole, without erasing the very contours enacting that which is complex.

This does not mean that researchers can only focus on small things. As Law points out, the global can still be a focus for research. The key is to focus on whatever thing is being studied as a specific, material effect of multiple specific, material connections. One example is Young's (2006) interest in precarious rural communities, an issue of importance to education related to the survival and support of rural schools, their access to resources, and educational equity and quality. Rural communities, their development, education and economy, are a large object of focus. However, in his ethnography, Young maintains his gaze on following the specific strategies employed by actors who are each trying to negotiate what he calls rural 'unruly environments' by accessing and connecting with networks. Actors are mostly hybrids. An automobile is an actor, a car/driver hybrid, a mechanical apparatus under some human control that also produces and constrains particular human actions and mobilities, even identifications. It is further hybridized by being embedded in infrastructures of roads, fuel stations, maps and bypasses. Distance is an actor, a material being that Young traces by examining in detail the various social, natural, and technological elements that link together to perform distance in highly variable ways that create inequity and power imbalances. In 'looking down', Young is able to recuperate the materiality of distance, showing the important insight for educators as well as for economic developers that rural communities are not disadvantaged by greater or lesser distance from major centres of expertise, resources and supply per se, but rather by how they perform distance.

Context in many educational studies is often treated as an abstract container. In a 'looking up' view of context we may carefully describe characteristics and various influences (social, economic, cultural, etc.) of a rural or urban region, a school, workplace, community event or college classroom. But such descriptions abstract the continual contingency and blurrings of people, action, learning and things. In their study of how literacy practices produce and organize space–time, Leander and Lovvorn (2006) set out to interrupt such conceptions of contexts of learning. The ANT approach, they argue, helps them focus on what texts do in different networks rather than what they mean in different contexts. This avoids a 'particular myopia in literacy studies of focusing on isolated texts or even textual practices' (Leander and Lovvorn 2006: 292). The study itself follows the engagements of one boy, Brian, in what the researchers call three different 'literacy networks'. Two of these literacy networks are at school, and one is a video game that he plays at home. Most of the article traces the moment-to-moment linkages among parts of boy and game. The researchers watch him closely, talking to him about the moves he makes, the objects he uses and the objects that act upon him, and noting what is produced through these interactions. This is what Leander and Lovvorn (2006) call a 'prepositional approach', seeking to spy the relations among actants – beyond, behind, before, between, backward, forward, in, on – as worked out in circulations.

For educational research, this is an important contribution of a 'looking down' ANT approach to gathering information. It can open conceptual black boxes, such as literacy, access, teaching and learning to examine how these phenomena actually, and often surprisingly, emerge in real-time among a whole series of heterogeneous relations. Barab *et al.* (1999, 2001) complain that learning, for example, is conventionally analysed post-activity, thus reinforcing received notions about what learning is and how it emerges. They created an ANT-based approach to focus instead upon what they call 'knowing in the making' in classrooms. Their method for gathering information is developed in painstaking detail, complete with suggested templates for researchers' records and technological means for graphically representing the networks that appear. For them, naturalistic observation is central. Human observers provide important insights into the group dynamics, and the many simultaneous interactions among people, resources and environmental elements. In addition, videotaping provides the necessary historic record to supplement this 'real-time, real-place observation' (Barab *et al.* 2001: 73). This is a record that can be viewed repeatedly by multiple viewers for analysis. They use multiple cameras directed at any one student learning group to capture 'fast-flying' interactions. Further information to support analysis is collected through field notes, student-generated artefacts, and interviews with students and teachers.

Observations are targeted towards documenting episodes of student activities including:

- practices such as tool use
- problem solving and use of resources such as tools and concepts
- discussions among students or students–teacher
- progress of student projects over time
- tracing a particular student, object, action or procedure over time.

An episode contains some information about the object of focus (material, conceptual or social), the initiators of the episode, the participants, the practices in which initiators are engaged, and the resources being used. Like Roth (1996), these researchers select and follow particular tracers to help focus their observations in an episode, where a tracer connects a path of events or network that enacts the development of a particular phenomenon that the researchers wish to understand. The researchers 'chunk', label, code and analyse these episodes. First, they describe the issue, initiator, participants, practice and resources, then they examine the different links that connect these nodes, asking: what links within a network address the underlying questions? Which links are most productive to represent graphically to understand these questions?

Gathering information in ANT-informed research often relies on approaches gleaned from ethnomethodology. The preoccupation is in exposing how actors come to be enacted and get things done. This involves examining the methods by which entities (actors and human/non-humans of all kinds) who participate competently in an activity conduct this participation. The methodology is not predetermined and imposed upon the site, but is largely directed by what emerges at the site. That is, members' practices are understood from within the members' practices. Human talk is an important part of the flow to which the researcher attends. However, as Laurier and Philo (2003) explain, the kind of talk that is most revealing for these purposes is not talk *about* the activity. These are the tips, tours and war stories of the sort that is most often offered through interviews conducted by social science researchers. It is rather the talk that occurs *within* the activity itself, talk that *is* the activity. Conversation analysis examines how the talk among all participants works to *achieve* particular understandings. An actor–network ethnomethodological analysis examines how the talk, action and other forces achieves the production not only of knowledge and social order but also of the very subjects, objects, bodies, and identities participating in a social order.

Fox (2008), who has shown the relevance of ANT to research in higher education and in organizational learning, adopts ethnomethodology in one study of a postgraduate class. Working from Garfinkel's texts, Fox reminds us that ethnomethodology has always described social order as not only practical and material, but also inextricable from moral order. Therefore, ethnomethodology was originally committed to explicating the ways that social and moral order, practice and facts are accomplished through practical, local activity. At every turn of a given activity, there are un-acted and unspoken possibilities. The ethnographer tracks the emerging activity in turn-by-turn detail, showing a projectable field of members' actions and talk. These are always constrained by moral expectations while also performing moral routines and transgressions.

Fox's conversational extracts from 'ordinary' class banter are analysed in delicate detail, highlighting the actors' complex positionings through humour and irony. In this banter, respect is extended or withheld, characters are realized, conflicts emerge and are negotiated, disruptions are attempted and repaired, and various accountabilities are performed. As Fox argues, this sort of emergent, turn-by-turn analysis of the ongoing performance of organizational routines shows how habituated practices or networks are achieved and continually held in place. It also, in distinction from other similar approaches to analysing social and educational processes, emphasizes members' methods of achieving these practices, in their own terms.

> Only ethnomethodology and conversation analysis actually yield such findings which explicate the ways in which *just these* members produce and recognize real and consequential moral facts of life as they come to know them in just these situated ways.
>
> (Fox 2008: 754, original emphasis)

However, there are problems with conventional ethnomethodology, pointed out in critiques of Garfinkel's work by writers such as Pleasants (1999). One is the assumption that individual human 'members' pre-exist activity as skilful agents, and further, that they are reflexive and independently interpretive actors regarding their own methods in producing social/moral order. This creates a series of anterior categories, ignores difference, and leans towards essentializing phenomena through notions of social order, accountability, the reflexive actor, and so forth. ANT approaches with ethnomethodology would begin by unsettling such assumptions and avoid privileging human members in any activity. A second potential problem is the researcher, who of course participates in bringing about any observed effects and who interpretively shapes the accounts. Traditional ethnomethodology has been accused also of lacking any reflexivity. This is only answered, as in all research, by researchers tracing and reporting their own implications and experiences in gathering information, and in their willingness to defer closure and step into ambivalence.

Acting in ambivalence

Much has been learned through experimentation with ANT in empirical research, and through researchers' reflexive attention to the ways they analyse and inscribe what they observe. One important caution that ANT researchers have generated is around the tendency of some early studies to treat the network as itself a static black-boxed object. Networks are a dynamic, ever-bubbling series of connections and failed connections. To treat the entities enrolled into the network as unitary identities rather than as fluctuating, partially unknown and often contradictory obviously takes research in a different direction. Researchers such as Singleton, Verran and Mol have argued that networks often are performed through ambivalence and ambiguity, marginality and multiple identities.

For example, in their study of a UK cervical screening programme implementation and coincident organizational learning, Singleton and Michael (1993) show how the general physician acts as both a pivotal enroller and detractor in the network. He translates equipment, women and assistants into the screening practice at the same time that he problematizes and subverts the network. The researchers became interested in the dual insider–outsider role that such participants can play in network assemblages. They concluded that network betrayal and defeat 'can be conceptualized as the congealment of a disparate array of ambivalences into a focused pattern of resistances. And that would be called "building an actor network"' (Singleton and Michael 1993: 259). It is through such insights that ANT researchers have tended to problematize the discourses of constructionism and social constructionism for their implied notions that networks and orders are built (Latour 1999a, Mol 2002).

This approach demands a certain willingness of the ANT researcher to not only notice ambivalence, but to dwell within it throughout the analysis process. This means suspending a need for explanation and resisting desires to seek clear patterns, solutions, singularities or other closure in the research. It is about noticing instead the strains, the uncanny, the difficult and the ill-fitting, allowing the messes of difference and tension to emerge alongside each other, rather than smoothing them into some kind of relation. As Mulcahy (1999: 100) explains, 'network analysis is a matter of showing the strain between the symbolic and the material, between representations of the body and embodiment as experience, of rendering the ambivalent character of the network more visible'. Her studies of vocational education (Mulcahy 1999, 2007) are particularly helpful examples for educational researchers. As shown in Chapter 6, she traces the simultaneous enactments of very different standards through work being performed in cooking classes by the texts, instruments, interactions, cultural history, and embodied craft knowledge. As she apprehends and begins following these ill-fitting meanderings of the networks, she also reveals her own shifting sense-making as she comes to recognize these ambivalences, then finds ways to represent them in writing without resolving them.

Another helpful example is offered by Hunter and Swan (2007). They are interested in what is actually achieved through diversity and equity work in the learning and skills sector in England. They explore the everyday routines of diversity workers, who they refer to as marginalized actors, within networks of contradictory equity policies and agendas, resources, learning materials and educational expectations. Specifically they follow one worker, Iopia, an African-Caribbean woman who teaches basic skills in an English prison. They focus on the micro-strategies and achievements of Iopia in her day-to-day work. What they illuminate is the multiple positionings that Iopia takes up. She is at once marginalized and racialized in the organizational networks, enrolled in a limited network *of* diversity while at the same time being central to a new network *for* diversity. This is a network that is both repressed and made powerful by narrow, decontextualized notions of diversity. The new network is sustained by non-human things that Iopia has enrolled, and that create types of agency and resources that might paradoxically be seen as racist. For Hunter and Swan's (2007) purposes, the study makes visible the complex multiplicities and contradictions of diversity as it is enacted in education, as well as the precarious movements and identity oscillations of educators who struggle to achieve particular agendas within this multiplicity. For our purposes, the study also demonstrates the patience and fine-grained reflexive attention demanded of researchers willing to dwell in ambivalence.

A final example comes from community education, where Singleton (2005) studied a UK programme intended to develop a community's capacity to deliver cardio-pulmonary resuscitation (CPR) to all residents. Singleton's starting point was personal. As a community resident, she was approached by a neighbour requesting contributions to the programme and enlisting individuals' participation. She writes that she became particularly curious in what appeared to be the programme's characterization of non-participants as lazy and ignorant, even inhumane. This curiousity led to the object of her study: 'to open a space to query a logic' (Singleton 2005: 779), where non-participation is negatively categorized as bad and participation as good, thus offering only one possible reconciliation of the tension between participation and non-participation. Here, we see that attention to ambivalence, or at least its possibility, is important from the moment the research question begins to come into focus. As she proceeds to examine the programme leaflets, take part in the community CPR training sessions in the local church basement, and talk with community members about their experiences, Singleton maintains this orientation to ambivalence. She questions the boundaries that are reproduced through conventional understandings of the world, such as medicalized care, active participation, and death as constant threat. She shows how, in the everyday enactments of such normative categories and their prescriptive effects, there are glimpses of tensions and alternate energies, the complex and heterogeneous messes of actual practice. These have potential to disrupt the press for coherence that stabilize particular categories, universalize what counts as health and care, and erase important distinctions and tensions. Her conclusion is suggestive of an important role for researchers working with ANT to help open the conditions of possibility for a new approach:

> This is an approach that lives in tense spaces in precarious categories and fluid boundaries: spaces from which modest notions of what it is to be healthy and to care emerge. The conditions of possibility include vulnerability, inevitable dissonance and inconsistency, and tremendous energy.
>
> (Singleton 2005: 785–6)

Allowing – and not reconciling – multiplicity

Dwelling in ambiguity is about confronting and allowing multiplicity. This is not about multiple perspectives or meanings of one world. Multiplicity does not just embrace multiple simultaneous identities, multiple networks, or multiple sources of agency circulating among multiple combinations of human and non-human elements. Multiplicity, or what Mol (2002) has called the problem of difference, is the important awareness in after-ANT-inspired analysis of different coexisting worlds. This is about research as primarily ontological practices and not primarily epistemological searches for truth. It is about research as intervention and experiment more than abstraction and representation (Barad 2007).

When researchers try to follow the everyday specific activities of practitioners, such as teachers or health care workers, they will often find confusing differences. Practitioners, even in the same general environment, might engage in very different activities that are all considered to be the same practice. Practitioners might talk about and work with common concepts, such as evaluation or learning, very differently. They might appear to be engaged in a common problem, such as enacting a science curriculum, in ways that bear little apparent relation to one another. Law (2004b) argues that, traditionally, analysts have tended to treat such differences as perspectival. That is, there is assumed to be a common, real object, or practice, or problem. The differences brought to bear among practitioners, including the observing researchers, are simple distinctions in their views of this object or practice. This is the one world, many interpretations/meanings approach to research. However, in much recent ANT analysis, these distinctions are often treated as different things. Two teachers enacting very different practices in the name of a shared science curriculum are not exhibiting different worldviews, but in fact, inhabiting different worlds. From a similar position, Rimpiläinen and Edwards (2009) have explored how two researchers observing the same classroom to address a particular research question produced two very different accounts due to their different hinterlands. They point to some of the pressures in the research team to produce a singular account from this multiplicity rather than represent the multiple ontologies of research practices. Different worlds may coexist, jostle with each other, and even contradict one another.

Mol (2002) was one of the first to propose that researchers need to appreciate how different objects and different worlds – multiple ontologies – can be enacted together in the name of one practice. This would include the reality of the account being constructed by the researcher to represent any of these ontologies and their intermeshing. In her detailed study of physicians' diagnoses and treatment approaches for lower-limb atherosclerosis in different locations, such as the pathology laboratory, the radiology department, the physician's clinic, the surgical theatre and so forth, she showed how very different methods and practices were being employed in each environment. Each was enacted through unique assemblages of instruments, routines and language. In each situation, Mol concluded, atherosclerosis itself was enacted as a different thing. For instance, in one environment it was a slide under a microscope showing a section of artery with thickened intima. In another, it was a set of X-ray pictures compared for percentage of lumen loss. In another it was a rubbery piece of theromatous plaque to be surgically removed and discarded. In analysing Mol's work and its implications, Law (2004b: 55, original emphasis) writes:

> And this is where the question of difference, of multiplicity, raises its head: when medicine talks of lower-limb atherosclerosis and tries to diagnose and treat it, in practice *at least half a dozen different method assemblages* are

implicated. And the relations between these are uncertain, sometimes vague, difficult, and contradictory ... We are not dealing with different and possibly flawed perspectives on the same object. Rather we are dealing with *different objects produced in different method assemblages.* Those objects overlap, yes. Indeed, that is what all the trouble is about: trying to make sure they overlap in productive ways.

In education, conflicting powerful views from government, industry, parents, students and professionals swirl around every major object from methods of reading instruction to purposes for a university education. It is commonplace to assume the problem to be one of managing these diverse perspectives or even reconciling them. The recent ANT switch to understand educational practices as multiple simultaneous ontologies opens a rich new approach to appreciating the fundamental differences afoot, and finding openings for their productive lashing up.

Who is writing whom?

In contemporary educational research that strives to embrace and appreciate multiplicity, emergence and ambivalence without colonizing it, a central question that has come to haunt every study is the researcher. Who chooses to study, and why? Where is this researcher? Who then speaks, who writes and who is written? And who speaks for the non-human? For, as Molotch (2005: 82, original emphasis) suggests:

> Scholars now understand that all objects tell a story, have a semiotics that people 'read'. Every material object thus works through its *semiotic handle* and that kind of handle, as much as any other type, affects what something can be making it attractive in the first place and specifically useful in practice.

The act of representing research can obscure the hand, eye and technologies of inscriptions of the representer. This is why, in any robust account of educational research these days, we expect a full description of the location and role of the researcher, the practices brought to bear, and the implications and limitations of the gaze. Ethical issues of representation are also wide-ranging and difficult. They range from presuming to write another's experience to assuming that any slice of imminent action can be meaningfully captured in fixed linear inscriptions.

For ANT, the issues of inclusion and exclusion discussed earlier become doubly difficult in representation, for the researcher is in effect enrolling both textual objects and readers into a single account. Everything left out is othered, becoming wild and monstrous in their absence. Everything included is potentially domesticated and purified into a network strategy of the researcher's own devices. Even the issue of inclusion in representation suggests that the ANT researcher is at the centre and enjoys the privilege of including others to this inside site, as if such others even desire such inclusion.

For non-representational theory such as ANT, a further critical issue in writing is the implicit separation of the research report produced *through* the study from the action *of* the study, as though the text functions as simply a reflection of this action. We write *about* or represent something, rather than write something. Yet:

> representationalism takes the notion of separation as foundational. It separates the world into the ontologically disjunct domains of words and things, leaving itself with the dilemma of their linkage such that knowledge is possible ... representationalism is a prisoner of the problematic metaphysics it postulates.
>
> (Barad 2007: 137)

In ANT, a text does not represent the real because words and things are not separate. It is the effect of a network that is actively attempting to perpetuate and extend itself in order to intervene and transgress limits. The network assemblages of which the text is a trace are continuing their work in the acts of writing, reviewing, and further circulations of the text on journal websites, etc. Further, writing itself is an embodied thing-entangled activity. Researchers:

> are writing as a practical embodied activity just like any other practical embodied activity, and to say that it is all doing representing is to miss the detail of whatever we are engaged in ... We are not always writing about something; in fact, we are usually writing something specific with purposes and motives that are part and parcel of the writing.
>
> (Laurier and Philo 2003: 90)

In ANT research accounts, even more issues emerge when considering non-humans and proliferating networks. Critics' cautions have been registered since the early ANT studies began to appear, and are usefully summarized by McLean and Hassard (2004, 2007). Concern is expressed about ANT's treatment of non-humans when it is only humans conducting and speaking in the research. However, when non-humans, such as technology, are granted such potency, they might overshadow, or even appear to determine, human subjectivities, imaginations and desires. The question of how to represent actors without reductionist or dehumanizing compressions is complicated further by things:

> For Callon, this relies on the observer being agnostic to ensure that 'no point of view is privileged and no interpretation is censored' (Callon 1986: 200). Latour similarly describes the need to make a 'list', no matter how long and heterogeneous, of those who do the work (Latour 1987: 258). Callon and Law (1997) call for the inclusion of the vast number of entities which, they argue, are missing from many social science stories (such as 'nature and animals', 'angels and fairies'). Perhaps one way is to recognize that 'things' can exist in many forms at the same time and can be mobilized through a variety

of ways (e.g. through instructions). However this again raises the question of how we represent those who are viewed as unrepresentable?

(McLean and Hassard 2004: 503–4)

The conventional ANT argument for symmetry suggests that the researcher ought to inscribe, represent and speak for the interests of actors, using a common vocabulary for things and people.

Law (2004b, 2007) wrestles with the question of representation on many issues. One is the persistent problem of any textual form, static and ordered, attempting the near-impossible: to make present the flickering nature of performance. Another is the problem of all qualitative research whose written accounts tend to collapse the multiplicity into one particular totality. Research accounts must struggle mightily to avoid reproducing notions of a world appearing to be definite, knowable, anterior and singular. A third problem of peculiar interest to ANT and related forms of inquiry, such as science and technology studies broadly, is the difficulty of handling the Otherness that has been excluded in the research – the unacknowledged absences that hover around the research site(s) as well as the absences created by the researcher's own limitations. Law frames this difficulty like this: What Othernesses – among those of which the researcher becomes aware, anyhow – can or should a researcher try to make manifest in representing the research? Law shows that even where the researchers can glimpse and attempt to portray vague, slippery and indefinite multiplicity, they confront the politics of the social science enterprise. Granting bodies, journal referees and policy-makers tend to seek findings and implications for utility. Certainly in education, we could add our many stakeholders in government, educational leadership and practice who want to ask researchers, so what? This is not reductionist, it is a reasonable and practical request to understand what the researcher has traced and how this can inform everyday educational activity that promotes things many educators care about: learning, creativity, equity, active participation, democracy and new possibilities.

The question is back to how to represent the mess that so often is eliminated in accounts of educational research, mess that educators are steeped in but often have no language for, mess that continuously erupts to play havoc with neatly ordered arrangements for curriculum implementation or educational reform or achievement measures. Law (2007) considers the use of arts based textual forms, such as poetry and fictional prose, which introduce issues about the imaginary into research representation. More useful, he decides, is using allegory in research accounts: descriptions of settings and events that embed more than one meaning at once without resolution. Such a description might be lyrical, it might be told from the researcher's dwelling place, it might choose to describe things that can symbolically reflect multiple meanings, and it would likely note incoherences among physical arrangements as well as things that happen.

Hamilton (2010) works with this approach in an article presenting her study of the Skills for Life policy implementation to promote literacy in the UK. She chooses three 'stories' that she writes from her data. The first describes the experience of the researchers making their way to a highly secured office to examine the International Adult Literacy Survey, and making notes for a critique that Hamilton ruefully notes will have little influence on the dense nodes of this powerful and pervasive policy network. The second story describes a 'Gremlin' television vignette to induce adults to join literacy education. This was part of a marketing campaign that was wildly successful even though many did not know what it was about. A third shows literacy teachers in a professional development session talking about the many difficulties, inspirations and contradictions in using the newly mandated 'Individual Learning Plans' with their students.

Each story reflects non-coherences and ambivalences. Each is followed by a commentary from Hamilton, which points out but does not resolve the undecidabilities. Overall, Hamilton works through the stories to show the assemblage of Skills for Life as a series of translations that become sedimented to form an increasingly powerful assemblage. She also shows, in this kind of educational policy context, the utility of Callon's (1986) notion of an obligatory passage point through which actions and resources come together, and discourses and debates are forced to pass. This narrative is useful for those seeking to understand how some educational initiatives, however problematic and widely critiqued, come to expand powerful influence – and where might lie the openings for its interruption. But alongside this analysis, the multiple non-coherent performances embedded in the stories leak out and gesture to the messy Otherness that bubbles within and all around the analysis.

McLean and Hassard (2007) point out that ANT does not deny unique singularities and political, cultural and subjective distinctions among things. It simply questions the assumption that these distinctions precede the relations that entangle them, arguing instead that distinctions are effects performed through these relations. The key is for researchers to explain the process through which they discern and articulate these effects. Part of this process that must be explained is the privilege through which a researcher is positioned within orderings of actor–networks to see and act and be seen and be responded to in particular ways. This positioning is not given and static, but produced through a history of enactments. It is continually maintained and disrupted through imminent relations unfolding in the here-and-now of the researchers' conversations, observations, note taking – as well as their exclusion from conversations and events. The best that can be achieved is through 'fractional ways of "knowing" and "telling" these distributions. This requires not only new skills but also new ways of knowing and telling which are comfortable with the uncertainties of minimalism' (McLean and Hassard 2004: 514). These ways of telling also need to explicitly disrupt the smooth narrative of much representation. They need to draw attention to the continuing network actively working through the text as a thing and demanding embodied activity in its production and consumption. They need to explicate the difficulties of inclusion and the violence of necessary exclusion. As Law (2007: 605) concludes:

our research methods necessarily fail. Aporias are ubiquitous. But it is time to move on from the long rearguard action which insists that reality is definite and singular ... We need new philosophies, new disciplines of research. We need to understand that our methods are always more or less unruly assemblages.

Chapter 11

Translating ANT in education

Latour draws no distinction between blind practical manipulation and privileged theoretical awareness. For Latour, we have nothing but our dealing with networks of objects; some may be nobler and others more base, but all are on the same ontological footing ... If philosophy is to make any progress in the decades to come, it is vital that we consistently oppose Heidegger and side with Latour: against the ontological/ontic distinction, against the theory/practice distinction, against the blanket contempt for mass-produced objects, against the idea that knowledge means transcendence of the world, against nothingness, and in favour of endless curiosity about all manner of specific beings.

(Harman 2007: 34)

We happen to agree with Harman that enormous potential is opened by the understandings of Latour and the many other writers in this book who are exploring these understandings. Even after raising severe questions about it, Harman (2009) concludes that Latour's metaphysics makes possible an object oriented philosophy. Latour's treatment of all things and concepts and feelings as networked actors, as effects of their alliances, banishes for good the divisions between human and world. While Harman focuses on philosophy, the dramatic influence of actor–network theory and its allies is evident across the social sciences. Our intent has been to point to the many ways that educators are exploring and exploding this potential to trace what are taken to be educational practices. These educational writers follow the material processes of attachments and translations that are continually assembling what appear to be distinct and self-evident things, people and concepts. They are showing the multiple heterogeneous layers and fragile connections that make up the 'actants' of education, the networks and politics that constitute curriculum, standardization, evaluation, teaching and learning. And in the process, these ANT-ish researchers are signalling new ways to frame educational problems, and new entry points for interventions. Further, we have become excited by the potential for future educational research that can be inspired through the work of social scientists like Law, Mol, Moser and

Hetherington pushing open ever-new questions of objects and values, different forms of coexistence among multiple ontologies, and ways to act and think within non-coherences. Much of this potential still awaits educators, and our project has endeavoured to gesture to what we believe are fruitful possibilities.

As anyone who has been involved in research knows, completing a project is also a trajectory into others. To conclude is therefore also to begin. To close is also to open. Therefore, as we reach the final chapter of this text, we are also aware that this is no ending. Consistent with ANT, we position this inscription of ANT in education as a temporary and fragile stabilization or punctualization. Indeed, as ANT commentators have pointed out (McLean and Hassard 2007), accounts of realities are performed at the same time as the realities they attempt to represent. As Law wrote in the early years of ANT's development (1992: 386):

> This, then, is the core of the actor–network approach: a concern with how actors and organizations mobilize, juxtapose and hold together the bits and pieces out of which they are composed; how they are sometimes able to pre-vent those bits and pieces from following their own inclinations and making off; and how they manage, as a result, to conceal for a time the process of translation itself and so turn a network from a heterogeneous set of bits and pieces each with its own inclinations, into something that passes as a punctu-alized actor.

In assembling this text and translating others within it, we have attempted to mobilize both ANT and its many uptakes in education into a punctualized actor or immutable mobile. It may even become an obligatory passage point for those who are seeking or are prepared to be enrolled in the network of those taking up ANT in education. Such uptakes are, of course, fragile, and the token may be dropped. The text may be enrolled in various networks in various ways. It may become part of a certain ontological politics, but it may also be taken up as a representation of a theory to be applied to educational issues. It may become part of the multiple ontologies of education that need to be lashed up in order for education to cohere, or it may be (re)presented as yet another perspective upon educational issues, alongside myriad others. For us, the text is a critical endeav-our, an attempt to gather.

> The critic is not the one who debunks but the one who assembles. The critic is not the one who lifts the rugs from under the feet of naïve believers, but the one who offers the participants arenas in which to gather.
>
> (Latour 2004b: 246)

Possibilities abound and cannot be truncated by authorial intent, not least because the text only exists as it becomes taken up in the networks of printing, publishing, marketing, etc. and the interests and pockets of the potential audi-ences it addresses. We do not claim it to be comprehensive as a text, even though it might be said to survey the existing terrain. Surveys rely on instruments and such instruments enact different forms of (in)visibility. We would position this text as an intervention and interruption into educational practices, an attempt to push at the limits or transgress, to provide a wedge. There is a materiality to the text and its inscriptions which attempt to portray both the mess that is education but also the mess which is ANT in education.

In relation to the latter, it is clear that ANT itself is not unified as a field or theory. We referred to ANT in the Preface as not an 'it', but a cloud: one that emerges through the objects being engaged with, thought about and spoken of as well as the words and identities doing the speaking. This still seems appropriate. After-ANT is a troubled and troubling space, always attempting to push at the limits of the attempts to bound ANT in certain ways, to domesticate it. This is ongoing work, not least as those working in this way respond to the many critics of it. We have pointed to some of these throughout this text, in particular those who criticize the attempt to treat the human and non-human symmetrically, or the challenges raised about where the limits of analysis lie when working with the concept of network. While attempting to reconfigure the material world as forms of assemblage and agency as effects, the pull to more conventional understandings of society being about the play of structure and agency remain strong(er). How successfully ANT enrols others in taking up ANT as an orientation is therefore open to question.

ANT progenitors have worried above all that ANT can become reified as an immutable research strategy, a fixed and singular standpoint for thinking about the world complete with methodological baggage that would inevitably reduce the phenomena it confronts to conform to its own theoretical content. For Law (1999), the fixity had already set in, partly through the very naming of ANT which he feared had black-boxed its strategy and sealed it off from its intentions to disrupt, open and experiment with the precarious. One can see in Law's writings since then a steady movement away from explicitly championing ANT or even mentioning it except in vague references within the broader rubric of science, technology and society or material semiotics.

In the field of educational research, where ANT approaches did not appear until the 1990s but have also actually enjoyed a surge of attention since 2000, the problem of singularity is not particularly threatening. ANT in education is a lumpy and messy series of uptakes. Studies exist which have adopted certain patterns identified in early ANT explorations, such as the 'obligatory point of passage' or Callon's four moments of translations, and wielded these patterns as a simplistic model against which observations of classroom life, educational policy, curriculum change and so forth are assessed. As we have seen in many studies in this text, concepts from ANT have been taken up and applied to educational phenomenon as a technology of representation.

However, there are also a profusion of educational studies that appear deeply committed to the difficulty of ambiguity, non-stability and transgression to fixed methodological approaches. This may be because education, as an impossible practice, is itself located within existential uncertainty and contradiction. Education as curriculum, as pedagogy, as language and as policy *is* an aporia of (un)becoming. Learning simultaneously enacts both a present activity, a past for un- and re-learning, and a deferred future, a future of imagined ideals as well as fearful anxieties. Learning activity embodies imminent actors (this teacher and this learner with these tools and texts) simultaneously with collective dreams and problems imprinted in all of its things. Educational research has hosted rich debates and experimentation about qualitative methods exploring what Lather (2007) has called its margins of intelligibility, working with feminist, post-colonial, narrative, emancipatory, anti-racist, post-structural and complexity analytical approaches. This may be why so many educational researchers working with ANT have combined it with other methodological approaches. With the many critiques of ANT now available, to which many of the educational studies reported in this book refer, researchers have struggled to avoid applying it as a rigid framework that tames theory, method and the life under observation. Leander and Lovvorn (2006: 295) state what appears to be rather a common orientation in educational research: 'we draw on ANT not as a stable body of work, but one that provides some tools and perspectives with which to think and analyse [literacy] as a social practice'.

For McLean and Hassard (2004, 2007), a primary issue to be confronted in engaging in ANT research is how to handle general symmetry. ANT researchers often find themselves in a paradoxical situation in field studies, charged to genuinely represent human and non-human entities as ontologically equivalent in potential power and importance in their connections and effects. However, this has to be done without erasing distinctions, flattening political hierarchies and inequitable distributions, or failing to account for interests, imagination and subjectivity. The challenge is 'to produce accounts that are sophisticated yet robust enough to negate the twin charges of symmetrical absence or symmetrical absurdity' (McLean and Hassard 2004: 516).

For Neyland (2006), the problem of ANT's discontent about becoming theoretically fixed can be addressed by re-engaging with what he calls its 'dismissed content'. This content is its patient and persistent tracing of mess: the local, the contingent, the decentred, ambivalent and multiple phenomena drawn into fluid relations. In this text, we have illustrated some of the ways in which that has been attempted in the study of education. The uptake of ANT has been particularly in tracing the many forms of reform, innovation and implementation that are at play in education. Positioning learning and knowledge production more generally as arising from the knowing locations of actors (human–non-human assemblages) in networks suggests alternative ways to enact pedagogy than those approaches which focus education on individual or collective cognition or consciousness. Tracing the work of standardization, accountability and audit and the mobilities and constraints they enact is also a powerful wedge in ANT-inspired educational research. And there are rich possibilities for exploring how education is assembled as a network of practices, appreciating the multiple ontologies that may be lashed together as temporary stabilizations in the process. We might also point to the ways in which education is dis- or re-assembled as, for instance, its work is more powerfully translated into the networks of the knowledge economy, or, for instance, when schools are enrolled as part of children's services, alongside social work, health, police and others. Here, there is a multiplication of the ontologies at play and needing to be lashed up in the enactment of 'children'. This inter- rupts some of the established work on inter-agency or inter-professional work and notions of 'joined up' policy and practice. It is often assumed that such approaches can smooth out differences and produce a singular intervention on behalf of, with and for the child. ANT suggest otherwise. The child is more than one and less than many in such enactments. Here, perhaps, moving into the discourse of the digital era, we might say that the child at the centre of these networks of practice is mashed up rather than lashed up.

Researchers need to interrogate ANT itself, 'to enable theoretical accounts produced by ANT to form a flow. This flow would offer opportunities for mul- tiple connections to be drawn together, connections that could dispute the content of the flow, question it, redirect it, and reassess it' (Neyland 2006: 42). Thus, throughout any research process employing it, ANT itself needs to be decentred through 'a constant questioning (and reformulation) of ANT sensibili- ties alongside a questioning' (Neyland 2006: 43) of the issues and language and assumptions at hand. Conditionality, fallibility and experimentation are therefore crucial to an ANT approach in the study of education. However, this also points to important implications for curriculum purposes for an ANT approach to edu- cation. A curriculum with more emphasis on experimentation, intervention and transgression, focussed on enacting matters of concern, than the representation of matters of fact may seem and is over simplistic. However, it is certainly one of the conclusions that has emerged from studies of curriculum and pedagogy draw- ing upon ANT. Questioning all things including ourselves and our knowledge as *effects*, as present mostly through various alliances in webs of different kinds of objects, is not a terribly comfortable space to inhabit. Even if we find problems with certain ANT tenets, even if we critique its logic or its applications on certain points, the questions it opens about the black boxes we tend to rely upon in edu- cational research are impossible to escape, and impossible to decide. And such undecidability places a major responsibility on the educator over what is gathered and excluded in the enactment of knowing locations.

However, we are somewhat suspicious of any such generalized conclusions to be drawn from ANT as a theory, as it is in the detailed analysis of specific edu- cational practices that we believe it offers most. For us, the value of ANT lies in its attention to mundane heaps of material and immaterial stuff and how they become stuck together (and unstuck). It turns out, despite our impatience to sweep them off the screen where we sometimes think the real drama is unfolding, that it is within these turbulent assemblages and how they do and do not move, endure or fall apart, that education is conjured into presence. This conjuring is uneven, lumpy and hungry, despite efforts to contain it – like this book.

References

Akrich, M. and Latour, B. (1991) 'A summary of a convenient vocabulary for the semiotics of human and nonhuman assemblies', in J. Law (ed.) *A Sociology of Monsters: Essays on Power, Technology, and Domination*, London and New York: Routledge, pp. 259–264.

Alberta Education (2008) 'AISI Facts'. Online, available at http://education.alberta.ca/admin/aisi/about/whatisaisi.aspx (accessed 20 October 2008).

Alberta Learning (2004) 'Improving Student Learning: Provincial Report for Cycle 1 (2000–2003)'. Online, available at http://education.alberta.ca/media/325050/AnnReoprtFull_2001.pdf (accessed 20 October 2008).

— (2001) *Annual Report 2000/2001*, Edmonton, AB: Alberta Learning, Government of Alberta.

— (1999) *Framework for the Alberta Initiative for School Improvement*, Edmonton, AB: Alberta Learning, Government of Alberta.

Angus, T., Cook, I. and Evans, J. (2001) 'A manifesto for cyborg pedagogy?', *International Research in Geographical and Environmental Education*, vol. 10, no. 2: 195–201.

Ball, S.J. (2000) 'What is policy?: texts, trajectories and toolboxes', in S.J. Ball (ed.) *The Sociology of Education: Major Themes*, London: RoutledgeFalmer, pp. 1830–40.

— (1998) 'Big policies/small world: an introduction to international perspectives in education policy', *Comparative Education*, vol. 34, no. 2: 119–30.

— (1994) *Education Reform: A Critical and Post-Structural Approach*, Buckingham: Open University Press.

Barab, S.A., Hay, K.E. and Yamagata-Lynch, L.C. (2001) 'Constructing networks of action-relevant episodes: an in situ research methodology', *Journal of the Learning Sciences*, vol. 10, no. 1: 63–112.

— (1999) 'Constructing networks of activity: an in-situ research methodology', paper presented at the annual meetings of the American Educational Research Association, Montreal, Quebec, 19–23 April.

Barad, K. (2007) *Meeting the Universe Halfway: Quantum Physics and the Entanglement of Matter and Meaning*, Durham, NC: Duke University Press.

Barton, D. and Hamilton, M. (1998) *Local Literacies: A Study of Reading and Writing in One Community*, New York: Routledge.

Barton, D., Hamilton, M. and Ivanič, R. (eds) (2000) *Situated Literacies: Reading and Writing in Context*, London: Routledge.

Belfiore, M., Defoe, T., Folinsbee, S., Hunter, J. and Jackson, N. (2004) *Reading Work: Literacies in the New Workplace*, Mahwah, NJ: Lawrence Erlbaum Associates.

Bigum, C. (1998) 'Solutions in search of educational problems: speaking for computers in schools', *Educational Policy*, vol. 12, no. 5: 586–601.

Bisset, S. and Potvin, L. (2007) 'Expanding our conceptualization of program implementation: lessons from the genealogy of a school-based nutrition program', *Health Education Research*, vol. 22, no. 5: 737–46.

Bloomer, M. (1997) *Curriculum Making in Post-16 Education*, London: Routledge.

Bloor, D. (1976) *Knowledge and Social Imagery*, London: Routledge & Kegan Paul.

Bosco, F. (2006) 'Actor-network theory, networks, and relational approaches in human geography', in S. Aitken and G. Valentine (eds) *Approaches to Human Geography*, London: Sage, pp. 136–46.

Bowers, J. (1992) 'The politics of formalism', in M. Lea (ed.) *Contexts of Computer-Mediated Communication*, Hemel Hempstead: Harvester Wheatsheaf.

Bowker, G. and Star, S.L. (1999) *Sorting Things Out: Classification and its Consequences*, Cambridge, MA: MIT Press.

Boyd, D. (2007) 'Why youth (heart) social network sites: the role of networked publics in teenage social life', in D. Buckingham (ed.) *Youth, Identity, and Digital Media*, Cambridge, MA: MIT Press, pp. 119–42.

Bruni, A., Gherardi, S. and Parolin, L. (2007) 'Knowing in a system of fragmented knowledge', *Mind, Culture, and Activity*, vol. 14, no. 1: 83–102.

Burger, J., Aitken, A., Brandon, J., McKinnon, G. and Multch, S. (2001) 'The next generation of basic education accountability in Alberta, Canada: a policy dialogue', *International Electronic Journal for Leadership in Learning*, vol. 5, no. 19. Online, available at http://www.ucalgary.ca/iejll/burger_aitken_brandon_klinck_mckinnon_mutch#top (accessed 25 October 2009).

Burgess, A. (2008) 'The literacy practices of recording achievement: how a text mediates between the local and the global', *Journal of Education Policy*, vol. 23, no. 1: 49–62.

Busch, K.V. (1997) 'Applying actor network theory to curricular change in medical schools', Proceedings of the Annual Midwest Research-to-Practice Conference in Adult, Continuing and Community Education, 16th, (15–17 October), Michigan State University, pp. 7–12.

Butler, J. (1992) 'Contingent foundations: feminism and the question of 'postmodernism'', in J. Butler and J.W. Scott (eds) *Feminists Theorize the Political*, New York and London: Routledge, pp. 3–21.

Callon, M. (1986) 'Some elements of a sociology of translation: domestication of the scallops and the fishermen of Saint Brieuc Bay', in J. Law (ed.) *Power, Action and Belief: A New Sociology of Knowledge?* London: Routledge & Kegan Paul, pp. 196–233.

Callon, M. and Law, J. (2005) 'On qualculation, agency, and otherness', *Environment and Planning D: Society and Space*, vol. 25, no. 5: 717–33.

Carmichael, P., Fox, A., McCormick, R., Procter, R. and Honour, L. (2006) 'Teacher networks in and out of school', *Research Papers in Education*, vol. 21, no. 2: 217–234.

Clarke, J. (2002) 'A new kind of symmetry: actor-network theories and the new literacy studies', *Studies in the Education of Adults*, vol. 34, no. 2: 107–22.

Cochran-Smith, M. and Lytle, S.L. (1999) 'The teacher research movement: a decade later', *Educational Researcher*, vol. 28, no. 7: 15–25.

Coughenour, C.M. (2003) 'Innovating conservation agriculture: the case of no-till cropping', *Rural Sociology*, vol. 68, no. 2: 278–304.

Cronin, A.M. (2008) 'Calculative spaces: cities, market relations, and the commercial vitalism of the outdoor advertising industry', *Environment and Planning A*, vol. 40, no. 11: 2734–50.

Crossan, M.M., Lane, H.W. and White, R.E. (1999) 'An organizational learning framework: from intuition to institution', *Academy of Management Review*, vol. 24, no. 2: 522–37.

Czarniawska, B. and Hernes, T. (eds) (2005) *Actor-Network Theory and Organizing*, Copenhagen: Liber and Copenhagen Business School Press.

Davis, B. and Sumara, D. (2003) 'The hidden geometry of the curriculum', in R. Edwards and R. Usher (eds) *Space, Curriculum and Learning*, Greenwich: Information Age Publishing, pp. 79–92.

Davis, B., Sumara, D.J. and Luce-Kapler, R. (2008) *Engaging Minds: Changing Teaching in Complex Times*, New York and London: Routledge.

de Laet, M. and Mol, A. (2000) 'The Zimbabwe bush pump: mechanics of a fluid technology', *Social Studies of Science*, vol. 30, no. 2: 225–263.

Dean, M. (1999) *Governmentality*, London: Sage.

DuFour, R. and Eaker, R. (1998) *Professional Learning Communities at Work*, Alexandria, VA: Association for Supervision and Curriculum Development (ASCD).

Dugdale, A. (1999) 'Materiality: juggling sameness and difference', in J. Law and J. Hassard (eds) *Actor Network and After*, Oxford: Blackwell Publishers/The Sociological Review, pp. 113–35.

Edwards, R. (2010) 'Translating the prescribed into the enacted curriculum in college and school', *Educational Philosophy and Theory* (in press).

— (2002) 'Mobilizing lifelong learning: governmentality in educational practices', *Journal of Education Policy*, vol. 17, no. 3: 353–65.

Edwards, R., Biesta, G. and Thorpe, M. (eds) (2009a) *Rethinking Contexts for Learning and Teaching: Communities, Activities and Networks*, London: Routledge.

Edwards, R., Ivanič, R. and Mannion, G. (2009b) 'The scrumpled geography of literacy', *Discourse*, vol. 30, no. 4: 483–500.

Edwards, R., Miller, K. and Priestley, M. (2009c) 'Curriculum-making in school and college: the case of hospitality', *The Curriculum Journal*, vol. 20, no. 1: 27–42.

Edwards, R., Nicoll, K., Solomon, N. and Usher, R. (2004) *Rhetoric and Educational Discourse*, London: Routledge.

Edwards, R. and Usher, R. (2008) *Globalisation and Pedagogy: Space, Place and Identity*, London: Routledge.

Emad, G. and Roth, W.M. (2009) 'Policy as boundary object: a new way to look at educational policy design', *Vocations and Learning*, vol. 2, no. 1: 19–36.

Farrell, L. (2006) *Making Knowledge Common: Literacy and Knowledge at Work*, New York: Peter Lang.

Fejes, A. (2008) 'Governing nursing through reflection: a discourse analysis of reflective practices', *Journal of Advanced Nursing*, vol. 64, no. 3: 243–50.

Fenwick, T. (2010a) '(Un)doing standards in education with actor-network theory', *Journal of Education Policy* (in press).

— (2010b) 'Reading educational reform with actor network theory: fluid spaces, otherings, and ambivalences', *Educational Philosophy and Theory* (in press).

Fenwick, T. (2009a) 'Making to measure? Reconsidering assessment in professional continuing education', *Studies in Continuing Education*, vol. 31, no. 3: 229–44.

— (2009b) 'Responsibility, complexity science and education: dilemmas and uncertain responses', *Studies in Philosophy and Education*, vol. 28, no. 2: 101–18.

— (2008) 'Understanding relations of individual-collective learning in work: a review of research', *Management Learning*, vol. 39, no. 3: 227–43.

— (2007) 'Towards enriched conceptions of work learning: participation, expansion and translation/mobilization with/in activity', *Human Resource Development Review*, vol. 5 no. 3: 285–302.

— (2003) 'The good teacher in neo-liberal risk society: a Foucaultian analysis of professional growth plans', *Journal of Curriculum Studies*, vol. 35, no. 3: 335–54.

— (1998) 'Managing space, energy, and self: beyond classroom management with junior high school teachers', *Teachers and Teacher Education*, vol. 14, no. 6: 619–31.

Fenwick, T. and Edwards, R. (2010) 'Reclaiming and renewing actor network theory for educational research', *Educational Philosophy and Theory* (in press).

Fountain, R.M. (1999) 'Socio-scientific issues via actor network theory', *Journal of Curriculum Studies*, vol. 31, no. 3: 339–58.

Fox, S. (2008) '"That miracle of familiar organizational things": social and moral order in the MBA classroom', *Organization Studies*, vol. 29, no. 5: 733–61.

— (2005) 'An actor-network critique of community in higher education: implications for networked learning', *Studies in Higher Education*, vol. 30, no. 1: 95–110.

— (2001) 'Studying networked learning: some implications from socially situated learning theory and actor-network theory', in C. Steeples and C. Jones (eds) *Networked Learning: Perspectives and Issues*, London: Springer-Verlag, pp. 77–91.

— (2000) 'Communities of practice, Foucault and actor-network theory', *Journal of Management Studies*, vol. 37, no. 6: 853–67.

Frankham, J. (2006) 'Network utopias and alternative entanglements for educational research and practice', *Journal of Education Policy*, vol. 21, no. 6: 661–77.

Fullan, M. (1993) *Change Forces: Probing the Depth of Educational Reform*, London: Routledge.

Gaskell, J. and Hepburn, G. (1998) 'The course as token: a construction of/by networks', *Research in Science Education*, vol. 28, no. 1: 65–76.

Gherardi, S. and Nicolini, D. (2000) 'To transfer is to transform: the circulation of safety knowledge', *Organization*, vol. 7, no. 2: 329–48.

Goodson, I.F. (2004) 'Understanding curriculum change: some warnings about restructuring initiatives', in F. Hérnandez and I. Goodson (eds) *Social Geographies of Educational Change*, London: Kluwer Academic Publishers, pp. 15–27.

Gorur, R. (2010) 'ANT on the PISA trail: following the statistical pursuit of certainty', *Educational Philosophy and Theory* (in press).

Gough, N. (2004) 'RhizomANTically becoming-cyborg: performing posthuman pedagogies', *Educational Philosophy and Theory*, vol. 36, no. 3: 253–265.

Greenhow, C., Robelia, B. and Hughes, J. (2009) 'Web 2.0 and classroom research: what path should we take now?', *Educational Researcher*, vol. 38, no. 4: 246–59.

Grek, S. (2009) 'Governing by numbers: the PISA "effect" in Europe', *Journal of Education Policy*, vol. 24, no. 1: 23–37.

Habib, L. and Wittek, L. (2007) 'The portfolio as artifact and actor', *Mind, Culture and Activity*, vol. 14, no. 4: 266–82.

Hall, E. (2004) 'Spaces and networks of genetic knowledge making: the 'geneticisation' of heart disease', *Health and Place*, vol. 10, no. 4: 311–18.

Hamilton, M. (2010) 'Unruly practice: what a sociology of translations can offer to educational policy analysis', *Educational Philosophy and Theory* (in press).

— (2009) 'Putting words in their mouths: the alignment of identities with system goals through the use of individual learning plans', *British Educational Research Journal*, vol. 35, no. 2: 221–42.

— (2001) 'Privileged literacies: policy, institutional process and the life of the IALS', *Language and Education*, vol. 15, no. 2–3: 178–96.

Hamilton, M. and Hillier, Y. (2007) 'Deliberative policy analysis: adult literacy assessment and the politics of change', *Journal of Educational Policy*, vol. 22, no. 5: 573–94.

Harman, G. (2009) *Prince of Networks: Bruno Latour and Metaphysics*, Melbourne: re.press books.

— (2007) 'The importance of Bruno Latour for philosophy', *Cultural Studies Review*, vol. 13, no. 1: 31–49.

Harris-Hart, C. (2009) 'Performing curriculum: exploring the role of teachers and teacher educators', *Curriculum Inquiry*, vol. 39, no. 1: 111–23.

Harrisson, D. and Laberge, M. (2002) 'Innovation, identities and resistance: the social construction of an innovation network', *Journal of Management Studies*, vol. 39, no. 4: 497–521.

Hassard, J., Law, J. and Lee, N. (1999) 'Preface: Organization's thematic issue on actor network theory', *Organization*, vol. 6, no. 3: 387–90.

Henare, A., Holbraad, M. and Wastell, S. (eds) (2007) *Thinking Through Things: Theorising Artefacts Ethnographically*, London: Routledge.

Hepburn, G.R. (1997) 'Working the network: initiating a new science and technology course', unpublished doctoral thesis, the University of British Columbia.

Hetherington, K. and Law, J. (2000) 'After networks', *Environment and Planning D: Society and Space*, vol. 18, no. 2: 127–32.

Hitchings, R. (2003) 'People, plants and performance: on actor network theory and the material pleasures of the private garden', *Social and Cultural Geography*, vol. 4, no. 1: 99–113.

Hunter, S. and Swan, E. (2007) 'Oscillating politics and shifting agencies: equalities and diversity work and actor network theory', *Equal Opportunities International*, vol. 26, no. 5: 402–19.

Hussenot, A. (2008) 'Between structuration and translation: an approach of ICT appropriation', *Journal of Organizational Change Management*, vol. 21, no. 3: 335–47.

I'Anson, J. and Allan, J. (2006) 'Children's rights in practice: a study of change within a primary school', *International Journal of Children's Spirituality*, vol. 11, no. 2: 265–79.

Ingold, T. (2007) *Lines: A Brief History*, London: Routledge.

ISO (2009) How are ISO standards developed? International Organization for Standardization. Online, available at http://www.iso.org/iso/standards_development/processes_and_procedures/how_are_standards_developed.htm (accessed April 2010).

Ivanič, R., Edwards, R., Barton, D., Martin-Jones, M., Fowler, Z., Hughes, B., Mannion, G., Miller, K., Satchewell, C. and Smith, J. (2009) *Improving Learning in College: Rethinking Literacies Across the Curriculum*, London: Routledge.

174 Actor–Network Theory in Education

Jöns, H. (2006) 'Dynamic hybrids and the geographies of technoscience: discussing conceptual resources beyond the human/non-human binary', *Social and Cultural Geography*, vol. 7, no. 4: 559–80.

Judah, M.L. and Richardson, G.H. (2006) 'Between a rock and a (very) hard place: the ambiguous promise of action research in the context of state mandated teacher professional development', *Action Research*, vol. 4, no. 1: 65–80.

Kenway, J., Bullen, E., Fahey, J. and Robb, S. (2006) *Haunting the Knowledge Economy*, New York: Routledge.

Knorr-Cetina, K. (1997) 'Sociality with objects: social relations in postsocial knowledge societies', *Theory, Culture and Society*, vol. 14, no. 4: 1–30.

Knox, H., Savage, M. and Harvey, P. (2006) 'Social networks and the study of relations: networks as method, metaphor and form', *Economy and Society*, vol. 35, no. 1: 113–40.

Kress, G. (2003) *Literacy in the New Media Age*, London: Routledge.

Kwa, C. (2001) 'Romantic and baroque conceptions of complex wholes in the sciences', in J. Law and A. Mol (eds) *Complexities: Social Studies of Knowledge Practices*, Durham, NC: Duke University Press, pp. 23–52.

Lankshear, C., Peters, M.and Knobel, M. (1996) 'Critical pedagogy and cyberspace', in H. Giroux, C. Lankshear, P. McLaren and M. Peters (eds) *Counternarratives: Cultural Studies and Critical Pedagogies in Postmodern Spaces*, London: Routledge, pp. 149–88.

Lanzara, G. and Morner, M. (2005) 'Artefacts rule!: how organizing happens in open source software projects', in B. Czarniawska and T. Hernes (eds) *Actor-Network Theory and Organizing*, Malmo: Liber and Copenhagen Business School Press, pp. 67–90.

Lather, P. (2007) *Getting Lost: Feminist Practices Toward a Double(d) Science*, Albany NY: SUNY Press.

Latour, B. (2005a) 'From realpolitik to dingpolitik: how to make things public', in B. Latour and P. Weibel (eds) *Making Things Public*, Cambridge, MA: MIT Press, pp. 14–41.

— (2005b) *Reassembling the Social: An Introduction to Actor-Network Theory*, Oxford: Oxford University Press.

— (2004b) 'Why has critique run out of steam?: from matters of fact to matters of concern', *Critical Inquiry*, vol. 30, no. 2: 225–48.

— (2004a) *Politics of Nature*, Cambridge, MA: Harvard University Press.

— (1999a) 'On recalling ANT.', in J. Law and J. Hassard (eds) *Actor Network and After*, Oxford: Blackwell Publishers/The Sociological Review, pp. 15–25.

— (1999b) *Pandora's Hope: Essays on the Reality of Science Studies*, Cambridge, MA: Harvard University Press.

— (1996) *Aramis, Or the Love of Technology*, Cambridge, MA: MIT Press.

— (1993) *We have Never been Modern*, Brighton: Harvester Wheatsheaf.

— (1991) 'Technology is society made durable', in J. Law (ed.) *A Sociology of Monsters: Essays on Power, Technology, and Domination*, London and New York: Routledge, pp. 103–31.

— (1987) *Science in Action*, Cambridge, MA: Harvard University Press.

— (1986) 'The powers of association', in J. Law (ed.) *Power, Action and Belief: A New Sociology of Knowledge?* London, Boston and Henley: Routledge & Kegan Paul, pp. 264–80.

Latour, B. and Woolgar, S. (1986) *Laboratory Life: The Construction of Scientific Facts*, Princeton, NJ: Princeton University Press.

— (1979) *Laboratory Life: The Social Construction of Scientific Facts*, London: Sage Publications.

Laurier, E. and Philo, C. (2003) 'The region in the boot: mobilising lone subjects and multiple objects', *Environment and Planning D*, vol. 11, no. 1: 85–106.

Lave, J. (1996) 'The practice of learning', in S. Chaiklin and J. Lave (eds) *Understanding Practice: Perspectives on Activity and Context*, Cambridge: Cambridge University Press, pp. 3–32.

Lave, J. and Wenger, E. (1991) *Situated Learning: Legitimate Peripheral Participation*, Cambridge: University of Cambridge Press.

Law, J. (2009) 'Actor network theory and material semiotics', in B.S. Turner (ed.) *The New Blackwell Companion to Social Theory*, Chichester: Wiley-Blackwell, pp. 141–58.

— (2007) 'Making a mess with method', in W. Outhwaite and S.P. Turner (eds) *The Sage Handbook of Social Science Methodology*, London and Beverly Hills: Sage, pp. 595–606.

— (2004a) 'And if the global were small and noncoherent?: method, complexity, and the baroque', *Environment and Planning D: Society and Space*, vol. 22, no. 1: 13–26.

— (2004b) *After Method: Mess in Social Science Research*, London: Routledge.

— (2003) 'Ordering and obduracy', *published by the Centre for Science Studies, Lancaster University*. Online, available at http://www.lancs.ac.uk/fass/sociology/papers/law-ordering-and-obduracy.pdf (accessed 15 November 2009).

— (2002) *Aircraft Stories: Decentering the Object in Technoscience*, Durham, North Carolina: Duke University Press.

— (1999) 'After ANT: topology, naming and complexity', in J. Law and J. Hassard (eds) *Actor Network Theory and After*, Oxford: Blackwell Publishers/ The Sociological Review, pp. 1–14.

— (1994) *Organizing Modernity*, Oxford: Blackwell Publishing.

— (1992) 'Notes on the theory of the actor-network: ordering, strategy, and heterogeneity', *Systemic Practice and Action Research*, vol. 5, no. 4: 379–93.

Law, J. and Callon, M. (1992) 'The life and death of an aircraft: a network analysis of technical change', in W.E. Bijker and J. Law (eds) *Shaping technology/building Society: Studies in Sociotechnical Change*, Cambridge, MA: MIT Press, pp. 21–52.

Law, J. and Hassard, J. (eds) (1999) *Actor Network Theory and After*, Oxford: Blackwell Publishers/The Sociological Review.

Law, J. and Hetherington, K. (2003) 'Materialities, spatialities, globalities', in M. Dear and S. Flusty (eds) *The Spaces of Postmodernism: Readings in Human Geography*, Oxford: Blackwell Publishing, pp. 390–401.

Law, J. and Mol, A. (2001) 'Situating technoscience: an inquiry into spatialities', *Environment and Planning D: Society and Space*, vol. 19, no. 5: 609–21.

Law, J. and Singleton, V. (2005) 'Object lessons', *Organization*, vol. 12, no. 3: 331–55.

Lawn, M. and Grosvenor, I. (eds) (2005) *Materialities of Schooling: Design, Technology, Objects, Routines*, Oxford: Symposium Books.

Leander, K.M. and Lovvorn, J.F. (2006) 'Literacy networks: following the circulation of texts, bodies, and objects in the schooling and online gaming of one youth', *Cognition and Instruction*, vol. 24, no. 3: 291–340.

Lee, N. and Brown, S. (1994) 'Otherness and the actor network: the undiscovered continent', *American Behavioral Scientist*, vol. 37, no. 6: 772–90.

Lepa, J. and Tatnall, A. (2006) 'Using actor-network theory to understanding virtual community networks of older people using the internet', *Journal of Business Systems, Governance and Ethics*, vol. 1, no. 4: 1–14.

Levin, B. (1998) 'An epidemic of education policy: (what) can we learn from each other?', *Comparative Education*, vol. 34, no. 2: 131–41.

Luck, J.T. (2008) 'Lost in translations: a socio-technical study of interactive videoconferencing at an Australian university', unpublished doctoral thesis, Central Queensland University.

— (2004) 'Technological agents?: exploring the ethics, risks and politics of researching non-human actants', in P.N. Coombes, M.J.M. Danaher and P.A. Danaher (eds) *Strategic Uncertainties: Ethics, Politics and Risk in Contemporary Educational Research*, Flaxton, QLD: Post Pressed, pp. 185–97.

— (2003) 'Performing teaching and learning using interactive videoconferencing', in B.A. Knight and A. Harrison (eds) *Research Perspectives on Education for the Future*, Flaxton, QLD: Post Pressed, pp. 83–97.

McEwan, N. (2008) *AISI – Seven Years of Enthusiasm: Improving Learning and Schools – Innovation, Renewal, Sustainability*, Edmonton, AB: Alberta Learning, Government of Alberta.

McGregor, J. (2004) 'Spatiality and the place of the material in schools', *Pedagogy, Culture and Society*, vol. 12, no. 3: 347–72.

McLean, C. and Hassard, J. (2007) 'Actor-networks and sociological symmetry', in J. Hassard, M. Kelerman and J. Cox Wolfram (eds) *Disorganisation Theory: Explorations in Alternative Organisational Analysis*, London: Routledge, pp. 45–71.

— (2004) 'Symmetrical absence/symmetrical absurdity: critical notes on the production of actor-network accounts', *Journal of Management Studies*, vol. 41, no. 3: 493–519.

Martinez, P. (2005) 'History of school desk development in terms of hygiene and pedagogy in spain (1838–936)', in M. Lawn and I. Grosvenor (eds) *Materialities of Schooling: Design, Technology, Objects, Routines*, Oxford: Symposium Books.

Massey, D.B. (2005) *For Space*, London and Thousand Oaks, CA: Sage.

Mathison, S. and Ross, E.W. (2002) 'The hegemony of accountability', *Workplace: The Journal for Academic Labor*, vol. 5, no. 1. Online, available at http://www.cust.educ.ubc.ca/workplace/issue5p1/mathison.html (accessed 4 May 2009).

Miettinen, R. (1999) 'The riddle of things: activity theory and actor-network theory as approaches to studying innovations', *Mind, Culture and Activity*, vol. 6, no. 3: 170–95.

Miller, D. (ed.) (2005) *Materiality*, Durham, NC: Duke University Press.

Miller, K.H., Edwards, R. and Priestley, M. (2009) 'Levels and equivalence in credit and qualifications frameworks: contrasting the prescribed and enacted curriculum in school and college', *Research Papers in Education*, vol. 24, no. 4: 1–19.

Mirchandani, K. (2004) 'Practices of global capital: gaps, cracks and ironies in transnational call centres in India.', *Global Networks: A Journal of Transnational Affairs*, vol. 4, no. 4: 355–74.

Mol, A. (2002) *The Body Multiple: Ontology in Medical Practice*, Durham, NC: Duke University Press.

— (1999) 'Ontological politics: a word and some questions', in J. Law and J. Hassard (eds) *Actor Network and After*, Oxford: Blackwell Publishers/The Sociological Review, pp. 74–89.

Mol, A. and Law, J. (2002) 'Complexities: an introduction', in J. Law and A. Mol (eds) *Complexities: Social Studies of Knowledge Practices*, Durham, NC: Duke University Press, pp. 1–22.

Mol, A. and Law, J. (1994) 'Regions, networks and fluids: anaemia and social topology', *Social Studies of Science*, vol. 24, no. 4: 641–71.

Molotch, H. (2005) *Where Stuff Comes from: How Toasters, Toilets, Cars, Computers and Many Other Things Come to be as they are*, New York: Routledge.

Mulcahy, D. (2010) 'Assembling the accomplished teacher: the performativity and politics of professional teaching standards', *Educational Philosophy and Theory* (in press).

— (2007) 'Managing spaces: (re)working relations of strategy and spatiality in vocational education and training', *Studies in Continuing Education*, vol. 29, no. 2: 143–62.

— (2006) 'The salience of space for pedagogy and identity: problem based learning as a case in point', *Pedagogy, Culture and Society*, vol. 14, no. 1: 55–69.

— (1999) '(Actor-net) working bodies and representations: tales from a training field', *Science, Technology and Human Values*, vol. 24, no. 1: 80–104.

— (1998) 'Designing the user/using the design: the shifting relations of a curriculum technology change', *Social Studies of Science (Sage)*, vol. 28, no. 1: 5–37.

Mullen, C.K. (2002) 'Nursing, technology, and knowing the patient', unpublished doctoral thesis, The University of North Carolina at Chapel Hill.

Murdoch, J. (2006) *Post-Structural Geography*, London: Sage.

— (1998) 'The spaces of actor-network theory', *Geoforum*, vol. 29, no. 4: 357–74.

Nespor, J. (2010) 'Devices and educational change', *Educational Philosophy and Theory* (in press).

— (2003) 'Undergraduate curricular as networks and trajectories', in R. Edwards and R. Usher (eds) *Space, Curriculum and Learning*, Greenwich, MA: Information Age Publishing, pp. 93–122.

— (2002) 'Networks and contexts of reform', *Journal of Educational Change*, vol. 3, no. 3–4: 365–82.

— (1994) *Knowledge in Motion: Space, Time and Curriculum in Undergraduate Physics and Management*, Philadelphia, PA: Falmer Press.

Neyland, D. (2006) 'Dismissed content and discontent: an analysis of the strategic aspects of actor-network theory', *Science, Technology and Human Values*, vol. 31, no. 1: 29–51.

Neyland, D. and Woolgar, S. (2002) 'Accountability in action?: the case of the database purchasing decision', *British Journal of Sociology*, vol. 53, no. 2: 259–74.

Nicoll, K. (2006) *Flexibility and Lifelong Learning*, London: Routledge.

Olssen, M. and Peters, M.A. (2005) 'Neoliberalism, higher education and the knowledge economy: from the free market to knowledge capitalism', *Journal of Educational Policy*, vol. 20, no. 3: 313–46.

OECD (2009) 'OECD Programme for International Student Assessment (PISA) homepage'. Online, available at http://www.pisa.oecd.org/pages/0,2987 ,en_32252351_32235731_1_1_1_1_1,00.html (accessed 30 October 2009).

— (2007) 'PISA 2006: Science Competencies for Tomorrow's World, Executive Summary'. Online, available at http://www.pisa.oecd.org/document/2/0,3 343,en_32252351_32236191_39718850_1_1_1_1,00.html#ES (accessed 30 October 2009).

Parsons, J., McRae, P., Taylor, L., Larons, N. and Servage, L. (2006) *Celebrating School Improvement: Six Lessons Learned from Alberta's AISI Projects*, Edmonton, AB: School Improvement Press.

Peterson, S. (2007) 'Mundane cyborg practice: material aspects of broadband internet use', *Convergence*, vol. 13, no. 1: 79–91.

Phelan, A. (2007) 'Critical response to standards – community web assignments for teacher education students', presentation to the Teacher Education Orientation, University of British Columbia, 28 August.

Pickering, A. (2001) 'Practice and posthumanism: social theory and a history of agency', in T. Schatzki, K. Knorr-Cetina and E. Von Savigny (eds) *The Practice Turn in Contemporary Theory*, London: Routledge, pp. 163–74.

Pinar, W.F. (2004) *What is Curriculum Theory?* Mahweh, NJ: Lawrence Erlbaum.

— (1976) *Autobiography, Politics and Sexuality: Essays in Curriculum Theory 1972–1992*, New York: Peter Lang.

Pinar, W.F. and Grumet, M.R. (1976) *Toward a Poor Curriculum*, Dubuque, IA: Kendall/Hunt.

Pleasants, N. (1999) *Wittgenstein and the Idea of a Critical Social Theory*, London: Routledge.

Pollock, N. (2005) 'When is a work-around?: conflict and negotiation in computer systems development', *Science Technology and Human Values*, vol. 30, no. 4: 496–514.

Popkewitz, T. (1996) 'Rethinking decentralisation and state/civil society distinctions: the state as a problematic of governing', *Journal of Education Policy*, vol. 11, no. 1: 27–51.

Power, M. (1999) *The Audit Society: Rituals of Verification*, 2nd edn, Oxford: Oxford University Press.

Resnik, J. (2006) 'International organizations, the "education-economic growth" black box, and the development of world education culture', *Comparative Education Review*, vol. 50, no. 2: 173–95.

Rimpiläinen, S. and Edwards, R. (2009) 'The ANT-ics of educational research: researching case-based learning through objects and texts', paper presented at the 5th Annual CRESC Conference, University of Manchester, 1–4 September.

Rizvi, F. (2009) 'Globalization and education policy', paper presented at the Institute of Education Policy and Policy Studies, Vancouver, BC, 5 August.

Rizvi, F. and Lingard, R. (2010) *Globalizing Education Policy*, London: Routledge.

Roberts, G. (2004) 'The new covert curriculum: a critical, actor-network approach to learning technology policy', Proceedings of the 4th International Conference Networked Learning 2004, University of Sheffield and University of Lancaster, 5–7 April.

Robertson, S. (2005) 'Re-imagining and rescripting the future of education: global knowledge economy discourse and the challenge to education systems', *Comparative Education*, vol. 41, no. 2: 151–70.

Robson, K. (1992) 'Accounting numbers as "inscription": action at a distance and the development of accounting', *Accounting, Organisations and Society*, vol. 17, no. 6: 685–708.

Rose, N.S. (1999) *Powers of Freedom: Reframing Political Thought*, Cambridge and New York: Cambridge University Press.

Roth, W.-M. and McGinn, M.K. (1997) 'Science in schools and everywhere else: what science educators should know about science and technology studies', *Studies in Science Education*, vol. 29, no. 1: 1–43.

— (1996) 'Knowledge diffusion in a grade 4–5 classroom during a unit on civil engineering: an analysis of a classroom community in terms of its changing resources and practices', *Cognition and Instruction*, vol. 14, no. 2: 179–220.

Samarawickrema, G. and Stacey, E. (2007) 'Adopting web-based learning and teaching: a case study in higher education', *Distance Education*, vol. 28, no. 3: 313–33.

Sarker, S., Sarker, S. and Sidorova, A. (2006) 'Understanding business process change failure: an actor-network perspective', *Journal of Management Information Systems*, vol. 23, no. 1: 51–86.

Sfard, A. (1998) 'On two metaphors for learning and the dangers of choosing just one', *Educational Researcher*, vol. 27, no. 2: 4–13.

Simpson, N. (2000) 'Diffusion theory and actor-network theory: two views on an innovation', in B.A. Knight and L. Rowan (eds) *Researching Futures Oriented Pedagogy*, Flaxton, QLD: Post Pressed, pp. 23–40.

Singleton, V. (2005) 'The promise of public health: vulnerable policy and lazy citizens', *Environment and Planning: Society and Space*, vol. 23, no. 5: 771–86.

— (1998) 'Stabilizing instabilities: The role of the laboratory in the United Kingdom cervical screening programme', in M. Berg and A. Mol (eds) *Differences in Medicine: Unravelling Practices, Techniques and Bodies*, Durham, NC: Duke University Press, pp. 86–104.

Singleton, V. and Michael, M. (1993) 'Actor-networks and ambivalence: general practitioners in the UK cervical screening programme', *Social Studies of Science (Sage)*, vol. 23, no. 2: 227–64.

Smyth, J., McInerney, P., Hattam, R. and Lawson, M. (1998) 'Teacher learning: the way out of the school restructuring miasma', *International Journal of Leadership in Education*, vol. 1, no. 2: 95–109.

Sørensen, E. (2009) *The Materiality of Learning: Technology and Knowledge in Educational Practice*, Cambridge and New York: Cambridge University Press.

— (2007) 'The time of materiality', *Forum: Qualitative Social Research/Sozialforschung*, vol. 8, no. 2. Online, available at http://www.qualitative-research.net/index.php/fqs/issue/view/6 (accessed 22 November 2009).

Spillane, J. (1999) 'External reform efforts and teachers' initiatives to reconstruct their practice: the mediating role of teachers zones of enactment', *Journal of Curriculum Studies*, vol. 31, no. 2: 143–75.

Star, S.L. (1995) 'The politics of formal representations: wizards, gurus, and organizational complexity', in S.L. Star (ed.) *Ecologies of Knowledge: Work and Politics in Science and Technology*, Albany, NY: SUNY, pp. 88–118.

— (1991) 'Power, technologies and the phenomenology of conventions: on being allergic to onions', in J. Law (ed.) *A Sociology of Monsters: Essays on Power, Technology, and Domination*, London and New York: Routledge, pp. 26–56.

— (1989) 'The structure of ill-structured solutions: boundary objects and heterogeneous distributed problem solving', in L. Gasser and M.N. Huhns (eds) *Distributed Artificial Intelligence, Volume II*, London: Pitman Publishers, pp. 37–54.

Star, S.L. and Griesemer, J.R. (1989) 'Institutional ecology, 'translations,' and boundary objects: amateurs and professionals in Berkeley's museum of vertebrate zoology, 1907–1939', *Social Studies of Science*, vol. 19, no. 3: 387–420.

Stelmach, B.L. (2004) 'Unlocking the schoolhouse doors: institutional constraints on parent and community involvement in a school improvement initiative', *Canadian Journal of Educational Administration and Policy*, no. 31, 18 June. Online, available at http://www.umanitoba.ca/publications/cjeap/articles/stelmach.html (accessed 25 October 2009).

Strathern, M. (1996) 'Cutting the network', *Journal of the Royal Anthropological Institute*, vol. 2, no. 3: 517–35.

Stronach, I., Corbin, B., McNamara, O., Stark, S. and Warne, T. (2002) 'Towards an uncertain politics of professionalism: teacher and nurse identities in flux', *Journal of Education Policy*, vol. 17, no. 1: 109–38.

Suchman, L. (2007) *Human-Machine Reconfigurations: Plans and Situated Actions*, 2nd edn, Cambridge, MA: Cambridge University Press.

— (2006) *Human-Machine Reconfigurations: Plans and Situated Actions*, Cambridge: Cambridge University Press.

— (2005) 'Affiliative objects', *Organization*, vol. 12, no. 3: 379–99.

Sumara, D. and Carson, D. (1997) 'Reconceptualizing action research as a living practice', in T. Carson and D. Sumara (eds) *Action Research as a Living Practice*, New York: Peter Lang Publishers, pp. xiii–xxxii.

Taylor, A., Neu, D. and Peters, F. (2002) 'Technocratic control and financial governance: the case of two school districts', *Educational Management and Administration*, vol. 30, no. 4: 469–86.

Thorpe, M. (2009) 'Technology-mediated learning contexts', in R. Edwards, G. Biesta and M. Thorpe (eds) *Rethinking Contexts for Learning and Teaching: Communities, Activities and Networks*, London: Routledge, pp. 119–32.

Thrift, N. (2005) 'Beyond mediation: three new material registers and their consequences', in D. Miller (ed.) *Materiality*, Durham, NC: Duke University Press, pp. 231–55.

— (2000) 'Afterwords', *Environment and Planning D: Society and Space*, vol. 18, no. 2: 213–55.

Timmermans, S. and Berg, M. (1997) 'Standardization in action: achieving local universality through medical protocols', *Social Studies of Science*, vol. 27, no. 2: 273–305.

Verran, H. (2007) 'Metaphysics and learning', *Learning Inquiry*, vol. 1, no. 1: 31–9.

— (2001) *Science and an African Logic*, Chicago, IL: University of Chicago Press.

— (1999) 'Staying true to the laughter in Nigerian classrooms', in J. Law and J. Hassard (eds) *Actor Network Theory and After*, Oxford: Blackwell Publishers/The Sociological Review, pp. 136–55.

Walsham, G. (1997) 'Actor-network theory and IS research: current status and future prospects.', Proceedings of the IFIP TC8 WG 8.2 International Conference on Information Systems and Qualitative Research, Chapman and Hall: 466–80.

Waltz, S.B. (2006) 'Nonhumans unbound: actor-network theory and the reconsideration of "things" in educational foundations', *Journal of Educational Foundations*, vol. 20, no. 3/4: 51–68.

— (2004) 'Giving artifacts a voice bringing into account technology in educational analysis', *Educational Theory*, vol. 54, no. 2: 157–72.

Webb, P.T. (2006) 'The choreography of accountability', *Journal of Education Policy*, vol. 21, no. 2: 201–14.

— (2005) 'The anatomy of accountability', *Journal of Education Policy*, vol. 20, no. 2: 189–208.

Weick, K.E. and Quinn, R.E. (1999) 'Organizational change and development', *Annual Review of Pyschology*, vol. 50: 361–88.

Wenger, E. (1998) *Communities of Practice: Learning, Meaning, and Identity*, Cambridge: Cambridge University Press.

Whatmore, S. (2002) *Hybrid Geographies: Natures Cultures Spaces*, London: Sage.

Woolgar, S., Coopmans, C. and Neyland, D. (2009) 'Does STS mean business?', *Organization*, vol. 16, no. 1: 5–30.

Yasukawa, K. (2003) 'Towards a social studies of mathematics: numeracy and actor-network theory', in S. Kelly, B. Johnston and K. Yasukawa (eds) *The Adult Numeracy Handbook: Reframing Adult Numeracy in Australia*, Broadway, NSW: NSWALNARC and Language Australia, pp. 28–34.

Young, N. (2006) 'Distance as a hybrid actor in rural economies', *Journal of Rural Studies*, vol. 22, no. 3: 253–66.

Index